THE GOALS OF
MACROECONOMIC POLICY

Since the time of Keynes, macroeconomists have been concerned with the effectiveness of stabilization policies in reaching full employment. However, no one has provided a convincing argument that this goal is universally desirable. Thus the book's main thesis is that Pareto optimality — the guiding principle of policy evaluation, because some gain and none lose — does not apply to macroeconomic policies and that full employment is essentially an arbitrary political aim.

The book is divided into three parts. The first part is historical: it examines the literature on the optimality of macroeconomic goals and the record of successive U.S. administrations in achieving the goals they have set. The second part presents a theory of the labor market, and an evaluation of welfare changes from rising or falling real wages.

The concluding part looks at public-choice decisions, especially those related to spending and taxation, from an individualistic perspective. Although originally intended to show what sacrifices are necessary in collective decisions, the aim is now to maximize one's own benefit from government spending and to avoid as much of the burden of taxation as possible. The resulting "free-rider problem" creates budget deficits which are no longer countercyclical but are tolerated because they have no adverse welfare consequences for the current population; instead they leave future generations saddled with extra interest payments on the accumulated debt. A number of possible ways of avoiding unnecessary budget deficits are explored without much hope of success.

Martin Prachowny is Professor of Economics at Queen's University, where he has taught since 1967, while holding visiting positions at MIT and LSE. He is the author of five previous books, the most recent of which is *Money in the Macroeconomy* (CUP, 1985), and many journal articles in the area of macroeconomic policy.

THE GOALS
OF
MACROECONOMIC
POLICY

Martin F. J. Prachowny

London and New York

First published 1994
by Routledge
11 New Fetter Lane, London EC4P 4EE

Simultaneously published in the USA and Canada
by Routledge
29 West 35th Street, New York, NY 10001

Typeset with TEX by the author.
The text is 10 on 12 point Computer Modern Roman.
Printed and bound in Great Britain by Mackays of
Chatham PLC, Chatham, Kent.

For permission to use copyrighted material appearing on p. 151
and p. 191, grateful acknowledgement is made to
The Economist Newspaper Ltd. Reprinted with permission.

British Library Cataloguing in Publication Data

*A catalogue reference for this book is available from the
Brtish Library*

Library of Congress Cataloguing in Publication Data
Prachowny, Martin F. J.
    The goals of macroeconomic policy/Martin F. J. Prachowny
        p. cm.
    Includes bibliographical references and index.
    ISBN 0-415-10763-6
        0-415-10764-4 (pbk.)

1. Macroeconomics. 2. Economic Policy. 3. Full employment
policies. 4. Inflation (Finance) I. Title

HB172.5.P7   1994
339.5–dc20   93-43158
                                                         CIP

Contents

List of Charts, Figures and Tables vii

Preface ix

Introduction 1

1 The Theory of Macroeconomic Goals **5**

1.1 The Pareto Optimality of Macroeconomic Goals 5
1.2 The Benefits of Full Employment 9
1.3 The Welfare Costs of Inflation 19
1.4 The Trade-off between Unemployment and Inflation 23
1.5 Summary 30

2 The Achievement of Macroeconomic Targets: U.S. Experience, 1948-90 **33**

2.1 U.S. Macroeconomic Performance, 1948-90 33
2.2 The Effectiveness of Stabilization Policy 40
2.3 Legislative Intent for Stabilization Policy 44
2.4 Implementation of Stabilization Policy 48
2.5 Concluding Remarks 88

3 The Market for Labor Services and the Macroeconomy **93**

3.1 The Supply of Labor 95
3.2 The Demand for Labor 103
3.3 Equilibrium in the Labor Market 109
3.4 Disequilibrium and Unemployment 112
3.5 Stabilization Policy and the Labor Market 115
3.6 Types of Unemployment 117
3.7 The Empirical Relevance of the Model 118
3.8 Conclusions about Labor-Market Characteristics 121

4 The Welfare Economics of Macropolicy **123**

4.1 Welfare Analysis in the Labor Market 123
4.2 The Possibility of Pareto Improvements 131
4.3 The Welfare Effects of Stabilization Policy 137
4.4 The Equity Argument 139
4.5 Democratically Determined Wages 140
4.6 Democratically Determined Macropolicy 146
4.7 Conclusions 149

5 Public Expenditures and the Private Interest **151**

5.1 Government Demand and Industry Welfare 152
5.2 The Welfare of Producing Agents 155
5.3 A Measure of Industry Welfare Changes 157
5.4 A Case Study of Federal Government Purchases 159
5.5 An Alternative Explanation 170
5.6 Conclusion 171

6 The Macroeconomic Policy Apparatus **173**

6.1 Individual Support for Public Choices 174
6.2 Government Activity as Zero-sum Games 177
6.3 Bias in Stabilization Policies 180
6.4 Improving the Policy Apparatus 184
6.5 Exploitation of Stabilization Policies 192
6.6 Conclusion 196

Epilogue **199**
Bibliography 203
Index 209

Charts

2-1   The U.S. inflation rate measured by GNP
      deflator, 1948-90   34
2-2   The U.S. output gap, 1948-90   39
2-3   The full-employment budget surplus
      and the output gap, 1948-90   41
2-4   The growth rate of real M1 money balances
      and the output gap, 1948-90   42
2-5   The period of a stable Phillips curve, 1948-68   61
2-6   The transition to higher inflation, 1969-73; the oil-price
      shocks, 1974-80; and the aftermath, 1981-90   67
3-1   Actual and natural rates of unemployment, 1948-90   95
5-1   The voting profile among U.S. workers, 1982   166

Figures

1-1   Phillips curves and reaction functions   25
3-1   Determining the reservation wage   98
3-2   Aggregating two individual labor-supply decisions   100
3-3   Adjustment and disequilibrium costs
      of employment   107
3-4   Equilibrium in the labor market   110
4-1   Welfare positions in the labor market   126
4-2   Welfare of the employed and the unemployed   129
4-3   Ranking workers by the security
      of their employment   130
4-4   Welfare and excess demand or excess supply   138
5-1   Welfare of two producing agents   156

Tables

2-1   Projected unemployment and inflation rates
      in *Economic Report of the President* for 1979-81   72
2-2   Projected unemployment and inflation rates
      in *Economic Report of the President* for 1982-90   87
5-1   Industry effects of reducing federal government
      expenditures, 1982   162-5
5-2   The effect of voting costs on the size of the
      electorate and the distribution of votes   168

Preface

"Why are so many people concerned about unemployment when so few ever experience it?" This was a question idly put by a participant at a long-ago conference and it has agitated my mind ever since. My tentative conclusion is that the majority of people really do not worry about unemployment but only say they do for public consumption, as indicated by a recent Gallup poll that reported an incredible 58% of those interviewed were "strongly worried" about losing their jobs. In any case, the idea that unemployment is concentrated in a small minority of labor-market participants has led me to think of macroeconomic problems in a conflict environment where policy changes favor one group over another. Because of the heterogeneity of the population I no longer think that it is possible to suggest Pareto-improving macroeconomic policy initiatives; but at the same time, differences in fundamental characteristics in the population help us to understand why any proposed policy is bound to attract heavy criticism from some element of the electorate.

This study is the culmination of many diverse efforts I have made to analyze the conflict environment in macroeconomics. There is still no grand generalization that allows us to predict behavior by groups in many different circumstances. Marx was convinced that the conflict between capital owners and workers was the all-important one, but there are many other instances of adversarial behavior in economic transactions. This study tends to concentrate on conflicts in the labor market as well because differences among individuals are most sharply drawn in transactions in that market: the major source of the conflict is between "secure" workers and "marginal" workers. But there are many ways of dividing the population into groups with contradictory economic interests. My first attempt to portray the conflict environment (Prachowny, 1981) was an analysis of a small open economy with two distinct sectors, tradables and nontradables, which had different views about the welfare effects of policy changes. There are many other potential conflicts: between the old and the young, between debtors and creditors, between regions or states, between those who work in private-sector industries and those who work for the public sector, between exporters and importers, between "inside" workers and "outside" workers and a whole host of other divisions. Because of the multiplicity of these conflicts, it is extremely difficult to predict how coalitions will be built to decide on policy issues, but it is also easier to understand the lack of a consistent approach to macroeconomic problems when they arise.

As with many of my previous projects I have received invaluable advice and suggestions from Professor Robert Solow; also Chris Sarlo gave me the benefit of his counsel. My wife, Marguerite, provided much useful editorial assistance. To all of these I am grateful for their help. Portions of this study have appeared previously in the following journals: *Zeitschrift für die gesamte Staatswissenschaft*, 1987, pp. 244–60; *Public Choice*, 1988, pp. 143–59. Publishers of these journals have kindly granted permission to reprint or paraphrase this material.

This book was typeset by the author using the TEX system invented by Donald E. Knuth. For those familiar with this revolutionary do-it-yourself publishing process the following details may be of some interest. The manuscript was typed in ASCII format with the TEX instructions and some customized macros incorporated. The resulting DVI files were printed on a laser printer for copy-editing and proofreading. The charts and figures were generated using *Freelance* and a laser printer and then reduced to size with PMTs. The final camera-ready copy was produced from the DVI files on a phototypesetter.

Introduction

The strand woven into the fabric of macroeconomic theory identified with stabilization policy has broken or has become so faint that its contribution to the strength of the whole cloth is now much in doubt. While business-cycle activity remains an important research topic, policies addressed to counter these cycles have received scant attention in the past decade. For example, in a path-breaking article on capital-market sources of economic fluctuations, Stiglitz (1992, pp. 294-96) devotes only a minor and incidental portion to a discussion of monetary policy.

We need to know why policy issues have become dormant. Is it because we have convinced ourselves that policy intervention is unnecessary or inoperative? Or is it, to the contrary, that these policies are effective and we have persuaded everyone that all the essential ingredients of such policy advice are well known and understood? The answer is that both reasons are partially to blame for the absence of academic interest in stabilization policy. Macroeconomists of the noninterventionist school are certain that the macroeconomy adjusts speedily and smoothly to shocks and does not require policy changes, while Keynesians are more concerned about finding microeconomic justification for continuing disequilibrium in the labor market than in policies designed to alleviate the problem. The purpose of this study is to change the focus of the debate from its past emphasis on the need — or lack thereof — for policy intervention to a new concern about effective policy implementation. With the evidence that unemployment remains well above the natural rate for many years, the interventionists have probably won the argument that there is room for activist macropolicy, but they have not yet addressed the next question:

Can such policies be made to work to improve national wellbeing? There are two reasons in addition to — or in place of — the traditional ones put forward by noninterventionists for reducing or eliminating countercyclical fiscal and monetary policies: (1) the welfare benefits of such policies are far from universal; and (2) the macropolicy apparatus is badly designed to achieve whatever goals are established by those in charge of policy decisions. Chapters 3 and 4 are devoted to the first of these topics, while Chapters 5 and 6 deal with the second topic. As preparatory material, Chapter 1 presents a review of the recent literature on the Pareto optimality of such traditional goals as "full employment" and "price stability" and Chapter 2 gives a historical perspective to U.S. macropolicy since the end of World War II in the light of these goals.

Macroeconomics, it is often said, is just microeconomics applied to a large number of people. There is, however, a crucial distinction: microeconomic theory must allow for diversity in tastes, endowments, and abilities in order to make predictions about their effects on prices, quantities, and welfare; macroeconomics, on the other hand, usually starts with the "representative agent" and then multiplies by n to obtain aggregates. While this emphasis on homogeneity of the population has some desirable properties, it hides the potential for conflict about policy choices. This is particularly true in the labor market: whether you favor expansionary policies depends very much on whether you are currently employed or unemployed. To highlight these conflicts, macroeconomic policy issues must be presented in a framework that allows for heterogeneity of economic agents in one or more dimensions.

To investigate these potential conflicts, it is really not necessary to abandon existing "old-fashioned" macromodels, although it is somewhat surprising that the overlapping-generations model, which has become the workhorse in "modern" macrotheory, has not been deployed for this purpose when it is immediately obvious that the "old" generation has different interests from the "young" generation. For this study, I tend to think in terms of the *IS-LM-AS* model enunciated in a previous book, *Money in the Macroeconomy*. What was missing there was a complete specification of the aggregate labor market, which is presented here in Chapter 3. Also, I tend not to take a monolithic position on the source of economic cycles (i.e., real business cycles *vs.* aggregate-demand shocks) except to suggest that the oil-price shocks in 1974 and 1979 were the only major instances of supply-side disturbances in the period 1948-90.

The presentation in this study is a mixture of theoretical, empirical, and historical analysis. On the theoretical front, the only contribution is in the labor market and it relies on the previously accepted notion of the reservation wage and on the observed fact that involuntary unemployment is not randomly distributed among existing workers. Despite the limited analytical apparatus, there is a powerful conclusion to be derived: optimality of equilibrium in the labor market can no longer be taken for granted. There are many individuals and firms that eagerly make exchanges every day even when the labor market is in disequilibrium, while there exist "naturally" unemployed persons in equilibrium who are unhappy because they want to work.

To compensate for the lack of novelty in theoretical discussions, a major effort is made to test specific hypotheses that are important to the conclusions of this study. In particular, it will be established that real wages move countercyclically and that the Phillips curve is quite robust. Moreover, an attempt is made to put policy discussions in a historical setting by examining the decisions that were made by various administrations in the context of received macrotheory at that time. It is useless to criticize policy in 1950 because it was inconsistent with rational expectations, but it is relevant to question the lack of appropriate estimates of the natural rate of unemployment in the 1960s.

Although this study was written in 1992-93, a conscious decision was made to end the tale in 1990. There are two major reasons for this choice. First, in the empirical aspects of the discussion, the emphasis is on long periods of history, rather than on recent macropolicy issues; hence the decision not to deal with events that are too close to the present. Second, in 1992, the U.S. Department of Commerce shifted from GNP to GDP accounting; although historical data for these new aggregates have been published, some related time series, such as potential output, will be years in the making and it is not possible to mix GNP and GDP data to measure the output gap.

Academic economists usually conclude their work by offering advice on how to improve the situation that they have identified, in this case the inability to identify unambiguous macroeconomic policy goals and the realization that existing macroeconomic policies are being exploited for private, self-interested reasons. The outcome is a classical case of the prisoner's dilemma with everyone being frustrated by everyone else's selfish desire for the government to meet their individualistic demands. One acknowledged escape from the dilemma is the biblical golden rule (Luke 6:26), but who will enforce this rule when all parties have an incentive to "do unto others as they have every reason to do unto me"? In these circumstances, it seems futile to preach self-discipline and impossible to find the price mechanism necessary to make collective choices that promote truly public needs.

1

The Theory of Macroeconomic Goals

Despite the genesis of macroeconomic theory as a scientific response to the Great Depression, very little effort has been directed since then toward the specification of precise goals for macroeconomic policy and toward the analytical basis for these goals. Defining and justifying macroeconomic goals is still shrouded in such amorphous terms as "full employment" and "price stability". Much of macroeconomic analysis has instead been devoted to arguing about the ability or inability of macroeconomic tools, such as fiscal and monetary policies, to influence macroeconomic performance towards exogenously chosen goals, without questioning the arbitrariness of these goals. This state of affairs seems to be tolerated even though there has been a prolonged pre-occupation in microeconomics with the evaluation of policies in terms of Pareto improvements, where at least one person is better off but no one is made worse off.

1.1 The Pareto Optimality of Macroeconomic Goals

To set the stage for the remainder of this chapter, contrast the inattention to optimality in macroeconomic-policy discussions with the rigorous approach on this issue prevailing in other areas, such as international trade theory and policy. The long tradition of debating the merits of free trade and the intellectual acceptance of the "optimum" tariff have been shaped by the clearly specified goal of maximizing a social welfare function. The difficulties in translating such abstract concepts into concrete actions are not to be minimized and less-than-optimal trade policies continue to be implemented by governments certain that they can justify their actions on the basis of *some* economic reasoning. Nevertheless, academic trade economists understand instinctively that policy intervention must be based on a clearly defined Pareto welfare improvement.[1]

Great advances have been made in macrotheory in predicting private behavior in various markets of an economy, but there is virtually nothing to determine the optimal behavior of government in providing stabilization-policy correctives. This chapter will review the limited state of our understanding of macroeconomic goals, starting with Keynes's view as expressed in *The General Theory*, advancing through the period of "fine tuning", the "rational expectations" revolution, to the current fascination with "games" between the public and its government as explanations of recent macroeconomic policy initiatives. The emphasis in this critical survey is not on what *can* be accomplished in the area of macroeconomic policy initiatives, but instead on what *should* be accomplished and *why*. The literature on analytical normative macroeconomics as such does not seem to exist; instead macroeconomics has been concerned either with purely descriptive topics or with prescriptive advice. This division of labor between theoretical and policy-oriented macroeconomics has been justified recently by Mankiw (1990, p. 1646): "The observation that recent developments [in macrotheory] have little impact on applied macroeconomics creates at least the presumption that these developments are of little use to applied macroeconomists." The lack of interest by theorists in the optimality properties of policies, however, remains puzzling. Instead of being able to survey a number of articles or monographs devoted to this specific subject, one must search for incidental discussion and unintentional asides in the whole of the literature.

The framework for this discussion is that macropolicy *should* use optimal intervention to remove a distortion, just as the optimal tariff is the best response to a country's monopoly power in international trade. When we find that tariffs are most often imposed because it is the best outcome for some special-interest group within the country, we are not at a loss to explain such

---

[1] Corden (1974) was able to write a tightly-argued 423-page book on the subject of welfare evaluations of trade policy; this present book, which attempts to perform the same function for macroeconomic policies, will be much shorter.

outcomes in a democratic society, even if the will of the majority should ensure otherwise. Moreover, in cases of repeated disappointment with governments that provide relief to small preferred groups or that are corrupt, there are only rarely demands voiced to impose constitutional restraints on politicians who do not carry out policies that are beneficial to the majority of citizens. The observed toleration of special-interest legislation or political corruption is not based on ignorance or self-deceit; instead, there is an awareness by most citizens that they must make an effort for *their* special-interest group to receive its rewards and that there is a payoff to that effort. With a heterogeneous population based on differences in tastes or endowments, there will be many special-interest groups vying for attention and preferred treatment. The government is an arbitrator in these public-choice decisions and it tries to avoid the conflict that this creates by attempting to please everyone. The outcomes of public-choice decisions are difficult to predict and are often entirely random, despite median-voter models, as we shall see in Chapters 5 and 6. In the political arena, we look for a voting equilibrium based on majorities within the population. However, if there are fixed costs to participation in the political process, then sheer numbers are not enough to determine the outcome. Typically, a policy change leads to a large number of people suffering small losses and a small group making large gains. If the transactions costs are sufficient to "disfranchise" the losers who do not have enough at stake to get involved in the political decision, the gainers will win the day by lobbying for their preferred result.

For example, from the Stolper-Samuelson theorem in trade theory, we know that owners of the scarce factor gain from a tariff at the expense of owners of the abundant factor. Also, we have convinced ourselves that the gains to the scarce factor are smaller than the losses to others; therefore, the imposition of the tariff makes the average person worse off. Government should not interfere with free trade even if it represents exclusively the owners of the scarce factor because it could implement a nondistortionary transfer payment that makes the owners of the scarce factor as well off as with the tariff but imposes a smaller loss on everyone else. On this basis, we would predict that governments always choose free trade. We also recognize that such nondistortionary taxes and subsidies are impossible to implement, so that these political decisions once again involve a conflict between losers and gainers.

In macroeconomic analysis, the emphasis is on the "representative agent" who has the average tastes and endowments of the economy as a whole. This reliance on homogeneity and universality in macroeconomic theory is only rarely acknowledged as a weakness. Kirman (1992, p. 134) suggests: "Only if we are prepared to develop a paradigm in which individuals operate in a limited subset of the economy, are diverse both in their characteristics and the activities that they pursue, and interact directly with each other, will economics escape from the stultifying influence of the representative agent." However, he does not provide practical guidelines for the construction of such a "paradigm" that also maintains the best features of current macrotheory. McCandless (1991, pp. 44-5) writes on the diversity of response to government policies:

> Almost all government policies involve the improvement of the utility level of some individuals and the reduction of the utility level of others when compared to their situation before the policy. Those who gain belong to the political pressure group that is supporting the policy and those who lose are in the pressure group that is against the policy... The macroeconomics of policy making ignores most of the above issues. With the aggregation of all goods into one good comes the aggregation of all individuals into the one 'individual' of the economy.

But the distinction between gainers and losers, as we shall see, is important if we are to understand the difficulties in defining and implementing macroeconomic goals. *Theoretical* advances on *policy* issues are necessary, despite Mankiw's contention to the contrary. For example, the theoretical emphasis on disequilibrium in the labor market involves the representative agent not being allowed to work "optimal" hours, but the policy problem involves some individuals being totally and involuntarily unemployed. To provide a theoretical foundation for involuntary unemployment requires the recognition that firms adjust their labor input primarily through alterations in the number of workers while they keep their hours of work relatively fixed. Excess supply in the labor market then creates winners (i.e., those who remain employed and receive a real wage that is too high to clear the market) and losers (i.e., those who are unemployed but willing to work).

1.2   The Benefits of Full Employment

John Maynard Keynes was probably the first economist to provide a justification for full employment as a macroeconomic target by showing that less-than-full employment was an equilibrium position but not an optimal one. He wrote in *The General Theory*, "The outstanding faults of the economic society in which we live are its failure to provide for full employment ..." (p. 372). He defined "full employment" in a number of ways, one of which is the following: "... a situation in which aggregate employment is inelastic in response to an increase in the effective demand for its output." (p. 26). This would be equivalent to an unemployment rate of zero percent, even though he acknowledges the existence of "frictional" unemployment "... being consistent with 'full' employment ..." (p. 16). In modern terminology, consider an increase in aggregate demand from a position of full employment; the rising price level in the face of a fixed money wage reduces real wages and provides a stimulus to extra output and employment, made possible with a pool of workers who are "frictionally" unemployed. Only if every potential worker is already employed will aggregate employment be inelastic and this requires that unemployment is completely eliminated. As a consequence, Keynes's view of the labor market would not admit to situations of excess demand, only excess supply, or, at best, full employment; otherwise, with equilibrium requiring zero unemployment, there would have to be a way of creating negative unemployment when demand exceeds supply.

In the 1930s, when 20% of the labor force was involuntarily unemployed, it was, of course, entirely excusable to concentrate on conditions of excess supply in the labor market. Nevertheless, the Keynesian prescription for curing this problem would have been severely biased because it takes a lot less additional aggregate demand to move from 20% unemployment to 5%, if that is the frictional unemployment rate, than to move from 20% to 0%. In fact, in the 1990s, it would probably take almost an infinite increase in aggregate demand to move from 7% unemployment to 0%.

Moreover, Keynes was not precise in detailing the benefits of the goal of "full employment" and seemed content to make generalized statements such as: "So long as a tolerable level of employment could be attained ..." (p. 309). At the time, the benefits were considered to be self-evident and did not need explanation: those who were unemployed were suffering a vast reduction in their standard of living, especially in the absence of modern-day unemployment insurance benefits, and putting them back to work would repair that damage. Despite the intolerable conditions of the day, Keynes was writing a *General Theory* applicable to all situations; explaining the sources of welfare improvements from aggregate-demand policies may have provided a firmer foundation for Keynesian macroeconomics. Such criticism that Keynesians do not worry about theoretical justifications for their policy conclusions is not new: Schumpeter (1954, p. 1171) accused Keynes of "... piling a heavy load of practical conclusions upon a tenuous groundwork, which was unequal to it yet seemed in its simplicity not only attractive but also convincing."

1.2.1   The Social Costs of Unemployment

What Keynes and his followers failed to provide was a clear indication of what was to be gained by using policy instruments to achieve full employment and by whom. It seemed merely to be taken for granted that full employment is Pareto superior to less-than-full employment because those who are already employed are unaffected while those who find employment as a result of these policies gain in welfare. It was not until Okun established his famous Law that we have an attempt to show that the benefits of full employment are widely shared. By arguing that policies designed to achieve full employment will bring about a substantial increase in output which allows the average person to increase his standard of living, Okun created an intellectual climate where full employment was seen as universally desirable. He wrote: "If programs to lower unemployment from $5\frac{1}{2}$ to 4 percent of the labor force are viewed as attempts to raise the economy's grade from $94\frac{1}{2}$ to 96, the case for them may not seem compelling. Focus on the [output] gap helps remind policymakers of the large reward [in terms of extra output] associated with such an improvement." (1970, p. 133) He then states his oft-quoted Law: "In the postwar period, on the average, each extra percentage point in the unemployment rate above 4 percent has been associated with about a 3 percent decrement in real GNP." (p. 135).

A numerical example of Okun's Law will illustrate the source of these "large rewards". In 1990, a reduction in the unemployment rate by one percentage point from the prevailing 5.4% would have created another 1.18 million workers. The increase in real GNP would have been 3%, which in 1990 amounted to $124.67 billion. On a per capita basis, these extra workers each produce $2,031.84 per week. At the time, the average weekly wage in 1982 dollars was $259.98; therefore, another $1,771.86 a week could be shared with everyone else in the economy. However, this extra output is not a windfall gain because other events are assumed to accompany the increased employment. Okun explained: "Clearly, the simple addition of 1 percent of a given labor force to the ranks of the employed would increase employment by only slightly more than 1 percent: $100/(100 - U)$ percent to be exact. If the workweek and productivity were unchanged, the increment to output would be only that 1+ percent. [This implies a constant marginal product of labor, which is not a sensible assumption for most production functions.] The 3 percent result implies that considerable output gains in a period of rising utilization rates must stem from some or all of the following: induced increases in the size of the labor force; longer average hours; and greater productivity." (p. 140). These additional factors are then quantified: "... an increase of nearly 0.5 percent in hours per man, or an addition of about 0.2 of an hour to the workweek ... perhaps a 1.8 percent increase in total labor input measured in hours ... manhour productivity must rise by 1.4 percent." (p. 142).

The extra workers and the additional hours that are devoted to work have to be paid out of this extra output. If 1.8% more workers are encouraged to participate in the labor market, then instead of 1.18 million there would have been 3.30 million more workers in 1990 who have to be paid the average weekly wage of $259.98. The additional 0.2 hours from all 121.22 million workers at $7.54 per hour amounts to $182.79 million per week. The residual comes from an assumed gain in productivity as unemployment falls. Okun is convinced that, "The record clearly shows that manhour productivity is depressed by low levels of utilization, and that periods of movement toward full employment yield considerably above-average productivity gains." (p. 142). Since these improvements do not have to be compensated by payments to additional factors of production, they can be treated as windfall gains and can be shared by everyone in the economy. Okun admits that he has "... little direct evidence to offer on the mechanism by which low levels of utilization depress productivity," but then enumerates a number of possibilities all of which "... could help explain why slack economic activity is accompanied by 'on-the-job underemployment,' reflected in depressed levels of manhour productivity." (p. 143).

To summarize this example, the additional output of $124.67 billion in 1990 from an assumed one percentage-point reduction in the unemployment rate is allocated as follows:

Compensation of 1.18 mil. previously unemployed	$15.95 bil.
Compensation of 2.12 mil. additional workers	$28.66 bil.
Compensation of extra 0.2 hours per week	$9.51 bil.
Residual productivity gain	$70.55 bil.

Such calculations, showing a significant portion of any output gains from lower unemployment being available as an extra dividend to all participants in the labor force, provided a powerful rationale for full-employment policies. Because the macroeconomy operates more efficiently at full employment, everyone has an interest in promoting activist stabilization policies. Of course, the productivity gain is calculated as a residual. If the extra hours have to be paid at overtime rates or if there is significant upward pressure on real wages, the residual becomes correspondingly smaller. Moreover, as Gordon (1984, Table 1) and Adams and Coe (1989, Table 12) document, the Okun coefficient has not been very stable in the postwar period. It is therefore quite possible that some expansions will have only very small or no productivity gains. Despite these uncertainties, Okun's seminal contribution was to provide an easily understood and widely applied justification for full employment as a welfare-maximizing situation.

Only subsequently, in Gordon's (1973) contribution, was account taken of the possible distortions caused by the full-employment policies which could overpower the benefits. Gordon explicitly tries to measure the benefits of reducing the unemployment rate in the United States by one percentage point in 1971. He takes Okun's Law as his starting point but mentions "... its failure to impute a positive value to nonmarket activity." (p. 138). Since consumers value "final commodities" which consist of both market goods and "home activity", the gains from employment in the market sector must be evaluated by the difference between the marginal product in market activity and the marginal product of home activity. Therefore, Gordon needs to establish prices for hours spent in non-market activity in order to calculate these differences. His Table 3 (p. 163) summarizes these estimates for a temporary reduction in the unemployment rate. The gain in market GNP is $28.36 billion, but the reduction in nonmarket activity is $3.58 billion. The net increase of $24.57 billion is put into the context of the Okun coefficient. Gordon writes, "The Okun's law elasticity, defined as the absolute change in final commodities divided by the level of market output, is reduced merely from 2.7 for the naive case that evaluates nonmarket activity at a zero price, to 2.3 when an appropriate price is applied to nonmarket activity." (p. 164).

Gordon also makes such calculations for a permanent reduction in the unemployment rate. The measured net gain is now only $7.97 billion as reported in his Table 4 (p. 166), mainly because the higher hours and productivity captured in Okun's Law cannot be sustained over the long run. From these calculations, Gordon suggests an optimal unemployment rate of 2.9% (p. 175) because the marginal contribution to market GNP is balanced by the negative effects on nonmarket time at that rate of unemployment. The spirit in which this exercise is done is one that recognizes the possibility of creating "involuntary" employment by tricking people to give up lucrative nonmarket activity for less valuable employment in the market economy. By measuring the costs of creating employment as well as the benefits, Gordon is trying to replicate for macropolicies what trade economists have long done for tariffs.

However Gordon has left out one group of losers and the costs that they bear from an attempt to follow expansionary policies that reduce the unemployment rate, even temporarily. In the face of such "surprise" policies, the real wage declines because the expected inflation is lower than actual inflation. This is what stimulates demand for labor and reduces the unemployment rate. For those workers who had secure employment before and who continue to work the same number of hours, including overtime, this attempted reduction in the unemployment rate causes them to have a lower standard of living as their real take-home pay declines. Yet Gordon explicitly assumes that the real wage is constant (p. 138) without suggesting how firms can be encouraged to hire more workers when the fiscal or monetary policy is unlikely to affect directly the marginal product of workers. This inconsistency in the analysis hides the possibility that there would be many people in the labor force who are made worse off by a reduction in the unemployment rate through expansionary policies. In that sense, not even the more sophisticated Okun's Law estimates allowed for the possibility that some individuals are made worse off when the unemployment rate is reduced, no matter what the increase in total output.

In an earlier contribution, Dobell and Ho (1967) try to determine the optimal amount of frictional unemployment by balancing the costs and benefits of reducing this type of unemployment. On the cost side they argue that, "Qualifying people to enter employment costs resources, and probably more resources the higher the present employment rate." (p. 675). The benefit is the extra stream of consumption available to everyone in society. The "optimal" number of people to be left untrained and therefore unemployable is obtained, just like the "golden rule" for investment, by equating the extra cost of training a potential worker to the discounted present value of higher future consumption from the additional employment. What this analysis fails to reveal is the repetitive nature of the costs required to fill vacancies. According to Dobell and Ho, once trained a person is always employable and therefore the frictional unemployment rate should fall over time, contrary to the experience in most industrial countries in the 1970s or 1980s. Nevertheless, by taking a cost-benefit approach, they have shown that there are some sacrifices that must be made in order to reduce unemployment. The determination of the frictional unemployment rate will be taken up again in Chapter 3.

While Keynes and his followers and Okun had a "vision of abundance through full employment ," (Hession, 1984, p. 298), the more recent contributions to the macroeconomics literature concentrate on the benefits of allowing all participants in the labor market to work optimal hours. An example is provided by Aizenman and Frenkel (1985). They ". . . define the equilibrium that replicates the performance of an economy in which labor markets clear without friction, as the social optimum." (p. 418). This implies the requirement that the marginal product of labor equal the marginal disutility of work, which in turn produces the equilibrium real wage and the level of the labor input that is consistent with this requirement, $\tilde{L}$. The quantity $\tilde{L}$ must be interpreted as hours per individual per unit of time (e.g., a week) since it ". . . is supplied by utility maximizing workers... In practice, due to a precontracted nominal wage, the realized real wage may differ from its full equilibrium level. Since by assumption employment is demand determined, $[L]$, it follows that the actual level of employment differs from $\tilde{L}$ ... The welfare cost of suboptimal employment is $[U(\tilde{L}) - U(L)]/\lambda$ where λ measures the marginal utility of money." (p. 419). In other words, the social cost arises from a discrepancy between the hours that an individual wants to work and the hours that he is allowed to work. This representation of the social cost of unemployment suffers from three deficiencies: (1) it assumes that all persons achieve the same results from their participation in the labor market; (2) it presumes that employment changes occur through individual adjustment of hours, when in fact most jobs specify a given number of hours and workers either supply these pre-specified hours or none at all; and (3) the analysis could not handle excess-demand situations without forcing involuntary exchange on the demand curve for labor. The last two criticisms of the Aizenman-Frenkel labor-market specification will be taken up in Chapter 3, but the first point can be dealt with here.

Arrow (1951) tried to translate individual preferences into social choices and found "the impossibility theorem" which proved that a social ordering of possible outcomes could not be found if five reasonable requirements were imposed. Of these, the one which insisted on a strong Pareto condition is the most likely to fail. This criterion involves no one being worse off and at least some people being better off as a condition for accepting that choice. There are numerous examples that clearly indicate that it is always possible to identify some losers from a policy choice if the cost of finding them is not made prohibitive.

In the Aizenman-Frenkel framework, once we allow for heterogeneity among workers, it is quite possible for some workers to have $\tilde{L} = L$, others $\tilde{L} > L$, and still others $\tilde{L} < L$, all at the same wage rate. An expansion of aggregate demand at that point will increase L for everyone, but this benefits only those suffering from $\tilde{L} < L$; the other groups become worse off. Thus such a policy cannot meet Arrow's criteria. In any case, such issues are quite jejune; one rarely hears about the "problem" of suboptimal hours in stabilization-policy debates, except to the extent that some individuals are not working at all.

Chapter 3 will develop a model of the labor market in which participants work either a fixed number of hours or none at all. This more realistic approach to observed behavior leads to a small group of people being involuntarily unemployed, while the large majority of workers may have the slight inconvenience of not working their optimal hours. Even in that setting, reducing unemployment will not benefit everyone, as mentioned above in the criticism of Gordon's study. Yet governments are always concerned about unemployment, but they are also concerned about other groups such as farm families and these concerns are not related to Pareto improvements; instead, they involve "entitlements" and the power to enforce them. Who wins these battles? Do farmers get more attention than unemployed workers? The widespread agricultural subsidy and marketing system adopted in most industrial countries is a prime illustration of government policies adopted and tolerated even though they benefit only a small proportion of the population and impose heavy but hidden costs of distortion on the vast majority. According to *The Economist* (July 11, 1992, p. 22; corrected August 8, 1992, p. 39), the U.S. farm sector received $81 billion in transfers in 1991, which worked out to $200 per taxpayer and $118 per consumer of food, despite the farm population being less than 2% of the total. Directly comparable data are not available for "subsidies" to the unemployed. In 1990, the farm population was 4.6 million while the number of unemployed persons was 6.9 million. "Transfers" from unemployment insurance programs amounted to $19.6 billion; the average weekly check from state programs was $161.56, compared to the weekly wage of $346.04. While it is not obvious that farmers are better able to promote their private interests in government policies than the unemployed, the impression remains that farmers are more politically powerful than the unemployed. Pareto optimality is not of prime importance to either group.

1.2.2   *Optimality and Symmetry*

There is a strange lack of symmetry in Keynesian arguments for full-employment policies because there does not seem to be a situation where excess demand in the labor market is ever envisaged. As pointed out earlier, by at least one definition of full employment, Keynes had in mind zero unemployment. Later, Okun advanced the notion that 4% unemployment was consistent with "potential output" but his Law still produced the above-mentioned windfall gains if the economy were driven to unemployment rates below 4%. He stated: "In the periods from which this relationship was obtained the unemployment rate varied from 3 to $7\frac{1}{2}$ percent; the relation is not meant to be extrapolated outside this range." (p. 137). From this statement, one could surmise that actual output would exceed potential output by about 3% when the unemployment rate was 3% and of this extra output more than a half would be identified as a productivity gain from a more efficiently operating labor market. There seem to be no costs attached to situations of actual output exceeding potential output. As a consequence, Keynes and his followers seem always to preach expansionary policy, never contractionary policy. While that emphasis may be forgiven when it is placed in the context of the Great Depression and its aftermath, Schumpeter's criticism that Keynesian macroeconomics is event-specific and only applicable to recessions brings out its asymmetrical relevance.

It was not until the development of the "natural rate of unemployment" by Friedman (1968) and Phelps (1967) that the needed symmetry for stabilization policy was firmly established. Since the natural rate was defined as the rate of unemployment with constant inflation, it could also be identified with a constant real wage since nominal wages and goods prices would rise in the same proportion. At that point, the labor market was in equilibrium. If there were excess supply, there would be falling inflation, but with excess demand there would be rising inflation. The dangers of trying to reach zero unemployment were now clear: the possibility of hyperinflation and the elimination of money as a medium of exchange.

1.2.3 Optimality of Policy Intervention

More recently, the development of the "rational expectations" approach to macroeconomics dealt a body blow to the whole notion of stabilization policy as a Pareto improvement. It was put forward by the neoclassical school of thought that the private sector can achieve the best results relying only on its own resources; the government has no advantage in reaching macroeconomic goals. Even if the government had "superior" information about impending shocks, it was argued that this does not open the door to intervention except of the limited kind of providing this information to the public who would use it for their own benefit.

During the 1980s the argument had come full circle to the prevailing view before the 1930s: that is, there was no reason why the government should pursue the goal of full employment. Although Keynesian and post-Keynesian economics is still attempting to provide an analytical foundation for macroeconomic interventionism, there now seems to be much less appeal of "fine tuning" the macroeconomy with active stabilization policy changes than in the 1960s. To the extent that the debate between interventionists and noninterventionists is still in progress, the difference of opinion is about the provision and use of information and who has a comparative advantage in these two activities — the government or the private sector. Keynesians would argue that the private sector provides useful information about macroeconomic developments which the government as a "social planner" uses to ensure optimal performance. The contrary view, taken by the rational-expectations proponents, is that the government should make its intentions known concerning such matters as the growth rate of the money supply and fiscal changes. This information is then incorporated into expectations about inflation and other future events by the public who maximize their utility subject to whatever constraints they face; nothing could improve on that outcome.

1.2.4 *Optimality and Commitment*

Keynes thought it was possible to generate enough aggregate demand, through expansionary policies, to allow those genuinely unemployed to find work, without any other group taking advantage of such a commitment to full employment for its own purposes. Keynes did not explicitly assume altruism in his theory, but it would not have been an unusual implicit presumption about human behavior at that time. Nevertheless, in a particularly scathing and generalized criticism, Barnett (1972, p. 63) wrote: "... in applying the qualities of gentleness, trustfulness, altruism, and strict regard for moral conduct to a sphere of human activity where cunning, cynicism, opportunism, trickery, and force, all in the service of ... self-interest still held sway, the twentieth-century British stood disarmed and blinded by their own virtues."

Keynes had a strong belief that the unemployed could not help their own cause since a reduction in money wages would not increase employment; instead, extra aggregate demand had to be provided by the government. While an analysis of this proposition must wait until Chapter 3, where the labor market is developed in full detail, this important departure from the classical view about market adjustments must be examined in relation to the behavior of participants in the labor market who are aware that the government has committed itself to full employment. Since a worker's welfare increases with the real wage, this group has an incentive to bargain for nominal wage increases that are larger than the rate of inflation; the normal counterforce to this incentive is the fear of losing one's job at which point welfare is reduced to the purchasing power of unemployment insurance payments and other nonwage income. If the commitment to full employment removes the possibility of ever being unemployed, the pressure to raise wages becomes unlimited. Furthermore, job-performance discipline is lessened in an environment without a threat of unemployment and productivity is likely to suffer with a consequent reduction in real wages. Therefore, a known commitment to full employment will alter the behavior of labor-market participants who are not reluctant to exploit this commitment for their own gains and to make its achievement less likely.

1.2.5 Summary

The case for full employment as a Pareto optimal outcome has not been made by macroeconomic theory to date. In the current literature, equilibrium in the labor market as a desirable position is based on the incorrectly assumed collective decision that offering opportunities for employment to the unemployed can have no adverse repercussions on those who currently have jobs. Once it is recognized that policies designed to achieve full employment have costs attached to them that are borne by those who do not benefit directly or indirectly from their implementation, the conflict environment in which macropolicies are made becomes evident and the supposed Pareto superiority of full employment vanishes.

1.3   The Welfare Costs of Inflation

An economic goal of even longer standing is zero inflation or price stability and we want to summarize the known benefits of this goal. There has been much more explicit discussion of the distortionary effects of inflation than was the case for unemployment.[2] By comparing economies with different rates of inflation, we can get some idea of the differences in performance which arise. If the decisions taken in the absence of inflation can be considered optimal, then decisions that are different in the face of inflation involve some additional constraint that is binding and that measures the "cost" of inflation. In an economy that is "fully indexed" decisions would presumably not differ and costs of inflation are zero. In such a world, the actual rate of inflation is immaterial to welfare. Some countries' inflationary experience seems to come close to this ideal: Israel's is often referred to as "useless inflation", while Fishlow (1974) labels Brazil's as "inflation without tears". No economy is able to have full indexation and therefore there will be some relative prices that will be distorted as one or more nominal prices are unable to rise at the overall rate of inflation. Most of the discussion of the costs of inflation then concentrates on particular examples of price rigidities. The most important class of nominal price rigidities involves contracts that set a price for some time into the future before all inflationary developments have taken place. Wage contracts come readily to mind. If wages are stipulated in nominal terms and goods prices rise at an unpredictable rate, the *ex post* real wage will differ from the *ex ante* real wage. The cost of inflation therefore can be interpreted as the cost of making an error in predicting the inflation rate. Since these errors will show up in adjustments in employment, a person's welfare depends on whether employment continues or not. We are, therefore, back to the issues raised in the previous section where we found both winners and losers.

There is one area in which inflation does not bestow a benefit on anyone and that is the imposition of "menu costs". These are transactions costs incurred in order to change prices periodically to keep relative prices correct.[3] One way to visualize these costs is to imagine that a monetary economy has a larger range of productive

---

[2] A very readable summary of the important results in this literature on the "costs of inflation" are contained in Howitt (1990).

[3] Even here there might be some groups that benefit: firms in the business of printing menus or of providing inflation hedges.

abilities than a nonmonetary economy because money is a techno-
logical improvement over barter trade. In other words, a monetary
economy has a production-possibility frontier that lies outside that
of a barter-trade economy. Inflation, in turn, lessens the benefits
of a monetary economy because it creates the need for nonmarket
activity (e.g., adjusting nominal prices more frequently, the higher
is the rate of inflation) and the use of factors of production in
these nonmarket activities pushes the production-possibility curve
inwards again. In the extreme case of hyperinflation, there are
strong incentives to resort to barter trade exclusively and avoid
completely the menu costs associated with continuous changes in
money prices. Although one is tempted to dismiss the importance
of such costs for countries with "mild inflation", Howitt (1988,
p. 94) is concerned about the dynamic impact of the diversion of
resources to cope with inflation. He writes:

> This ... aspect of the cost of inflation may indeed be the most
> important of all. All of the other adverse effects of inflation
> affect the level of productivity of the economy — the level of
> output attainable with the use of a given stock of factors of
> production. But if inflation diverts entrepreneurial talent and
> inventiveness away from productive applications, then it im-
> pairs not just the level but the rate of growth of productivity,
> the ultimate source of which is the growth of useful knowledge
> brought about by investment in human capital, on-the-job ex-
> perience, fundamental research, and industrial innovations.

Okun (1975, p. 383) pinpoints the psychological effects of inflation
on economic activity:

> Prolonged and intense inflation upsets many habits of eco-
> nomic life, confronting consumers with price increases and
> price dispersions ... and forcing them to compile more in-
> formation and to try to predict the future — costly and risky
> activities that they are poorly qualified to execute and bound
> to view with anxiety. The recognition by the consumer that
> economic institutions are gravely disturbed by inflation is an
> appreciation of reality — not money illusion.

An alternative view of the transactions costs of inflation is that they represent a tax on money holdings as the purchasing power of money is reduced over time by the rate of inflation. As with any other tax, there is a dead-weight loss and a reduced demand for the commodity in question. The production cost of fiat money is virtually zero, but its opportunity cost is the nominal rate of interest, which through the Fisher effect will rise with the rate of inflation. Therefore, the higher is the rate of inflation, the larger is the discrepancy between the social cost of money, which is essentially zero, and the private cost which is the nominal interest rate when money balances are defined as cash and demand deposits. The social and private costs of money can be equated or the social cost of inflation can be eliminated by forcing the real return to money to equal its marginal cost, which in turn requires a rate of *deflation* equal to the real interest rate.[4] This would lead, as Friedman (1969) has suggested, to optimal money holdings which would, of course, be larger than in a situation of positive or even zero inflation. Further refinements would recognize that eliminating the inflation tax on money holdings would require other, probably distortionary, taxes to keep government revenue unaffected and that negative, as well as positive, inflation rates create menu costs. These considerations move the optimal inflation rate toward zero.

Trying to reach the goal of optimal inflation has greater implications for appropriate monetary policy than for fiscal policy. Friedman's (1969) rule of a constant — or at least predetermined — rate of money growth would be calculated by finding the amount of extra money needed to sustain real growth in the economy. No deviations would be allowed from this announced money rule. In the face of shocks to the system, output and inflation would adjust temporarily, but on average this is the best that the monetary authorities could achieve. Because the only goal that is set for the policy maker is the elimination of the social costs of inflation, there is no incentive to tinker with the growth rate of the money supply to influence output or unemployment. However, with the recent instability of money demand, it would still be difficult to find a money-growth rate that did not systematically impinge on real growth and keep inflation in check.

---

[4] This requirement can be stated as $i = r + \pi = 0$ where i is the nominal interest rate, r is the real rate and π is the rate of inflation. Therefore, $\pi = -r$.

Comparing the goals of "full employment" and "optimal inflation", it is quite evident that the latter has been derived from explicit welfare comparisons, but the former is merely the result of the presumption that equilibrium is "good" and disequilibrium is "bad". This lack of a symmetrical basis for the two macroeconomic goals does not necessarily suggest that one is more important than the other. There are times, such as during the Great Depression, when almost all the emphasis in macroeconomic models is on the achievement of full employment; at other times, inflation is the primary target. Moreover, there are opposing schools of thought that differ in their goals for macroeconomic policy; Blinder (1988) suggests that ardent Keynesians and uncompromising neoclassical economists can be distinguished by their undivided attention to one or the other goal. Nevertheless, many middle-of-the-road macroeconomists are concerned about both unemployment and inflation and even have put forward an objective function that assigns weights to the achievement of employment and inflation goals. We now turn to an examination of our current understanding of these multi-target goals.

1.4 The Trade-off between Unemployment and Inflation

After the appearance of the Phillips curve that initially showed a systematic negative relationship between unemployment and inflation, it was only logical to try to find the one point on the Phillips curve that maximized someone's utility. To find this point analytically we need to specify the Phillips curve and the objective function. The expectations-augmented Phillips curve can be written as

$$\pi = \pi^e - \beta(u - u^*), \tag{1.1}$$

where π and π^e are actual and expected inflation, respectively, while u and u^* are actual and "natural" rates of unemployment. The coefficient β is the slope of the Phillips curve for a given value of π^e, but to the extent that π is completely predictable, the Phillips curve becomes vertical and $u = u^*$. The objective function can be written as

$$L = \alpha_1(u - \bar{u})^2 + \alpha_2(\pi - \bar{\pi})^2, \tag{1.2}$$

where α_1 and α_2 are the weights attached to the unemployment and the inflation goals, respectively, while $\bar{u}$ and $\bar{\pi}$ are the "optimal" values of unemployment and inflation.

These two relationships have been the basis of a number of policy issues in macroeconomics: (1) reaction functions for the authorities to find how they respond to deviations from unemployment and inflation targets, (2) the outcome of policy changes when they are predictable, and (3) games between the private sector and the government authorities, including political business cycles. These three areas will be explored shortly, but first we need to look at the analytical derivation of the objective function in equation (1.2).

Blanchard and Fischer (1989, p. 568) feature an objective function similar to equation (1.2) in their review of macroeconomic policy, but they do not suggest how α_1 and α_2 are to be derived from first principles or whose choices they represent. They indicate the *ad hoc* nature of these weights by stating:

> Evaluating the full-fledged social welfare function, which is likely to depend on the utilities of current and prospective members of society, under alternative policies, rapidly becomes analytically untractable (sic). Thus we often have to rely on a simpler objective function, a *macro welfare function*, defined directly over a few macroeconomic variables such as output, unemployment, inflation, or the current account. This approach goes back explicitly to Tinbergen (1952) and implicitly much further, to earlier authors who discussed policies to stabilize the trade cycle.

It will be remembered that Tinbergen's main contribution in the cited reference was to show that the number of independent policy instruments must be equal to the number of goals that were to be achieved, rather than an analytical justification for these goals.

The choice of $\bar{u}$ and $\bar{\pi}$ in equation (1.2) has been summarized by Blanchard and Fischer. The first term ". . . can be interpreted as a quadratic approximation to the welfare loss of being away from $\bar{y}$, the equilibrium level of output absent distortions and rigidities." (p. 568). Since the distortions are in the labor market, the choice of $\bar{u}$ or $\bar{y}$ is almost irrelevant; however, they do not explicitly show that $\bar{y}$ is related to the output available at the natural rate of unemployment, namely that $u^* = \bar{u}$.

The costs of inflation enumerated by Blanchard and Fischer are

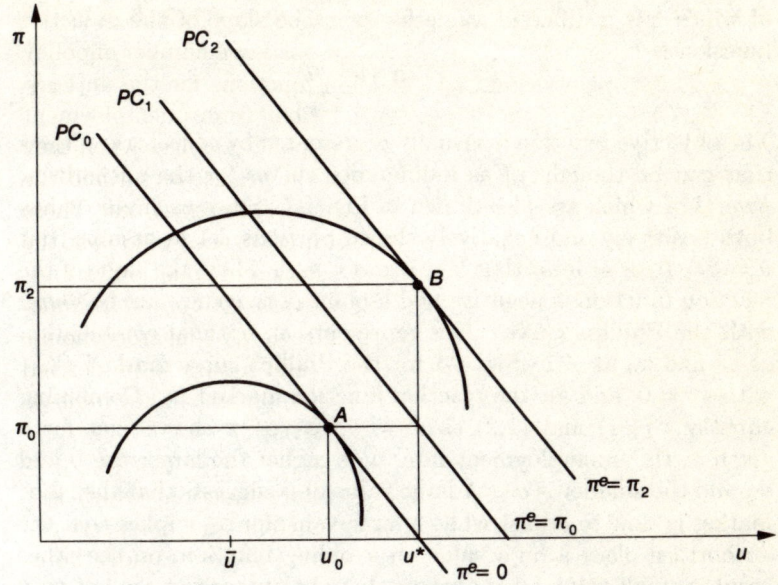

Fig. 1-1.   Phillips curves and reaction functions.

closely related to those presented in the previous section, but the
possibility that $\bar{\pi} < 0$ as optimal deflation is not discussed. They
conclude however, that, "Despite an impressive array of models in
which inflation is socially costly, there appears to be professional
consensus (which we believe is less justified than it was a decade
ago) that economics cannot justify the weight put on low inflation
as a goal of policy." (p. 569).

1.4.1   Reaction Functions

If the Phillips curve of equation (1.1) represents a menu of choices
of attainable rates of inflation and unemployment, the objective
function of equation (1.2) allows one to make the "optimal choice"
from that menu. In the early days of the Phillips curve, before
the realization that expectations of inflation played a role in the
position of the curve, the "trade off" between inflation and unemployment was given by the slope of the Phillips curve, namely,

$d\pi/du = -\beta.$[5] Several Phillips curves are shown in Fig. 1-1, each of which has a different value for π^e. The slope of the objective function is

$$\frac{d\pi}{du} = -\frac{\alpha_1(u - \bar{u})}{\alpha_2(\pi - \bar{\pi})}. \tag{1.3}$$

The objective function is visually represented by concentric ellipses that can be thought of as indifference curves for the authorities, several of which are also drawn in Fig. 1-1. Since each ellipse has both positively and negatively sloped portions, let us assume that $\bar{u} = \bar{\pi} = 0$, or at least that $u > \bar{u}$ and $\pi > \bar{\pi}$. Then, the slope of the reaction function is negative and a point of tangency can be found with the Phillips curve. This represents an optimal combination of u_0 and π_0 at A in Fig. 1-1 for the Phillips curve marked PC_0, with $\pi^e = 0$, and for the reaction function marked L_0. Combining equations (1.1) and (1.2) as $u = -\beta(\alpha_2/\alpha_1)\pi$ shows that for a given π, the unemployment rate, u, is higher the larger are β and α_2 and the smaller is α_1. A large value of β suggests that the labor market is slow to adjust while a large value for α_2 implies that the authorities place a high value on avoiding inflation; on the other hand, a small value for α_1 means that the authorities are not very concerned about unemployment.

Reuber (1964, p. 132) estimated such reaction functions and optimal choices for the Bank of Canada in the 1950s and found that:

> Were the economy freed from international constraints, the evidence suggests that the relative economic costs of price inflation and unemployment would be approximately equal at a policy combination of $1\frac{1}{2}$ per cent unemployment and $3\frac{3}{4}$ per cent annual increase in prices... In order to stabilize prices and thereby avoid [a] deterioration in the balance-of-payments position ... a level of unemployment of about 5 per cent would have to be endured.

Such "optimal" combinations of inflation and unemployment are now only fond memories for reasons that will become obvious shortly.

---

[5] This indicates that the Phillips curve is a straight line, but if it were convex from below the remainder of the discussion would still be relevant.

1.4.2   Predictable Policy Changes and their Effects

After the realization that expected inflation could not be treated
as exogenous in the face of variations in actual inflation, the optimality of point A in Fig. 1-2 could not be sustained. What Phelps
(1967) and Friedman (1968) essentially showed is that the private
sector will choose the optimal point on the Phillips curve, namely
a point where $u = u^*$. In other words, the objective function
reflects preferences of the authorities which are in direct conflict
with those of the public that they presumably represent, but the
public's wishes will ultimately prevail.

Starting from point A in Fig. 1-1, where the authorities have
created inflation equal to π_0, we must allow expectations to incorporate that information; therefore, the Phillips curve will shift
upward from PC_0 where $\pi^e = 0$ to PC_1 where $\pi^e = \pi_0$. Optimizing by the authorities against this new constraint would involve
a new tangency (not shown) with a lower level of welfare. The
only long-run equilibrium that can be maintained is on a vertical
line above u^*. Thus the authorities can have any inflation rate
that they desire including $\pi = 0$, but the private sector gets the
unemployment rate that it wants at $u = u^*$. Once the authorities
recognize the limitations of their actions they should force α_1 to
zero or, alternatively, they can choose $\bar{u} = u^*$.

Thus, the new classical macroeconomics has curtailed the role
of activist policy quite severely: the government cannot choose $\bar{u}$
independently of u^*.

1.4.3   Games between the Public and the Authorities

Governments and central banks continue to make major policy
decisions as if their actions mattered and without any apparent
awareness of their impotence. Since policy makers are unlikely to
make random changes in the variables that they control merely
to "trick" private agents for some vague purpose, it becomes vital for new classical macroeconomists to find predictable elements
in macropolicy *without* allowing a systematic effect on output or
employment. One model of such behavior is described in the influential paper by Barro and Gordon (1983) about games between
the private sector and the government.

Barro and Gordon devise a model of the economy that incor-
porates two of the major tenets of the neoclassical school: (1) a

policy-invariant natural rate of unemployment and (2) rational expectations. Since they are concerned with predicting government behavior they also specify that, "The policymaker's objectives reflect the public's preferences." In fact, they "... allow for unanimity about desirable governmental actions." (p. 590). In their specification of the objective function, similar to equation (1.2) above, they chose the target rate of unemployment, $\bar{u}$, to be less than the natural rate, u^*, because of "... some existing distortions in the economy." (p. 591). The cause of the distortion is based on the following argument: "In the presence of unemployment compensation, income taxation and the like, the natural rate will tend to exceed the efficient level — that is, privately chosen quantities of marketable output and employment will be too low." (p. 591). In turn, "... given that some government expenditures are to be carried out, it will generally be infeasible to select a fiscal policy that avoids all distortions." (p. 594). Then monetary policy is used as the instrument to overcome this distortion by trying to make $u = \bar{u}$ instead of $u = u^*$.

The outcome is also shown in Fig. 1-1. Starting from a position of $u = u^*$ and $\pi = \pi^e = 0$, the authorities try to minimize their loss by reaching point A. But since this action generates inflation equal to $\pi_0 > 0$, the public reacts by raising its expected inflation to $\pi^e = \pi_0$ shifting PC_0 to PC_1. The end result of the "game" between the public and the government is a point such as B which is vertically above u^* at a point of tangency between PC_2 and L_2 with a positive rate of inflation and a loss to the government of $\alpha_1(u^* - \bar{u})^2 + \alpha_2(\pi_2 - \bar{\pi})^2$. This outcome frustrates both sides: labor-market participants want to be at u^* while the government wants to be at $\bar{u}$ because it is more efficient than u^*. A superior alternative is a cooperative solution that would ensure $u = u^*$ and $\pi = 0$. Both sides would be better off than at B since the public moves to its preferred point while the government moves to a lower indifference curve through u^* (not shown). This could be accomplished by the authorities following a prestated rule for monetary growth, but an announcement of such a regime would not be credible unless the government renounced its objective function.

There are two important issues that are not and cannot be resolved in the Barro-Gordon model: (1) If the government has rational expectations and can therefore predict the final outcome of the game, why does it persist in trying to reach $\bar{u}$ instead of accepting u^* as a second-best solution or using optimal intervention to reach a first-best as suggested by the literature on distortions pioneered by Bhagwati and Ramaswami (1963); and (2) Knowing that the government has an incentive to trick them, why do voters not insist on a constitutional framework that prevents the monetary authorities from exercising discretionary power? There are no satisfactory answers to these questions.[6]

Such inconsistencies are also contained in models of the political business cycles pioneered by, among others, MacRea (1977). Here, governments stimulate the economy just before an election to reduce the unemployment rate and the inflationary effects are delayed until after the election. Therefore, while private agents normally optimize over an entire lifetime in their economic decisions, in the political arena these same agents are assumed to have very short memories that do not extend beyond one election.

The extensive literature on macroeconomic games is misconceived by putting into an otherwise rational and optimizing framework one group of actors, the government, that has the *power* to frustrate private actions, but is, at the same time, an *agent* of the public. This inconsistency seems to be taken for granted by Alesina (1988, p. 13) who presents "... games in which a single policy maker plays 'against' the private sector of the economy [by attempting] to surprise the public with an unexpected shock to reduce unemployment." In a democratic society where the government is the servant of the public, this kind of relationship is inconceivable. Therefore, to make sense of the conflict over macroeconomic policy we need to postulate identifiable groups formed by citizens who have incompatible aims; the government then acts as arbiter between these groups. But this type of conflict is virtually impossible in neoclassical macroeconomics because the public is assumed to be composed of identical agents. In the Barro-Gordon model that assumption is explicit.

In the related literature on reputations of government, there may be some recognition of the conflict between factions within the public. In Backus and Driffill (1985, p. 536) there are "hardnosed" and "wet" governments that have different tolerances for inflation. Backus and Driffill conclude:

---

[6] The material up to this point in the section is taken from Prachowny (1987).

First, it is commonplace to hear politicians reassure us that they are serious about beating inflation. These statements are correctly regarded with skepticism since both hard-nosed and wet governments have an incentive for being tough ... Conversely, governments frequently complain that their actions are thwarted by the 'mistaken' expectations of labor unions, big business, and the gnomes of Zurich. Second, the model provides an account of the political business cycle without relying on voter myopia ... It works, on average, because the public is uncertain about the government's true character. Voters are not myopic; they simply do not have all the information.

While there are many and divergent views concerning what governments should do about inflation and unemployment, the main emphasis in these reputation models is still on a homogeneous population that gets "tricked" because a government's reputation is only an imperfect predictor of its actions. One is therefore forced to ask: Why tolerate such a political system? Why not impose a constitutional restraint on the authorities' actions? The answer, as we shall see, is because important groups benefit from the *status quo* and even the losers hope to be winners the next time.

1.5 Summary

The common thread in the macroeconomics literature that specifies policy objectives is that the objectives are self-evident and universally desired. To question the goal of full employment is almost sacrilegious and to suggest that special-interest groups benefit from unemployment is at least curmudgeonly. While macroeconomic theory distinguishes itself from microeconomics on the basis of its emphasis on aggregates and its de-emphasis of individual markets, the use of "representative agent" models, where all individuals are essentially the same and have identical demands for government action, has blinkered the profession to the existence of heterogeneity and conflict and their impact on policymakers. It is not necessary to abandon macrotheory in order to incorporate these features into evaluations of policy changes; instead, what is needed is a Pareto apparatus to detect individuals with certain characteristics who might not benefit from such policy initiatives and to think of ways in which their opposition might be overcome. Also, in lieu of characterizing governments as either wise social planners at one extreme or as cynical exploiters of infrequent or indecisive elections at the other extreme, macroeconomists should recognize the role of government as arbiters between conflicting private groups.

This selective and critical survey of the macroeconomics literature that explores optimal policy intervention has set the stage for an attempt to improve our understanding of stabilization policies and their Pareto-improving qualities. Since these policies are primarily aimed at the labor market, using the goods market or the money market only to transmit the effects of fiscal or monetary policies, it is the market for labor services that must be analyzed in detail. This will be done in Chapter 3, after which it will be possible to investigate welfare changes in that market in Chapter 4. Before embarking on that task however, it will be useful to complement this chapter with a historical perspective of stabilization policies and their evolving commitment to fighting unemployment and inflation.

2

The Achievement of Macroeconomic Targets: U.S. Experience, 1948-90

Although governments have intervened in economic activity for centuries, macroeconomic policy and the institutions that have been created to carry out such policies are relatively new. In the United States, stabilization policy was initiated with the "New Deal" of the first Roosevelt administration in 1933. The Federal Reserve System, created twenty years earlier, initially had a limited role in preventing panic in the banking system that had occurred in 1873, 1884, 1893, and 1908. Perhaps indirectly and primitively the Fed may have generated some countercyclical forces in the provision of an "elastic currency" as the Federal Reserve Act of 1913 required. That it did not perform this function at the time of the Great Depression has been argued by Friedman and Schwartz (1963). Their contention is that the depression would not have been nearly as severe or as prolonged if the real money supply had not fallen by more than a third between 1929 and 1932. Before we continue with a historical discussion of the major U.S. legislation concerning macroeconomic intervention and its implementation, it is useful to pause and analyze the performance of the economy with respect to inflation and output during the postwar era.

2.1 U.S. Macroeconomic Performance, 1948-90

Leaving out of account the period 1945-47 because these were the years of demobilization and adjustment, we will concentrate on the period starting with 1948 to determine how well the U.S. macroeconomy performed relative to what was achievable. Of interest will be the overall performance for the 43-year period rather than individual episodes. The variables that will be charted are the inflation rate and real output relative to potential output.

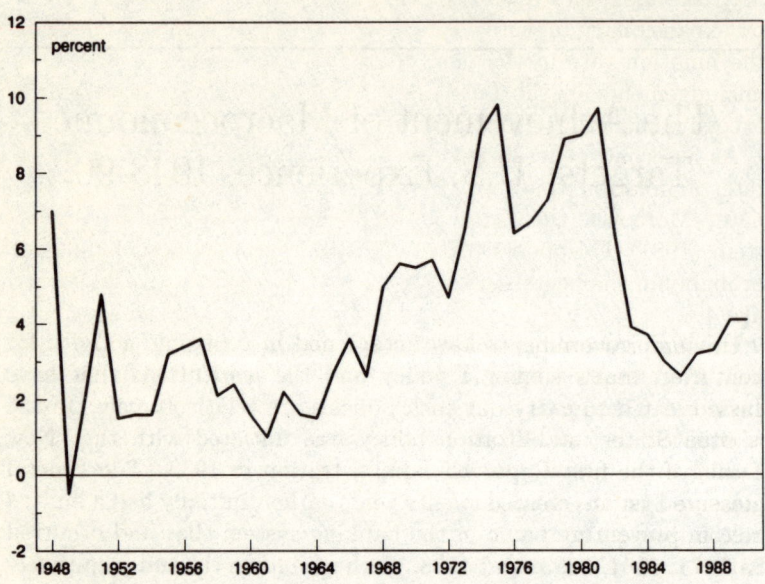

Chart 2-1. The U.S. inflation rate measured by GNP deflator,
1948-90. Source: *ERP*, 1991.

2.1.1   *Inflation Performance*

Immediately after World War II, inflation in the United States was
high, reaching 22.9% in 1946 and 13.9% in 1947. Chart 2-1 then
shows the inflation rate for the remainder of the period, 1948-90.
The average for this period was 4.27%, with a standard deviation
of 2.58%. If the oil-price shocks of 1974 and 1979 are eliminated
because they are exogenous causes of inflation, the average for the
remaining years is 4.04%.

As a first generalization, it could be argued that every postwar
inflationary episode was triggered by an exogenous change in relative prices (i.e., war or OPEC), that was not accompanied by
any absolute price reductions. On the other hand, these relative-
price battles were not prolonged as inflationary pressures abated
relatively quickly after the initial shock. For example, the 1979 oil-
price increase caused the inflation rate to hit 9.7% in 1981, but by
1983 it was down to 4% once more. In other words, while inflation

may be a monetary phenomenon, these episodes were not "caused" by expansionary monetary policy. Even the upward movement in the inflation rate in the period 1968-72 was largely the result of misjudgements in the financing of the Vietnam war and not of excessive monetary growth *per se*.

As a second generalization, there is also a positive underlying rate of inflation that not even the severest recession can eliminate. Moreover, this "core inflation rate" — as labelled by Eckstein (1981) — appears to be getting larger: in the 1960s it was probably in the neighborhood of 2%, but in the 1980s, it was more like 4%.

Having presented the basic evidence on postwar inflation we can now examine its costs.[1] The "optimal" rate of inflation, as discussed in Chapter 1, is found where the rate of return on money is equated to that of other interest-bearing assets. The cost of having an inflation rate that is other than optimal is normally measured as the area under the demand curve for money. This method was suggested by Bailey (1956). The welfare effects of inflation that measure the transactions or "shoe-leather" costs have typically been found to be negligible. Fischer (1984) estimated that 10% inflation in the United States created costs that were equal to 0.25% of GNP. Earlier, Fischer and Modigliani (1978, p. 814, fn. 3) thought that every one percent of inflation costs about 0.06% in output so that 10% inflation would yield 0.6% of GNP. By way of comparison, Howitt (1990) calculated the cost for Canada in 1988 to be less than 0.1% of GNP,when short-term interest rates were 9%.

In situations of hyperinflation the costs can be quite alarming, even if they are difficult to quantify. In a series of articles *The Wall Street Journal* described in detail some of the activities that were elicited by the existence of 50,000% inflation in early 1985 in Bolivia. Nevertheless, with "mild" inflation as experienced by the United States during the postwar period, people continue to use money as a medium of exchange and the shoe-leather costs of inflation remained acceptably low.

Next we turn to an evaluation of the welfare costs of inflation

---

[1] Fischer and Modigliani (1978) present a catalogue of the real effects of inflation, of which only a few are explored here because estimating some of these costs is virtually impossible.

that come through the tax system. Although tax-reform advocates have stressed the importance of indexing the tax system to eliminate distortionary effects of inflation, the Tax Reform Act of 1986 did not implement across-the-board indexation. As a result, there is at least the possibility that the existence of inflation changes the marginal tax rate faced by individuals or corporations and alters their decisions. That is particularly true for capital income, which is taxed on a nominal basis and therefore includes purely inflationary gains. Halperin and Steuerle (1988) estimate that average inflationary gains in net worth were 16.1% of NNP for the period 1948-85. They argue that, "If [this] era portends likely future changes in the value of individual net worth, a tax on nominal ... income would expand the tax base far beyond economic income and result in a large increase in the tax rate on capital." (p. 351). However, they find many hidden forms of indexation, which they summarize as follows:

> ... almost all forms of capital income receive some form of special treatment or ad hoc indexing under current law. The realization principle prevents current taxation of many capital gains, while various exclusions and deferrals prevent much tax from being imposed on the inflationary component of capital income. The major exception is interest income, but there taxable interest receipts are more than matched by the deduction of interest payments, so that net taxes on private interest income are actually negative. The other exception is short-term capital gains, which benefit neither from significant deferral nor from any form of exclusion at death. Most inflationary returns, however, are not received as either taxable interest receipts or taxable short-term capital gains (p. 356).

Although Halperin and Steuerle then propose better methods of indexation they do not calculate the losses from the present *ad hoc* system. The implication is that these costs are not high. In fact, it would be surprising if they were. Congress is under constant pressure to provide tax relief to various "disadvantaged" groups. While it is difficult to predict to which requests Congress succumbs, it would be impossible to argue that legislators intended deliberately to put inflationary distortions into the tax system; therefore, requests for relief from specific inflationary effects are likely to meet with approval as they arise, leading to the piece-meal system now in place.

The previous discussion was concerned with the costs of predictable, steady-state inflation. Now, we must ask: How predictable was the inflation rate during this period? If we assume that the inflation rate evolves according to a simple second-order autoregressive equation:

$$\pi = \beta_0 + \beta_1 \pi_{-1} + \beta_2 \pi_{-2} + \epsilon, \tag{2.1}$$

and then let the predicted inflation rate, π^e be a one-period-ahead forecast from the just-estimated equation, we can use the technique of "rolling regressions" to estimate the appropriate parameters and not rely on any information unavailable at the time that the prediction is made. The first regression was run for 1949-52 and the first prediction was made for 1953; then the second regression covered the years 1949-53 to make a prediction for 1954, and so on. For the period 1953-90, the predicted value of π had a mean value of 3.78% with a standard deviation of 1.77% while actual π had a mean of 4.44% and a standard deviation of 2.52%. The root mean square error of prediction was 1.82%. The largest positive error was 4.57% in 1974 and the largest negative error was −2.13% in 1982. Of the 38 observations for $(\pi - \pi^e)$, 16 were negative or 42% of the total. An even more simple expectations process that involves no resource use at all stipulates $\pi^e = \pi_{-1}$. The mean value of the error of prediction is only 0.068%. The largest positive error is 2.6% in 1974 and the largest negative error is −3.4% in 1976. The root mean squared error is even smaller at 1.30%.

These prediction errors, although relatively small, lead to winners and losers from inflation. When inflation is unpredictably high, workers will lose purchasing power from their wage income while firms gain from lower real wages; also previously unemployed workers may now find a job. Furthermore, debtors gain from underpredicted inflation if interest rates are also lower; by the same token, creditors lose under these conditions. For the economy as a whole many of these effects cancel out at any point in time and they probably also cancel out over time as periods of overprediction are followed by periods of underprediction.

While there are admitted costs of tolerating inflation, there are also costs attached to the process of disinflation in terms of lost output or employment. This was particularly evident during the recession of 1982 which was largely the result of tight monetary policy imposed to bring down the rate of inflation inherited from the 1979 oil-price shock.

To assess the output costs of disinflation we need an aggregate-supply curve of the following form:

$$\pi - \pi^e = \alpha(y - y^*) + e, \qquad (2.2)$$

where π and $\pi^e = \pi_{-1}$ have been defined and measured previously, while $(y - y^*)$ is the output gap measured as the percentage deviation of actual real GNP from potential output. Equation (2.2) was estimated for the period 1953-90 and using the output gap plotted in Chart 2-2. The results are as follows:

$$\pi - \pi_{-1} = 0.225 \ (y - y^*) \quad \bar{R}^2 = 0.30,$$
$$(.065)$$

where the bracketed term is the standard error.[2] This implies that if inflation were reduced by 1% while predicted inflation remained at its previous value, a negative output gap would appear equal to 4.44% which in 1982 would have amounted to \$141 billion. Since the relationship between $(\pi - \pi^e)$ and the output gap is linear, the output gap would be 4.44 times the reduction in inflation. Therefore, a fairly flat *AS* curve imposes quite large costs of disinflation.

Nevertheless, such costs could be avoided altogether, if the counterinflationary policy also influenced expectations directly. Thus a pre-announced and credible policy that aimed to reduce inflation by a stated amount, could lower π and π^e equally, leaving the output gap unchanged. The difficulty in making such a policy credible can be seen by imagining the effect of the announced policy not actually being implemented. Then π^e falls but π does not and workers will have been "tricked" into a reduction in the real wage, which they can avoid by not accepting the promise of disinflation until it actually materializes.

2.1.2   Output Performance

At this point in the discussion the emphasis shifts to an overview

---

[2] Other diagnostic tests are: test for first-order serial correlation of the residuals, using the test equation (48) in Pindyck and Rubinfeld (1991), produced $t = -0.640$; Chow test for structural break between 1974 and 1975, $F = 0.850$. The unconstrained coefficient on π_{-1} was 1.031 with a standard error of 0.40.

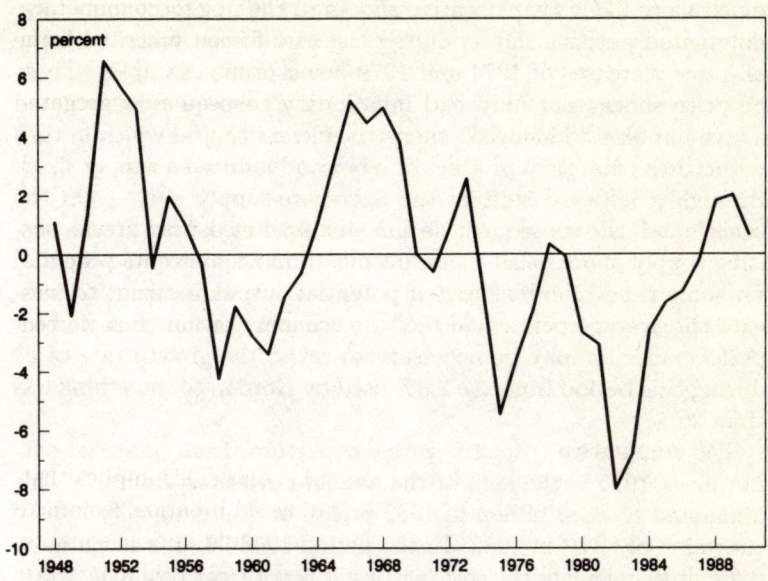

Chart 2-2. The U.S. output gap, 1948-90.
Sources: *ERP*, 1991 and Gordon (1990).

of the output gap for the years 1948-90. Potential output has been measured by the time series provided by Gordon (1990). Other estimates of potential output also exist, such as those computed by Adams and Coe (1989), but they tend to cover shorter time periods. Since Gordon's data end with 1988, his assumed growth rate of 2.3% for 1987-88 has been extended to 1989-90. Both real GNP and potential output are measured in billions of 1982 dollars.

Chart 2-2 shows the output gap for 1948-90. The mean value of $(y - y^*)$ for this period was -0.07%, with a standard deviation of 3.29%; the largest positive value was 6.57% in 1951 and the largest negative value was -8.01% in 1982. While the early period indicated some symmetry, since 1975 there have been only four positive values for $(y - y^*)$ and the mean value for 1975-90 has fallen to -2.04% with a standard deviation of 2.90%. It is possible that Gordon's measure of potential output is idiosyncratically optimistic, but the mean value of the output gap obtained by Adams and Coe for 1975-88 is also negative at -2.09%. It is therefore much more likely that negative shocks to the macroeconomy have dominated positive shocks during the past fifteen years, with the oil-price increases of 1974 and 1979 being prime examples. These oil-price shocks not only had inflationary consequences as noted above but also "destroyed" energy-inefficient capital which in turn reduced the marginal product of labor and induced a supply shock through a leftward shift of the aggregate-supply curve. On the other hand, the subsequent decline in oil-prices did not create positive supply shocks that cause output to move above its potential for some time. Nevertheless, if potential output is meant to indicate the average performance of the economy rather than its best performance, it may be necessary to revise the growth rate of y^* during this period from the 2.3% used by Gordon to something less than 2%.

The cumulative cost of negative departures from potential output since 1975 is the sum of the annual deviations from y^*. This amounted to $880 billion in 1982 prices, or approximately 28% of the value of GNP in 1982. In the period 1948-74, it is much more difficult to calculate the cost because it is not clear how to evaluate positive departures from y^*. Is the extra output produced desirable or is it the result of substituting lower-valued goods consumption for higher-valued leisure? It will be argued later in Chapter 3, that there is no sacrifice of leisure but that instead some of those previously unemployed are producing the additional output.

2.2   The Effectiveness of Stabilization Policy

The macroeconomic performance of the U.S. economy in the postwar period must be judged against the stabilization policies that were implemented during this time. Both fiscal and monetary policy instruments will be analyzed. Chart 2-3 shows how federal government fiscal policy has evolved. Gordon's (1990) measure of the full-employment budget surplus in 1982 dollars has been divided by his potential GNP series to obtain a ratio of the surplus or deficit to potential output. Since Gordon's data are not available after 1988, the series for 1989-90 uses a nominal cyclically-adjusted surplus published periodically in the *Survey of Current Business* first divided by the GNP deflator. The output gap from Chart 2-2 is superimposed to see how successful countercyclical fiscal policy has been. If stabilization policy succeeded in stabilizing output

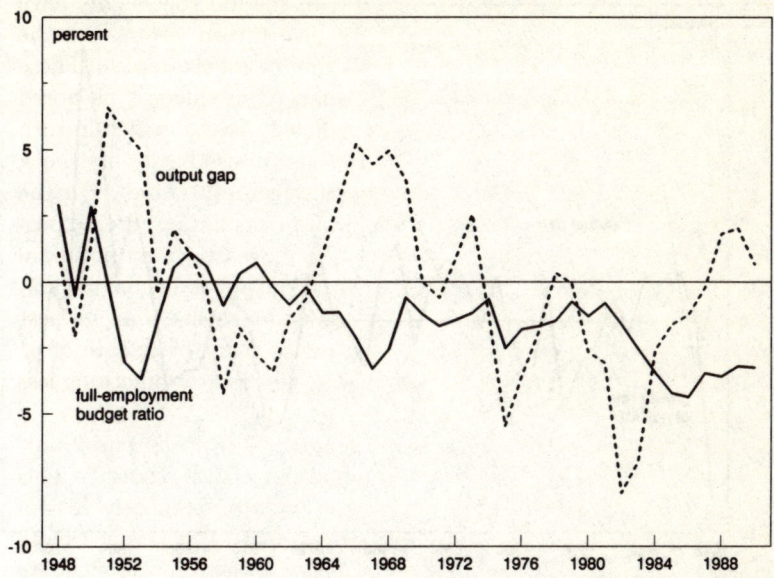

Chart 2-3. The full-employment budget surplus
and the output gap, 1948-90. Sources: Gordon (1990),
Survey of Current Business and Chart 2-2.

completely, one would see very small or no deviations from equilibrium output but possibly substantial variations in the budget surplus ratio to achieve this result. If, on the other hand, both series displayed a fairly smooth path, one would ascribe the stabilization of the macroeconomy to some other cause. Finally, if both series have a lot of variability then stabilization policy was attempted but not successful or fiscal policy was used for some other purpose.

The surplus ratio had a mean value of −1.39% for 1948-90, with a standard deviation of 1.69%. The largest positive value was 2.90% in 1948 and the largest negative value was −4.38% in 1986. There were only seven years of budget surpluses out of the 38 years in that time period and the last one was in 1960. As to timing of budget changes, one would want to see a surplus during periods of a positive output gap and a deficit during negative output gaps. There is a noticeable absence of such a relationship. The simple

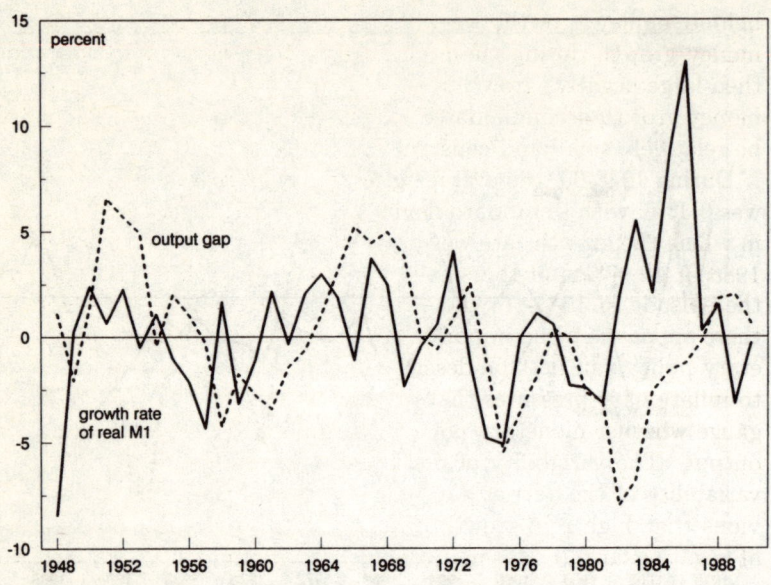

Chart 2-4. The growth rate of real M1 money balances
and the output gap, 1948-90. Sources: *ERP*, 1967, 1991
and Charts 2-1 and 2-2.

correlation between these two variables is −0.03 and if the fiscal-
policy variable is lagged by one year the correlation coefficient is
−0.04. Moreover, during 1953 and again in 1967, we can observe
fairly large positive output gaps but also sizable deficits. Then in
the 1980s, the deficit ratio became larger and totally unrelated to
economic activity. In a sense that has been widely acknowledged,
the federal budget ceased to be a policy instrument and became
an untamed behemoth with a will of its own.

To analyze the contribution of monetary policy to macroeconomic performance,   Chart 2-4 presents the annual percentage
change in real money balances, using M1 as the monetary aggregate since M2 or M3 became available only more recently. By subtracting the inflation rate, as shown in Chart 2-1, from the growth
rate of nominal M1, the resulting time series gives a good indication of whether monetary policy initiated inflationary episodes
or accommodated them. In the former case, since inflation lags

behind money growth, we would observe large increases in real money growth during the preliminary stages of the inflation and then large negative growth rates of real M1. If, on the other hand, money growth accommodated inflation, real money growth should be relatively small and constant.

During 1948-90, the average growth rate of real money balances was 0.35%, with a standard deviation of 3.62%. There are 23 years in which the growth rate was positive; the largest observation is in 1986 at 12.99% and the smallest in 1948 at −8.43%. Except for the episode in 1985-86 where real money grew at 10% or more,[3] there appear to be no important cycles in this time series and monetary policy can best be described as imperfectly accommodating to inflationary pressures that are initiated elsewhere. We can also gauge whether monetary policy contributed to the stabilization of output. The variability of real money growth is greater than the variability of the output gap, but in terms of timing, it is not obvious that high real growth of money takes place during periods of negative output gaps and *vice versa*. The simple correlation between these two variables is again quite low at −0.04. Even if the growth rate of M1 is lagged by one year, the correlation coefficient is now positive at 0.35 which is actually procyclical.[4]

While it is tempting to criticize specific policy errors since the end of World War II, when stabilization policy was put in place, it is more useful to look at the whole period to determine whether fiscal or monetary policies have contributed to smaller or fewer business cycles. The evidence from Charts 2-3 and 2-4 does not show that either monetary or fiscal policy was timely or appropriate. While automatic stabilizers such as the progressive nature of the income-tax system or unemployment-insurance benefits may have played a role in reducing economic fluctuations, it is difficult to find that discretionary budget changes or Federal Reserve policy-making were such as to increase demand for goods and services at times when output was below its potential or to reduce

[3] The blame has been placed on unpredictable movements in the velocity of M1 at that time.

[4] Regressions were run for the period 1948-90 with the growth rate of nominal money as the stochastic variable and π and $(y - y^*)$, both current and lagged, as independent variables. Both constraint-free lags and polynomial-distributed lags were used. The results were uniformly disappointing.

demand that otherwise pushed output above its full-employment level.

Although many neoclassical macroeconomists have been critical of active stabilization policy in the past, what is argued here is that such policies were never systematically used. To see what was possible, given will power and resources, consider the short history of the Civil Works Administration (CWA) during the Great Depression. According to Schlesinger (1959, p. 270), the CWA was an outgrowth of the Public Works Administration from which it received some appropriations. On November 15, 1933, Harry Hopkins, the Administrator of the CWA, announced that on December 15, there would be 4,000,000 persons employed under his jurisdiction. Although the target was not reached until January 1934, the CWA managed 400,000 projects mostly in the area of highways, roads, schools and airports. It was estimated that the cost was nearly a billion dollars, which was approximately 1.8% of GNP in 1933. By the end of 1934, CWA was phased out despite pleas for its continuation from such unlikely sources as Governor Alfred M. Landon of Kansas.[5] Nothing on this scale has been tried since despite the fact that Congress had an apparently much stronger resolution to deal with unemployment after World War II than it did during the Great Depression.

2.3   Legislative Intent for Stabilization Policy

The Employment Act of 1946 is often thought to provide the mandate for active stabilization policy in the United States. Partly in fear of a repeat of the Depression of the 1930s as the process of demobilization and conversion lead to large-scale labor adjustments, Congress committed itself and the Executive Branch to a goal of full employment. It stated, "The Congress hereby declares that it is the continuing policy and responsibility of the Federal Government to use all practicable means ... for the purpose of creating and maintaining ... conditions under which there will be

---

[5] Brown (1956) has often been cited as providing evidence that fiscal policy was not expansionary during the 1930s, but this is based on an aggregation of all levels of government. He writes, "The federal government's fiscal action was more expansionary in the 'thirties than it was in 1929." (p. 866).

afforded useful employment opportunities ... for those able, willing, and seeking to work, and to promote maximum employment,
production, and purchasing power." (U.S. Congress, 1946, Section
2). Also, in the Act the President is required to submit what is
now called the *Economic Report of the President* annually, "...
setting forth [in part] ... (4) a program for carrying out the policy declared in section 2, together with such recommendations for
legislation as he may deem necessary or desirable." (Section 3).

A literal application of the law would require the President to
"act" as long as the unemployment rate is positive, because there
would still be some "seeking work" and because maximum employment and production could be achieved only when everyone in the
labor force has a job. However, nothing in the Act specifies that
the federal government would become the employer of last resort.
In fact, the Employment Act does not deal with stabilization policy or the role of budgetary decisions in that framework, probably
with good reason. From the vantage point of current macrotheory, we know that a policy of zero unemployment would lead to
virtually unlimited deficits, since it is impossible to move the unemployment rate to zero in the face of a positive natural rate of
unemployment. Perhaps Congress understood and circumvented
its predicament by declaring the desirability of "full" employment,
without forcing any actions to achieve this result. In other words,
after the Act was passed in 1946, it was cited frequently in support
of many policy initiatives but scant attention was paid to its strict
requirements.

At the time that President Truman signed the Employment Act
of 1946, Secretary of the Treasury Vinson prepared the following statement for the signing ceremony: "Occasionally, as we pore
through the pages of history, we are struck by the fact that some
incident, little noted at the time, profoundly affects the whole subsequent course of events. I venture the prediction that history,
someday, will so record the enactment of the Employment Act of
1946." (Truman, 1955, Vol. I, p. 494). It was perhaps some powerful foresight that persuaded Truman not to utter those words.

Truman himself never seemed to understand the purpose of the
legislation that he urged Congress to pass. The President noted
that he "... particularly wanted swift action, because the problem
promised to grow as soon as wartime production was curtailed and
demobilization was stepped up." (pp. 491-2). However, before

the Act was even passed, he saw a brighter future, because by January 1946, 52 million people out of a labor force of 53.5 million had jobs. The rationale for the legislation now became: "The real problem was not how to *achieve* full employment. It was how to *maintain* it." (p. 493, italics in the original). He praised the provisions that established the Council of Economic Advisers and a joint congressional committee to study the presidential reports sent to Congress, but he did not indicate how the legislation is to be implemented and how success is to be judged.

Some forty year later, Congress felt the need to amend the Employment Act of 1946 with the Full Employment and Balanced Growth Act of 1978, popularly known as the Humphrey-Hawkins bill. This new legislation was designed: "To translate into practical reality the right of all Americans who are able, willing, and seeking to work to full opportunity for useful paid employment at fair rates of compensation." (U.S. Congress, 1978, preamble). Although Section 2 of the 1946 Act was reiterated, further goals were added: "... increased real income, balanced growth, a balanced Federal budget, adequate productivity growth, proper attention to national priorities, achievement of an improved trade balance, ... and reasonable price stability ..." (Section 102(a)). Despite such vague and incompatible aims, the 1978 Act specified very precise goals for both unemployment and inflation. The unemployment rate for individuals twenty years and older and the inflation rate were both to be reduced to 3% within five years. Because a conflict was possible between these two goals, the former was to have priority over the latter. (Section 104).

Furthermore, the stabilization function of budgetary proposals was strengthened. The new Act required that, "Both the expenditure and revenue elements of the President's Budget shall be developed to promote the purposes, policies, and goals of the Full Employment and Balanced Growth Act of 1978. The size of the President's expenditure and revenue proposals ... shall be determined in a manner which gives consideration to the needs of the economy ... and the relationship between the President's expenditure and revenue proposals shall be guided accordingly." (Section 107).

Finally, not only was fiscal policy to be used to achieve these goals, but also monetary policy was to make a contribution to stabilization. The Act specified that the Board of Governors of the

Federal Reserve System report to Congress annually, "... setting forth ... (2) the objectives and plans of the Board ... with respect to the ranges of growth or diminution of the monetary ... aggregates ... taking account of past and prospective developments in employment, unemployment, production, investment, real income, productivity, international trade and payments, and prices ..." (Section 108).

In an unusual expression of congressional frankness, Section 201 of the Act states: "The Congress recognizes that general economic policies have been unable to achieve the goals set forth in this Act related to full employment ...". Section 202(a) therefore mandates the President to implement specifically "countercyclical employment policies" which include "... accelerated public works, including ... public service employment, ... procurement programs which are targeted on labor surplus areas ...". Presumably to ensure that these programs are geared to their specified purpose and not for pork-barrel projects, a provision that requires the President to use a "... triggering mechanism which will implement the program during a period of rising unemployment and phase out the program when unemployment is appropriately reduced ..." is required in Section 202(b).

Because the objectives that Congress set forth and the specification of the means to achieve them were so clearly stated, this legislation probably elicited greater expectations of success than could in fact be achieved. With respect to the unemployment goal, since 1978 the lowest unemployment rate for males and females over 20 years of age was 4.2% and 4.7%, respectively; therefore, the unemployment target has never been reached. The inflation target, on the other hand, was not reached until 1986 when the "all items CPI" increased by 1.9%. In the five years after 1978, the inflation rate averaged 8.9%. Whatever Congress had in mind for presidential action with respect to the budget and for Federal Reserve action with respect to monetary aggregates, it is quite clear that neither Presidents Reagan and Bush nor Chairmen Volcker and Greenspan have been guiding the policy instruments under their control to achieve the full-employment targets established by the 1978 Act. While we all recognize that such legislation cannot foresee new developments that hinder the attainment of the targets or that compromise is often necessary when goals conflict, it is also patently obvious that the Employment Acts of 1946 and

1978 really had no chance of success. There was then and still is
now insufficient political will power in the executive and legislative
branches of the federal government to make full employment a serious and over-riding concern. Since Congress and the President are
democratically elected, one has to conclude that the public at large
does not want the federal government to put much effort or many
resources into job creation. Nevertheless, in a process that must
involve some self-delusion, voters want governments to "pretend"
that full employment is a national objective and they show their
displeasure to politicians who fail to keep recessions at bay. Stein
(1988, pp. 217-18) comments on the commitment to the explicit
targets of the 1978 Act: "Every informed person knew that the
whole idea — including the 4 percent unemployment — was non-
sense and that the bill could be stomached only on the assumption,
which proved to be correct, that it would be forgotten as soon as
enacted. But no political person ... found the courage to say so."[6]

2.4   Implementation of Stabilization Policy

Herbert Stein, who has watched and participated in many policy
decisions, has a pessimistic view of the process of macroeconomic
policy-making. He writes (1988, p. 24) from an "insider" perspective that, "Much of the history of presidential economics is
the history of trying to cope with the unemployment and inflation problems without recognizing or being able to manage these
relationships. This failure has led to many serious mistakes and
aberrations of policy, from Roosevelt's NRA to Nixon's price and
wage controls."

In terms of contemporary assessments of macroeconomic policy,
the *Economic Report of the President*, especially the *Annual Report of the Council of Economic Advisers* contained therein, has
shown shifting views of what stabilization policy can and should
achieve. Sometimes, unemployment is more important than inflation, sometimes the priorities are reversed; during some periods
policy-making is assertive, during other periods the administration takes a defensive posture. Not only because they are politi-

---

[6] It is noteworthy that President Carter in whose administration the 1978 Act
was passed and who made full employment a cornerstone of his economic
policy, does not even mention the Act in his memoirs, *Keeping Faith*.

cal documents, but also because the most recent problems seemed paramount, these *Economic Reports* have very short-time horizons, placing blame on previous administrations for the economic woes prominent in voters' minds at that time and promising to cure them very soon. Far removed from robust macroeconomic theory, there is no "time-invariant natural rate of unemployment" with a consistent commitment to reach it nor is there an announced "optimal inflation rate" and a uniform pledge to achieve it. Nevertheless, a chronological review of these *Reports* serves a useful function: to indicate the shifting priorities and the current justification for actions taken or not taken.

2.4.1 The Period of a Stable Phillips Curve: 1948-68

In retrospect, the period 1948-68 represented two decades of business cycles that were dominated by demand-side shocks, which had their primary influence on employment and output and only marginal effects on inflation. In other words, the Phillips curve was relatively flat and stable. In that environment one would expect stabilization policy to find the "optimal" point on that Phillips curve and to use monetary and fiscal policies to reach it. While this optimal point may differ from one administration to another, we should still be able to observe consistency in the application of these policies. Instead, there are very few announced targets, relatively erratic swings in priorities and no admissions of failure to achieve the goals established by the Employment Act of 1946. Before making a critical assessment of the period as a whole it is useful to provide a year-by-year chronology of the most important statements concerning stabilization policy in the annual *Economic Report of the President.*[7]

The Truman Administration

In the early postwar period, the emphasis was on avoiding the

---

[7] Hereafter, references to the *Economic Report of the President* will be to the *Report* or to the acronym *ERP* and the date of publication, which is January or February of the year following the period covered by the *Report*. During the first few years there were two reports published annually, the *Midyear Economic Report* being published in July.

possibility of duplicating the Great Depression. In the July, 1947 *Midyear Report*, President Truman asserted that, "It is of the utmost importance that we be prepared to take prompt action should a downturn in business activity appear imminent." (p. 37). By early 1950, when fears of massive unemployment had passed, there is a weakening of resolve to use aggressive policy measures: "... we do not now believe that current and proposed Government programs should be expanded above their contemplated rate merely in order to take up the slack in employment. We should instead rely upon the recuperative forces now at work." (1950, p. 104). This also points to the continuing debate about relying on automatic stabilizers against new discretionary initiatives.

In the 1949 *Report*, the relative strength of fiscal policy over monetary policy is enunciated, recognizing that the Fed's main task was to provide orderly markets for the immense federal debt left over from war finance (p. 40). By 1951, economic mobilization for the Korean war was the main topic. However, macroeconomic targets need not be sacrificed. The build-up of inflationary pressures resulting from large increases in defense expenditures was to be countered not only by temporary price controls but also by tax increases. In the July 1951 *ERP*, President Truman stated: "There is no more important single measure for combatting inflation, under present circumstances, than the maintenance of a balanced budget. The substantial increases in taxes adopted by the Congress since the Korean outbreak have helped to stabilize the economy and aided in halting the price rise." (p. 14). Again, in the July, 1952 *ERP*, the President is urging a tax increase: "There should be no need at this late date to discuss again the superiority of taxation over borrowing as a means of distributing the financial cost of the defense program." (p. 93). Later, the political will-power to raise taxes during the Vietnam conflict was much weaker, as we shall see.

The January 1952 *ERP* sees the first of many misunderstandings about the nature of inflation and its causes. During 1951, the labor market exhibited very low unemployment and the inflation rate was high by historical standards. The policy choice should have been simple: contraction of aggregate demand would, if implemented in time, reduce the inflation rate by allowing the unemployment rate to increase. Instead there is a general ambivalence about policy changes because their net effect cannot be estimated. For example, "Wage advances means higher costs of production, and higher costs of production are a powerful force in raising prices. Wage increases also expand consumer buying power ..." (p. 140). We now recognize that the wage rate has its effects on the supply-side of the economy and that predictions of consumption demand should rely on total disposable income rather than on the functional division of that income. The same argument is made about the supply and demand effects of monetary policy: "General credit policy ... is designed to dampen business investment generally, and thereby to stabilize prices. But the increase in interest rates ... is an increase in the cost of capital, and this involves an increase in costs of production and may tend to press prices upward." (p. 140). This seemingly unchallenged ability to raise prices even if demand is falling was often ascribed to a lack of competitive behavior in goods and labor markets. Later, as we shall see, a number of Presidents tried to use their persuasive powers to moderate or rescind bell-weather price increases in non-competitive industries. This moralistic approach to the problem of inflation obscured the role that stabilization policy has in the inflationary process, but fortunately inflation rarely became a serious intrusion on the macroeconomic performance of the first two postwar decades.

In his last *Report* in 1953, President Truman makes a retrospective assessment of the Employment Act of 1946 and the performance of his administration under it. Not surprisingly he is pleased with the result. "I submit that in no previous period have the economic programs of Government shown so high a degree of internal consistency, or so clear a relationship to the needs of the over-all economy." (p. 11). He is particularly proud of the tax increases legislated to pay for the Korean war. But nowhere is there an attempt at a quantitative evaluation of how these policies have reduced the variations in employment or in the inflation rate. Success is measured merely by avoidance of another Great Depression. Nevertheless, he restates his commitment to countercyclical fiscal policy: "Since public spending diverts resources from private use, except in times of depression, the burden of this diversion is borne by the people whether or not taxes are imposed. But taxation serves to impose the burden more equitably, and in a manner least detrimental to the whole economy ... If a substantial part of our productive resources were lying idle because private enterprise could not utilize them, it would do good rather than harm to utilize them through public action even though this occasioned some deficit." (p. 19). One member of the Council of Economic Advisers, John D. Clark, wrote a strange, dissenting note: "Many fluctuations will develop within our free, erratic economy during the next 3 years, but I am not able to see changes in business conditions which would bring about a recessionary trend threatening enough to require new counterdeflationary action by Government." (p. 102). He may have been the first non-interventionist, neoclassical macroeconomist in a policy-making role.

The Eisenhower Administration

In his first *Report* of 1954, President Eisenhower committed his administration to the goals of the Employment Act of 1946, but stressed that monetary policy was more flexible than fiscal policy and that if there were to be changes in expenditures or taxes, they would have to be implemented on the basis of predictions of future developments (p. 52 and pp. 111-14). He also wanted to rely more heavily on the built-in stabilizers derived from the income-tax system (p. 81).

The reluctance to engage in "pump-priming" is accentuated in the 1954 recession. The *Report* for 1955 says, "Instead of ... initiating new spending programs, the basic policy of the Government in dealing with the contraction was to take actions that created confidence in the future and stimulated business firms, consumers and States and localities to increase their expenditures." (p. v). In 1956, this more passive role is explained: "... soundly conceived and well-timed governmental policies, aided by private stabilizing influences, can prevent a minor contraction from turning into a spiraling depression; ... neither direct controls over prices and wages, nor huge public spending programs, are needed to achieve a reasonably stable prosperity." (p. 11). Although the 1958 recession was more severe than previous postwar downturns, the 1959 *ERP* discusses the virtues of automatic stabilizers. "In many respects, the most important lesson taught by the recent recession is that a competitive economic system has remarkable power to resist contractive pressures and, without an extended interruption of growth, to stage a good recovery." (pp. 1-2). He continues by stating that part of the credit for this goes to "the Federal-State unemployment insurance system ... and our system of graduated personal income taxes ..." (p. 2).

Furthermore, Eisenhower was afraid that lags in the implementation of expenditure and tax changes would in fact create more instability than it cured. He stated in the 1959 *ERP*, "Though a useful contribution can be made by the acceleration of public works projects that are already under way or are ready to be started, little reliance can be placed on large undertakings which, however useful they may be in the longer term, can be put into operation only after an extended interval of planning." (p. 2). On the other hand, "... monetary and credit policy, used vigorously, can produce prompt and significantly helpful results." (p. 2). This statement was made in advance of Friedman's (1969, pp. 249-50) admonition that monetary policy has long and variable lags.

The reluctance to commit to an activist fiscal policy is justified on a number of grounds. The 1957 *ERP* states, "... this experience [the recent boom] suggests that fiscal and monetary policies must be supported by appropriate private policies to assure ... a high level of economic activity ..." (p. 44). These private policies are not spelled out but imply strong self-equilibrating forces. The 1960 *Report* takes an even more laissez-faire approach: the role of government is to enhance the functioning of competitive markets, provision of a stable currency and "the moderation of fluctuations in employment and output," (p. 5) rather than the elimination of these fluctuations.

The 1956 *ERP* also contains a prescient remark: "Governmental measures of monetary and fiscal restraint are not as readily accepted as measures of economic stimulation." (p. 43). This lack of symmetry between responses to booms and recessions later lead to spiraling budgetary deficits that not even the Gramm-Rudman-Hollings legislation could overcome. It also helps to explain the more cautious use of countercyclical fiscal policy than under Truman because Eisenhower was wary of stimulating the economy in a recession, realizing that it is difficult to reverse course later. In his last *Report* of 1961, President Eisenhower assesses the operation of the Employment Act of 1946. He noted that the framers of the Act, "... wisely omitted ... any requirements that economic goals be publicly stated as fixed quantitative targets, ... [because] such a requirement could invite broad, irreversible intervention by the Federal Government if the projected targets are not reached."

(p. 47). Although "... experience has proved the Employment Act to be a helpful instrument for achieving important common economic goals ..." (p. 55), he recommended an amendment "to make reasonable price stability an explicit goal of national economic policy ..." (p. 67). Overall, one is left with the strong impression that the Eisenhower administration did not make a literal interpretation of its responsibilities under the Employment Act and that it was content to rely on automatic stabilizers to deal with business cycles.

Stein (1988, p. 87) applauds the "... fiscal-monetary policy aimed at economic stabilization, but in a moderate way ... [T]he performance of the economy did not seem to require a more active, ambitious, interventionist policy on the part of the government." Also, Stein notes that the "liberation of monetary policy" (p. 82) from its role of supporting the government debt after the Accord of 1953, allowed the burden of stabilizing the economy to be spread between monetary and fiscal policies. Nevertheless, the idea of a stable *LM* curve which could be manipulated by changes in the money supply was not, at that time, part of the conventional wisdom. Instead, the focus was on the "availability doctrine" which de-emphasized the cost of credit or interest rates as determinants of investment expenditures and emphasized the rationing of the quantity of funds available to borrowers. These views received important backing from the Radcliffe Committee Report in the U.K. (1959, p. 131) and the Commission on Money and Credit in the U.S. (1961, p. 52). It was only later realized that the insensitivity of investment to changes in interest rates was found because the interest rate tended to be relatively constant in the early postwar period. As a result, monetary policy was contrived to be a rationing device, with explicit controls on specific interest rates, variations in reserve requirements, and adjustments in margin requirements for stock transactions as the major policy instruments.

The Kennedy-Johnson Administration

In his initial *Report* of 1962, President Kennedy took the occasion to "re-emphasize [his] dedication to the principles of the Employment Act" (p. 3) and promised to do better than his predecessors. He pointed out that, "In the past fifteen years, the economy has spent a total of seven years regaining previous peaks of industrial production." (p. 4). To be able to react more quickly to a recession he requested legislation that would allow: (1) stand-by power to reduce income taxes temporarily, (2) immediate starts on public-works projects, and (3) strengthening the unemployment insurance system. (p. 4). Moreover, he set a target for unemployment of 4% and for GNP of $600 billion in 1963. Also, by labelling involuntary unemployment as "an economic waste of leaving productive resources idle" (p. 40), the *Report* took to heart the operation of Okun's Law as shown in its Chart 2. In the 1963 *ERP* the cost of unemployment is broadened: "Unemployment is an important index of economic slack and lost output, but it is much more than that. For the unemployed person it is often a damaging affront to human dignity and sometimes a catastrophic blow to family life. Nor is this cost distributed in proportion to ability to bear it." (p. 39).

Furthermore, there was the explicit recognition of the Phillips curve in that "... a serious attempt to push unemployment close to zero would produce a high rate of price inflation." (1962, p. 44). Full employment is defined as "frictional" unemployment and the role of stabilization policy is to eliminate "aggregate-demand" unemployment (pp. 45-6). Choosing a desirable point on the Phillips curve is also discussed: 4% unemployment is mentioned but the accompanying inflation rate is not. A year later, the *ERP* suggests that the *price* Phillips curve is relatively flat: "Although wage pressures undoubtedly would be somewhat stronger at lower rates of unemployment, unit labor costs need not be higher because a considerable improvement in productivity would be the direct consequence of return to higher rates of capacity utilization." (p. 85).

Although the 1963 *Report* admits: "Each of the four postwar recessions — 1948-49, 1953-54, 1957-58, and 1960-61 — has been both short and mild," (p. 67) and credits the automatic stabilizers in place at the time for this success, there is an earlier reference to these stabilizers being "blindly symmetrical in their effects." (1962, p. 71). Hence, Kennedy wanted to speed up expenditure and tax changes in response to business-cycle developments. Although public-works projects would be phased in or out as needed, the major innovation was to be a temporary tax cut in a recession. "An across-the-board variation in the basic individual income tax rate can be a potent stabilization measure." (1962, p. 75). This assessment was made without any awareness that the permanent-

income hypothesis or life-cycle hypothesis of consumption dictated
that a *temporary* increase in disposable income would have virtually no effect on current consumption expenditures. In the 1963
ERP, a marginal propensity to consume of 0.92 − 0.94 is used to
calculate the effect on aggregate demand since, "Additions to after-
tax incomes resulting from tax reductions are likely to be spent in
the same way as other additions to income," (p. 45) even though
the incorporation of these additions to life-time income will involve
an uncertain and subjective evaluation of future tax changes. In
1964 this theme is repeated: "... tax and expenditure policies cannot be adjusted with sufficient speed to cope with the swift changes
in private demand that bring recession or inflation. Greater flexibility would be desirable." (p. 41).

The "full-employment budget surplus" and "fiscal drag" made
their first appearances in the 1962 *ERP* as concepts and problems.
"The full employment surplus rises through time as tax rates and
expenditure programs remain unchanged." (p. 80). Thereafter,
there is an obsession with the need for almost continuous tax cuts
to prevent asymmetrical business cycles, where booms are cut short
by virtually automatic budget surpluses that reduce aggregate demand.

Throughout the Kennedy-Johnson administration there is an additional macroeconomic problem to worry about: large balance-of-
payments deficits. Initially, monetary policy was assigned to deal
with these deficits, as Mundell's (1962, 1963) principle of Effective
Market Classification suggested. Therefore, the influence of monetary policy on inflation is minimized. Instead, inflation is generated
in goods and labor markets because firms and workers are not be-
having competitively. For example, the President announced in
September 1961 that "A rise in steel prices would force price increases in many industries and invite price increases in others."
(*ERP*, 1962, p. 182). Inflation was to be tackled by moral suasion,
even though earlier in the report there is a clear understanding of
the location of the Phillips curve. Perhaps, the "jaw-boning" was
designed to move the Phillips curve downward. Although formal
wage and price controls were to be avoided, wage "norms" were
established which were limited to the rise in productivity growth
and prices would thus remain constant (p. 188).

In the 1963 *Report*, for the first time there is an awareness of the
co-ordination between fiscal and monetary policy needed to achieve

stabilization goals. In discussing the financing of the government deficit, "A more expansionary method of financing is needed when unemployment is substantial and considerable excess capacity is available than under conditions when the economy is closer to its potential. Thus, the 'proper' way of financing a deficit is that which contributes to the goals of increased output, growth, price stability and payments balance." (p. 54). Of these, the first two or three are more important than the last: "Monetary policy as well as debt policy must be coordinated with fiscal policy to secure the objectives of higher employment and growth without inflation." (p. 55). "But monetary and debt management policies are formulated in the context of an open economy, and must continue to aim at external balance as well as domestic expansion." (p. 57). The inconsistency between eliminating a balance-of-payments deficit and stimulating aggregate demand was to be avoided by "Operation Twist" whereby the term-structure of interest rates was to be adjusted to achieve higher short-term rates to attract capital flows and lower long-term rates to generate extra investment expenditures. This can be successful only if future short-term rates are expected to fall from their present level, a situation that cannot be maintained for long. Moreover, monetary policy seems to be overloaded with too many goals and Mundell's principle of Effective Market Classification, enunciated the previous year, has already been abandoned.

In 1965, the "War on Poverty" was in full swing but aggregate-demand policies are still receiving much attention. In discussing the basic thrust of the Kennedy-Johnson approach to stabilization policy the 1965 *ERP* says, "These policies were not laid down in one master plan early in 1961 and then carried out on a predetermined schedule. There have been delays, surprises, and a need to adapt policies to changing events; but policies have had a unified direction and strategy." (p. 61). "The basic task of Federal fiscal policy is to help to provide a total market demand for goods and services that neither exceeds nor falls short of the economy's productive capacity at full employment." (p. 62).

By 1966, the conflict between full employment and price stability is becoming more obvious, but the causes of inflation are still not understood. After asserting that price determination is best explained by individual goods-market performance, "When markets are roughly in balance, the sequence and magnitude of price changes is less predictable." (p. 65). Moreover, President Johnson was still trying to maintain his Great Society programs and simultaneously finance the Vietnam war without major tax increases. His vision involves a much greater involvement of the government in economic affairs. He justifies this as follows: "The nature of that share [of responsibility of the Federal government for the performance of the economy] has been more and more clearly defined over the years ... " (p. 5) and then lists six "main tasks" for economic policy, many of which are in conflict (i.e., full employment and price stability). In the 1967 *ERP* this overambitious program continues: "How can we steer between these dangers [recession and inflation], and — at the same time — supply the needs of national defense, strengthen our overseas payments, relieve the inequities of tight money and high interest rates, maintain the momentum of social progress, and provide the growth of incomes which lets each of us move toward fulfilling his private aspirations? I am confident that we can find such a course ... The tools of economic policy are not perfect; but they are far better understood and accepted ... than ever before." (p. 25). Still, there is a need "to sharpen and improve these policy tools ... so that short-term policy can respond efficiently and flexibly to economic fluctuations ..." (p. 65).

As inflation becomes more pronounced there is a new misunderstanding of the role of monetary policy: "... if monetary policy is used repeatedly and in large doses to restrain inflation, it may be difficult to avoid a long-term upward trend in interest rates." (1967, p. 65). This clearly shows a lack of appreciation for the difference between real and nominal interest rates and the effects of inflation on nominal rates. Temporary tax changes are still thought to be a powerful fiscal instrument to influence aggregate demand. "The very fact that tax rates are less stable than in the past helps to make for a more stable economy. Far from being a source of increased uncertainty — as is sometimes alleged — the flexible and coordinated use of stabilization policies should enable both business firms and individuals to make their economic decisions in a climate of greater confidence." (p. 68). The debate about the role of expectations and the performance of the macroeconomy is still in the future.

In the 1968 *ERP* the usefulness of automatic stabilizers is raised once more. "It is no accident that this most successful period of sustained growth in our economic history has coincided with a new and determined commitment to apply economic policies in active pursuit of the goals of the Employment Act." (p. 62). "The short-comings of our policy record under the Employment Act reflect inaction or inadequate action far more often than excessive or in-appropriate action." (p. 88). Nevertheless, "The limitations of the economist's ability to predict the future argues for prudence in policy decisions ..." (p. 89).

The Phillips curve is no longer stable because "... an accelera-tion of wage and cost increases would provide the impetus to keep the wage-price spiral turning long after the excessive demand had vanished." (1968, p. 83). Also, as more of the stabilization policy role falls on the Federal Reserve, there is also concern that mone-tary policy has unequal effects on the macroeconomy. "As in 1966, the mortgage market and the homebuilding industry would, in all probability, be more seriously restricted than other sectors of the market." (p. 84). To allow fiscal policy to make a contribution to a reduction in aggregate demand, President Johnson wanted a temporary 10% surcharge on income taxes of corporations and in-dividuals, but there is continued worry that the tax increases will be passed through prices. (p. 87). Also, the required symmetry in fiscal policy is given some attention: "Congressional response in the weeks ahead will demonstrate the political feasibility of mak-ing fiscal policy work in the unpleasant task of restraint, as well as in the more welcome task of providing tax cuts and added public programs. The proof that taxes can be raised when necessary will strengthen the ability of the Nation to resume a long-run policy of tax reduction when the defense emergency ends." (p. 87).

Although inflation was now running at 3-4%, there is the stated aim to achieve price stability defined as a 1 to 1.5% increase in consumer prices because, "Such a moderate rate of price increase ... does not represent a significant erosion in the purchasing power of the consumer's dollar." (p. 100). Despite the recognition that the labor market was in excess demand at that time (p. 107), the reduction in inflation was to be accomplished through incomes policy, namely the "Guideposts" introduced in 1962. In the 1969 *Report*, notwithstanding earlier arguments about the virtues of dis-cretionary policy changes, there is the fear that, "Price stability could be restored unwisely by an *overdose* of fiscal and monetary restraint." (p. 10, emphasis added).

In summing up the achievement of the Kennedy-Johnson administration, the 1969 *Report* states, "... during the past 8 years, national policy has been designed not merely to counter cyclical fluctuations but to promote steady expansion of economic activity in pace with productive potential. While fiscal and monetary policies have not always been appropriate to the needs of the day, their general success in fulfilling the lofty promises of the Employment Act is clearly demonstrated ..." (p. 61). Despite the continuing concern about "fiscal drag" and the need to cut taxes (p. 73), there is also the opposite worry that the tax surcharge needed in 1966-67 to bring the boom under control took so long to be enacted (p. 77). There is also some initial discussion of the role of monetary growth targets but dismissed because, "Given the complex role of interest rates in affecting various demand categories and the likely variations in so many other factors, any such simple policy guide could prove to be quite unreliable." (p. 92).

For the first time, the 1969 *ERP* contains a Phillips-curve diagram and associated discussion (p. 95). But instead of choosing an "optimal point" on that Phillips curve and directing policies to achieve it, there is still the belief that both full employment and price stability can be reached by applying microeconomic policies that eliminate frictional unemployment and the forceful application of "voluntary restraints" (pp. 98-121).

Overall Assessment of the Period

If there ever was a period in which stabilization policy could be successful, the first two decades of the postwar era had the best chance. By 1948, the Keynesian model of the macroeconomy should have been understood by the policy makers and its application should have virtually removed business cycles. Inflation, on the other hand, probably could not be eliminated, but an average performance of 2% should have been possible.

The Phillips curve for 1948-68 is shown in Chart 2-5. The horizontal axis shows both excess demand (i.e., to the left of zero) and excess supply by subtracting the natural rate of unemployment, as estimated by Gordon (1993), from the actual rate. The inflation rate on the vertical axis is measured by the percentage change in the GNP deflator. Following the identification of each year in the chart, the plus or minus signs in the parentheses are

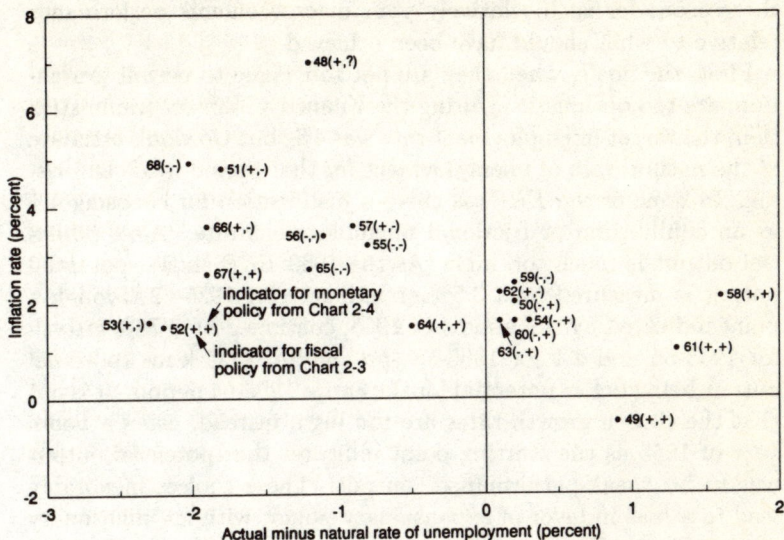

Chart 2-5. The period of a stable Phillips curve, 1948-68.
Sources: *ERP*, 1991, Gordon (1993) and Charts 2-3 and 2-4.

indicators of the fiscal or monetary policy stance that year, taken
from changes compared to the previous year as shown in Charts 2-
3 and 2-4. For example, a decrease in the full-employment budget
surplus is taken to be expansionary fiscal policy. If the Keynesian
prescription had been applied uniformly, one would expect $(+, +)$
to dominate those positions to the right of the chart and $(-, -)$
to the left. That prediction is verified for the "worst" years, such
as 1949, 1958, 1961, and 1968. However, it is also obvious that in
many years both fiscal and monetary policy are inappropriate for
the prevailing conditions or that the two policies are in conflict.
For example, in the 12 years of excess demand in the labor market, there are three years in which both fiscal and monetary policy
are expansionary and there are a further four years in which the
two policy instruments are working against each other. Only 1956,
1965 and 1968 meet the Keynesian criteria. On the excess supply
side, there are five years in which the two policies are in conflict.

On the basis of this evidence and statements in the *Economic
Report of the President*, one can reach some conclusions about

the reasons for such relatively poor macroeconomic performance relative to what should have been achieved.

First, the goals, when they are not too vague to permit evaluation, are too optimistic. During the Kennedy-Johnson administration, the target unemployment rate was 4%, but Gordon's estimate of the natural rate of unemployment for that period is 5% and rising. In none of the *ERP*s is there a justification for choosing 4% as an equilibrium or frictional unemployment rate. Also, potential output is much too high. As the 1969 *ERP* shows, potential output is measured by a 3.5% growth rate for 1955-62 through a point indicated by the middle of 1955, continued by 3.75% growth for 1963-65 and 4% for 1966-68 (pp. 64-5). This leads to actual output being below potential for the entire 1956-64 period. It is not that the chosen growth rates are too high; instead, using a boom year of 1955 as the starting point indicates that potential output was to be "peak-performance" output. These choices inexorably lead to a bias in favor of expansionary policy, with its inflationary consequences. This crucial error is especially noticeable for fiscal policy which is too strong in its stimulus in 1964, 1966 and 1967, when excess demand already prevailed.

Second, the debate about the adequacy of automatic stabilizers is never resolved. There is the possibility of a generalization that Democrats thought them to be inadequate while Republicans placed heavy reliance on them. But even within a particular administration there are inconsistencies, as the quotes from the various *ERP*s above indicate. In any case, there seems to be no clear evidence that one party or the other had a better system. Both Democratic and Republican administrations had periods in which the labor market was badly out of equilibrium and neither party made a consistent effort either to strengthen these stabilizers or to get rid of them entirely and rely only on discretionary action, let alone to devise some optimal combination of the two.

Third, it is easy to criticize with the benefit of hindsight, but in many cases the theoretical analysis of an issue is incorrect even by contemporary standards. A simple *IS-LM* model of the macroeconomy with a properly chosen level of potential output would have been a sensible apparatus to employ throughout the period, but such a model never makes an appearance. Alternatively, because the *IS-LM* model does not determine inflation, a Phillips-curve approach would have been useful, but its properties are only infrequently invoked. Instead, one has the impression that the analysis is geared to the conclusions already reached. The temporary tax cuts in the early Kennedy-Johnson years are a case in point. By the early 1960s the Council of Economic Advisers should have been aware of the permanent-income hypothesis of Friedman, whose influential book was published in 1957, and the life-cycle hypothesis of Modigliani-Brumberg-Ando, which received much attention in an 1963 article in the *American Economic Review*. By that time, the difference between a temporary and a permanent tax cut in its effect on current consumption expenditures should have been better understood than seems to be the case. It was not until the 1977 *ERP* (p. 61) that the life-cycle model is acknowledged. Also the inflation process should have had better theoretical grounding. Although there was still considerable debate about the slope of the *LM* curve at that time, the notion that inflation was a monetary phenomenon was not novel and should have received more attention. Expectations of inflation and their role in a macro model were not incorporated into macro analysis at the time and it would be unfair to criticize the lack of early recognition of the problem in 1965 when inflationary pressures began in earnest.

The amazing truth is that the entire 21-year period fits into a robust Phillips curve of the most rudimentary form:

$$\pi = 2.158 - 0.707\,(u - u^*) \quad \bar{R}^2 = 0.23, \ D.W. = 1.77, \atop (0.35) \quad (0.27) \qquad\qquad F = 6.94 \tag{2.3}$$

where u^* is the natural rate of unemployment. Both coefficients are significantly different from zero at the 98% confidence level; there is no evidence of serial correlation or a structural break in the relationship. Thus, the various administrations would have had to tolerate an average inflation rate of about 2% if they kept the labor market in equilibrium and were not able to influence expectations of inflation. In fact, if that outcome were consistently aimed at, policy makers would not need any information, such as the slope of the Phillips curve, that is available only after the fact. The only crucial estimate in this exercise is the value of the natural rate of unemployment and there is no evidence that the Council of Economic Advisers put any effort into obtaining this information, despite its importance in calculating potential output — an exercise carried out annually by the Kennedy-Johnson administration.

2.4.2   The Transition to Higher Inflation: 1969-73

The Nixon Administration

This period covers the four years between the 1964-68 era of excess demand in the labor market which initiated the high-inflation environment and the first of the oil-price shocks in late 1973 which worsened the situation even more. It is entirely within the Nixon administration.

In his first *Economic Report*, President Nixon announced his "Seven Basic Principles" of economic policy, in which price stability seemed to take precedence over full employment. Moreover, he dictated that, "Government must say what it means and mean what it says." (1970, p. 10). To put that dictum into practice the *Report* warns that, " ... we cannot ignore the possibility that joblessness will rise in the period immediately ahead. But we cannot avoid this problem by allowing the current inflation to continue, for that would harden the expectations of inflation and make subsequent policies to curb it more difficult and harsh." (pp. 21-22). Nevertheless, there is still the promise of meeting all goals: "There is no inherent reason why a high employment economy must be an inflationary economy — even a mildly inflationary economy." (p. 71).

Since this was the 25th anniversary of the Employment Act of 1946, the 1971 *Report* tries to compare the performance of the economy before and after the Act. It finds that the average unemployment rate was 4.6% in the preceding 25 years and 4.7% in the 25 years before 1929. It concludes therefore that, "This suggests that we have not appreciably reduced the incidence of small departures from *maximum* employment but that we have reduced the incidence of large departures, which is just what one would expect aggregate economic policy to be able to do." (p. 21, emphasis added). There is also the first hint of the role of inflationary expectations in wage negotiations and contracts: "After so many years of rising prices there was also a strong desire to incorporate in wage increases some protection against cost-of-living increases expected for the future." (p. 61).

The New Economic Policy — flexible exchange rates and a 90-day wage and price freeze — was introduced in 1971. The 1972 *Report* states on several occasions that aggregate-demand policies will be expansionary, but that inflation will be restrained by the controls, as if the aggregate-supply curve could suddenly become horizontal: "The policy of restrained expansion of demand, coupled with ... controls of prices and wages, will finally eradicate the continuing inflationary consequences of the boom that started in mid-1965." (p. 27). "Reduction of the unemployment rate in 1972 is a primary objective of this year's economic policy. It is to this end that the Government is pursuing a highly expansive fiscal policy. And it is in large part to this end that prices and wages are controlled, so that expansion of demand will generate more jobs, not more inflation." (p. 108). However, the *Report* also admits that, "The problems of managing fiscal policy or monetary policy or both have apparently been underestimated. It may well be that more has been promised than can be delivered with existing knowledge and instruments." (p. 112).

In 1973, the *ERP* stated, "The goal of policy in 1971 and 1972 ... was not only to reduce the probable rate of inflation but also to reduce the general fear of continued or rising inflation ... The controls have made a substantial contribution to this." (p. 62). Evidence from interest rates was used to substantiate the claim that expectations of inflation fell (p. 64). The Council of Economic Advisers also suggested that predicted inflation for 1972, based on previous relationships, was higher than actual inflation, indicating that this was proof that the controls had beneficial effects. Although their inflation model is not specified and their estimates are not provided, if we estimate a Phillips curve of the form:

$$\pi = 0.535\,\pi_{-1} - 0.895\,(u - u^*), \quad \bar{R}^2 = 0.08, \atop (0.09) \qquad\qquad (0.30) \qquad\qquad F = 2.91 \tag{2.4}$$

for 1948-71 and use the coefficients to predict inflation for 1972, we obtain $\hat{\pi} = 3.2\%$ against $\pi = 4.7\%$, which is the exact opposite to what was claimed. Of course, $\hat{\pi}$ would have been higher if u^* was assumed to be too low; in fact if

$$\pi = 0.423\,\pi_{-1} + 0.294\,u \quad \bar{R}^2 = 0.02, \atop (0.12) \qquad\qquad (0.11) \qquad F = 1.42 \tag{2.5}$$

is taken as the Phillips curve, $\hat{\pi} = 4.0\%$ for 1972, but this is still lower than actual inflation for the year.

In the 1972 *Report*, a "hypothetical unemployment rate", based on demographic changes since 1956, was estimated to be 4.5% in

1971 (p. 115). Then in the 1973 *ERP*, there was an admission that the target rates for unemployment and output during the 1960s were no longer applicable in the 1970s. The target for the end of 1973 was 4.5% unemployment, without any indication of how such a figure was reached (p. 73). In fact, there is still no recognition of the role of the natural rate: "It is worth repeating that the policy goal is a condition in which persons who want work and seek it realistically on reasonable terms can find employment ... it must seek to eliminate obstacles that prevent willing workers and willing employers from getting together, insofar as these obstacles can be overcome without excessive cost." (p. 74). Subsequently, Stein (1988, p. 150) has written that, "The administration considered a public report to try to alter the conventional notion that 'full employment' was 4 percent unemployment. The idea was discarded on the ground that it would be interpreted as an effort to conceal the true economic condition." Nevertheless, a publicity campaign to justify a 4.5% unemployment rate was not as useful as an internal study that would have established more realistic estimates of the natural rate, which Gordon calculated to be 5.8%. Had this information been available at the time, the whole controls episode may not have been necessary; in retrospect, traditional contractionary aggregate-demand policies were still the best weapon.

The 1974 *Report* acknowledges the crucial event of 1973 as the oil-price rise late that year, but also blames the inflationary pressures on food prices that also rose substantially. Even at this early stage there is some evidence that the oil-price rise was recognized as a supply shock: "The current and prospective oil situation will at the same time raise prices, limit production in some industries, and reduce demand in others." (p. 6). "Looking at it in this way, it seems reasonable to say that the conditions peculiar to 1973 held 'actual potential' below the trend [rate of increase of potential output] ... " (p. 65). To counter the inflationary pressures from the earlier food-price increases, another freeze on prices was implemented for two months between June and August 1973 (p. 96). But the *Report* is fairly critical of the freeze as a method of halting inflation: "There is much *prior* evidence that price and wage controls of the kind tolerated during peacetime in free societies cannot significantly restrain inflation under the supply and demand conditions experienced in 1973." (p. 109, emphasis added).

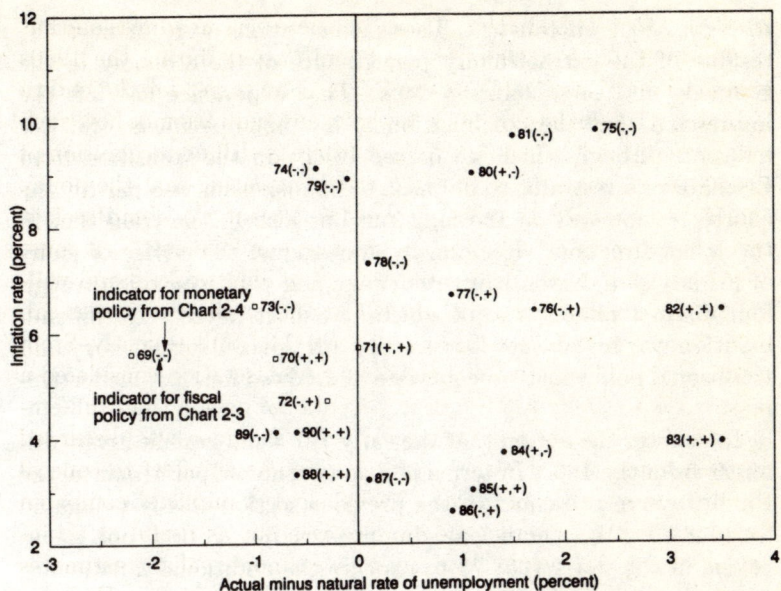

Chart 2-6.   The transition to higher inflation, 1969-73;
the oil-price shocks, 1974-80; and the aftermath, 1981-90.
Sources: *ERP*, 1991, Gordon (1993) and Charts 2-3 and 2-4.

Assessment of the Period

All five years, except for 1971, exhibited excess demand in the
labor market as shown in Chart 2-6, which follows the same format as Chart 2-5. The inflation rate is now substantially higher
than in the 1960s, because aggregate demand has been too strong
continuously since 1964. Sooner or later, inflationary expectations
will try to catch up to actual inflation and even though the period
ended without any improvement in the unemployment rate, the
inflationary pressures were much stronger.

Standard policy requirements in this environment would be contractionary fiscal and monetary actions, but as Chart 2-6 shows,
only 1969 and 1973 fit that mold, with 1971 and 1972 having both
policies expansionary and 1972 having conflicting policy initiatives.

Stein (1988, p. 158) places the Nixon efforts to curb inflation
without creating a recession in a historical context: " ... performance was measured against a set of expectations which, in ret-

rospect, seem unrealistic. These expectations were in part the residue of the extraordinary performance of the economy in the Kennedy and early Johnson days. That experience had left the impression that the combination of low unemployment and low inflation through which we passed briefly in the transition from Eisenhower's restraint to Johnson's expansionism was par for the course — not only in the long run but also in the transition in the other direction." Reluctantly and against the advice of many of his advisers, Nixon instituted wage and price controls through four distinct phases, two of which had short freezes. In the end, inflation was higher, not lower, and both the controls strategy and traditional policy instruments were discredited for their ineffectiveness.

To counter the notion that the early 1970s were qualitatively different from the 1960s in terms of macroeconomic performance, the Phillips curve presented in the previous section was re-estimated for 1948-73 with an additional dummy variable, D, that took values of one in the years 1968-73 to capture the additional inflationary pressures at that time.

$$\pi = 2.183 \ - 0.536\,(u - u^*) + 2.745\,D \quad \bar{R}^2 = 0.52, \ D.W. = 1.81.$$
$$\quad (0.32) \quad (0.24) \qquad\qquad (0.26) \quad F = 14.74$$

$$(2.6)$$

Again, the empirical results are robust. This suggests that during the 1969-73 period, the rate of inflation that would have to be tolerated at equilibrium in the labor market would now be close to 5%, but even that could have been lowered by working on expectations directly, a process that was beginning to be understood.

In conclusion, the structure of the policy environment had not changed even though the Phillips curve had shifted upwards. The policy response was more difficult to implement for political reasons because contractionary policies required to remedy the excess demand in the labor market would have had to be applied more strenuously and for longer, but the inability to pinpoint the natural rate of unemployment made the policy choices more difficult than they needed to be.

2.4.3   The Oil-Price Shocks: 1974-80

Twice during the 1970s the price of crude oil was dramatically raised by OPEC, once in late 1973 and again in 1979. In September

1973, the price of a barrel of imported crude oil was $4.54; a year later it was $12.53 and by 1979 it was well over $20.00. Given their importance in the economy, these price increases spilled over into other energy costs so that the producer price index of fuels and related products rose from 134.3 in 1973 to 208.3 in 1974 and to 408.1 in 1979. The ripple effect on all other prices meant that the all-items CPI rose by 50% between 1973 and 1979. In addition, food shortages around the world, although less dramatic than the cartel-inspired actions of OPEC, had similar effects on overall prices in that time-frame.

Moreover, the oil-price increases "destroyed" energy-inefficient capital and reduced the potential output of the economy until new investments could be made in capital that used energy more efficiently. Alternatively viewed, profit maximization by firms dictates that at current prices of final products, output must fall if a substantial input price has increased and if rising marginal-cost conditions prevail. In the macroeconomy, these were supply-shocks that shifted the aggregate-supply curve upwards, instead of the previous aggregate-demand shocks. Now both inflation and unemployment would rise together, contrary to prior experience which had a trade-off between inflation and unemployment along a fairly stable Phillips curve. To set the stage for an assessment of policy during this critical period, relevant sections from the *Economic Report of the President* for these years will be quoted and analyzed.

The Ford Administration

The 1975 *Report* recognizes the existence of a supply shock: "The story of the past year was one of inflation and recession. Several of the forces that added to the rate of inflation also exerted downward pressure on economic activity." (p. 19). The policy dilemma is also acknowledged by, "... the concern that a too expansionary budget carries the risk of worsening the inflation," (p. 24). As to monetary policy, "... this one-time increase in prices will require additional financing, so as to avoid a contractive effect on the real economy. However, rapid monetary growth would run the risk that inflationary pressures would once again be increased ..." (p. 26).

In the chapter on unemployment, there is a discussion of the Phillips curve, both the short-run version and the long-run vertical line through the natural rate: "Much evidence suggests that in the long run the rate of unemployment is consistent with any fully anticipated rate of inflation." (p. 97). There is then a listing of factors that may have changed the natural rate over time without any quantification of their effects (pp. 96-7). There is also criticism of trying to find the "optimal point" on the Phillips curve because of the recent instability of the trade-off, without finding the natural rate that would provide a stable inflation rate (p. 137). The 1976 *Report* mentions full employment output, "... a condition which is estimated to move the unemployment rate below 5% by the end of the decade." (p. 42). By that time, Gordon's estimate of the natural rate was 5.9%. Another chapter on inflation finally recognizes the monetary aspects of the phenomenon: "Rapid and sustained inflation requires a continual increase in the supply of money." (1975, p. 131). Hence target growth rates of various monetary aggregates begin to receive attention (p. 132). The following year, however, there is already some worry that M1, the preferred aggregate till then, has shown some unstable velocity. (1976, pp. 37-8)

With a recovery underway, the 1976 *Report* warns of the dangers of trying to overstimulate the economy and once more suggests that lags in the implementation of discretionary policy make such changes possibly procyclical. It recommends a "... steadier course in macroeconomic policy ... broadly consistent with sustainable long-term noninflationary growth," (p. 21) without specifying what that growth rate might be.

There is a *post mortem* on the effects of supply shocks and possible responses: "When such external shocks as the rise in international oil prices or other cost push factors increase the rate of inflation, Government authorities are faced with a painful dilemma. If they do not accommodate cost push factors ... then real output will fall and unemployment will increase to the extent that other prices resist downward pressure. On the other hand, if these shocks are accommodated, forces may be set in motion which perpetuate or even increase the inflation rate." (p. 31).

In the 1977 *ERP*, there is finally an awareness that temporary tax cuts do not stimulate demand by consumers (p. 26). By aiming policy toward steady expansion there is less risk of overstimulus especially since, "There is also some uncertainty about the unemployment rate that should be used to represent a constant degree of tightness in the labor market at full employment either now or in the future." (p. 31). The *Report* then discusses the factors that have changed the natural rate from the earlier 4% to the current 4.9%, one whole percentage point lower than Gordon's subsequent calculation (p. 51). Moreover, the Council of Economic Advisers revised downward the previous estimates of potential output (p. 54), but that number is still too optimistic as can be seen by the fact that between 1969 and 1976 only one observation, 1973, has a small negative output gap. By using a constant growth rate for potential output of 3.6% for 1962-76 (p. 53), no attempt is made to allow the oil-price increases to have even temporary effects on the economy's ability to produce goods and services at equilibrium.

Because of room for error in these new estimates, the Council of Economic Advisers cautions against aggressive policies in the coming years. "Policy makers ... should watch closely for signs of accelerating wage inflation when the overall unemployment rate falls to about $5\frac{1}{2}$ percent." (p. 56). There is then a whole chapter enumerating "Policies to Increase Supply," mostly microeconomic in nature. "Reduction of the implicit subsidies currently built into the unemployment compensation system would lead to a more efficient utilization of labor resources." (p. 139). "A substantial body of research suggests that minimum wage legislation tends to diminish employment opportunities for teenagers, but does not have a significant net effect on adult employment." (p. 141). "Thus far, training programs for adults with employment difficulties have not shown to have more than very limited benefits and they have incurred substantial costs." (p. 146).

The Carter Administration

In his first *ERP* in 1978, President Carter was heartened by the continuing recovery. However, there was renewed worry that monetary policy will be ineffective because of unpredictable changes in the velocity of M1. The *Report* acknowledges "The principal cause [of the rise in velocity] appears to be changes in cash management techniques of businesses and individuals" (p. 63) through NOW accounts and overnight repurchase agreements.

The Carter administration approved of the revised estimates of potential output and the natural rate of unemployment of the previous year. It then predicted that actual output will finally reach potential in 1981 after seven years of above-average growth follow-

Table 2-1. *Projected Unemployment and Inflation Rates in* Economic Report of the President *for 1979-81* [†]

Year of ERP	1979	1980	1981	1982	1983	1984	1985	1986
	unemployment rate, percent							
1979	6.2	6.2	5.4	4.6	4.0			
1980		7.5	7.3	6.5	5.6	4.8	4.0	
1981			7.7	7.4	7.0	6.6	6.2	5.9
actual[*]	5.8	7.0	7.5	9.5	9.5	7.4	7.1	6.9
	inflation rate (CPI), percent							
1979	7.5	6.4	5.2	4.1	3.0			
1980		10.7	8.7	7.9	7.2	6.5	5.8	
1981			12.6	9.6	8.2	7.5	6.7	6.0
actual[#]	11.3	13.5	10.3	6.2	3.2	4.3	3.6	1.9

[†] Source: 1979, Table 22; 1980, Table 19; 1981, Table 26.   [*] From 1991 *ERP*, Table B-39.   [#] From 1991 *ERP*, Table B-62.

ing the first oil-price shock in 1974 (1978, Chart 3, p. 85). This estimate supports the contention that potential output is still being considered to be "high-performance output" which can be reached only after a long period of expansion.

During this year, the Full Employment and Balanced Growth Act of 1978 was passed and the 1978 *Report* thinks that it is a useful amendment to the original Act of 1946: "... the economy has changed in many respects since 1946; the task of making economic policy has become more complex; and the standards for acceptable economic performance have been raised." (p. 93). It does not discuss what programs will be necessary to reach the goal of 4% unemployment by 1983, stated in the Act, but it does see a possible inconsistency: "A 4-percent rate of unemployment in 1983 is a very ambitious objective, for it would imply that actual GNP would exceed our present estimates of potential GNP." (p. 95).

In 1979, as required by the new Act, the President must stipu-late goals for unemployment and inflation rates for the next five years. By 1983, the unemployment rate is to fall to 4% and the inflation rate (CPI) will be 3% (1979, Table 22, p. 109). "By any criterion these are ambitious goals. Achieving all of them simultaneously would demand not only a performance by the American economy that is unprecedented in peacetime history, but also government programs that can deal effectively with some of our most intransigent problems, particularly inflation and structural unemployment ... The likelihood of achieving rapid and sustained economic growth while inflation remains high is very small." (p. 110). The policy decisions needed to achieve this herculean task are not provided: "The course of economic policies that would ensure sufficient aggregate demand growth ... and still avoid excess demand that would interfere with the unwinding of inflation can only be described in very general terms." (p. 111). Beyond predicting that the Federal budget will move into surplus by 1982, there is a recognition that aggregate-demand policies alone cannot simultaneously reduce inflation and unemployment. To influence both variables requires a shift downward of the aggregate-supply curve. This is to be done by voluntary guidelines on wage and price increases that are supposed to reduce inflationary expectations: "... the anti-inflation program announced by the President on October 24 is based on the premise that braking the momentum of inflation will require widespread compliance by business and labor in reducing the rate of private price and wage increases." (p. 117). "Measures to address the structural sources of unemployment have been an ingredient of government economic policies for more than a decade, but differential unemployment ratios among groups in the labor force are greater today than they were 10 years ago. Unless these differentials can be reduced, the prospects are dim for making substantial further reductions in the unemployment rate without creating additional inflationary pressures." (p. 118). Despite such pessimistic results, the Carter administration plans to try four new strategies: (1) public service jobs designated for those who are structurally unemployed, (2) welfare reform, (3) youth employment programs, and (4) employment subsidies (pp. 120-1).

In the 1980 *ERP* President Carter had to deal with the second oil-price shock, which is now characterized as follows: "Oil price increases affect the broad performance of the economy in two principal ways. First, the overall price level is raised because of the higher prices of petroleum products and the higher costs of products incorporating petroleum. Second, income is transferred from users of petroleum to foreign and domestic producers and also to the government through increased tax collections." (p. 64).

This suggests a combined aggregate-demand and aggregate-supply shock.

It is interesting to compare the five-year projections for unemployment and inflation in a number of *ERP*s as the realization sinks in that the Humphrey-Hawkins goals are too ambitious. Table 2-1 summarizes this information. As the goals become more unrealistic there is a reluctance to abandon them; it is more acceptable to postpone them. "The target for achieving 3 percent inflation has been postponed until 3 years beyond [i.e., to 1985]." (1980, p. 94). "Progress toward the goals of the Humphrey-Hawkins Act will also require policies that reduce structural unemployment through carefully targetted jobs programs, especially for minorities and youth." (p. 96).

The dilemma for aggregate-demand policies after a supply shock is a nagging worry:

> To suppress even the direct inflationary consequences of an abrupt increase in food or oil prices, fiscal and monetary policy would have to be sufficiently tightened that the reduction in price and wage inflation outside the affected sector would offset the price shock within the sector. But given the relative insensitivity of wages and prices to economic slack, such a policy would lead to unacceptably severe reductions in output and employment. On the other hand, an effort to avoid any loss in output and employment from the supply shock would require supporting aggregate demand to the point where no resistance would be offered to the wage-price spiral triggered by the price shock. Such a policy would raise the underlying rate of inflation, setting back for many years the long-term goal of reducing inflation. A practical alternative would be to accommodate the direct inflationary effects of the shock but, through a combination of monetary and fiscal policies and wage-price guidelines, to seek to stabilize the rate of wage and price inflation elsewhere in the economy ... Such a policy would lead to some temporary loss of output (pp. 103-4).

After this assessment of aggregate-demand policies, the *Report* turns to supply-side remedies, but since these are only imperfectly understood at this time it is not surprising to find only generalities being proposed: "Supply-side policies do not produce quick and dramatic results. They operate slowly and sometimes only after a considerable lag. But unless we successfully pursue them, we cannot achieve the high rates of economic growth, stable prices, and full employment set forth as goals in the Humphrey-Hawkins Act." (p. 105).

The inability to make headway with the anti-inflation fight is the chief source of frustration in President Carter's last *ERP* in 1981. "The most troublesome feature of the inflation of the past 15 years ... has been the fact that after each of the three inflationary episodes the underlying rate of inflation did not fall back to its earlier level." (p. 39). To explain the downward insensitivity of wages and prices, the *Report* argues that, "During the past several decades the vast majority of firms, labor unions, and workers have come to expect that expansionary government policies will be applied sooner or later to reverse recessionary tendencies in the economy." (p. 44). Also, long-term contracts and COLA clauses are blamed. The cost of the anti-inflation battle is high: "... reducing inflation by 1 percentage point would require a sacrifice of $100 billion in lost output (in 1980 prices) and a one-half percentage point rise in the unemployment rate over a period of 3 years." (p. 46). No evidence is cited for these calculations. The issue of policy credibility is then raised:

> Some observers have suggested ... that the government could show its resolve by announcing a target path for nominal GNP or for money supply growth (or both) and by committing itself to pursuing those targets whatever the consequences for unemployment and production ... But simply announcing a set of targets does not guarantee that they will steadfastly be pursued in the face of mounting losses in employment, profits and sales. (pp. 48-9) To the extent that the credibility of government policies can be strengthened, the reduction in inflation will come more quickly and the social costs will be reduced ... But it would be imprudent to expect entrenched expectations to be changed quickly. (p. 50)

To supplement aggregate-demand policies and their effect on expectations, the 1981 *Report* delves into tax-based incomes policies to help slow the rate of inflation (pp. 60-7).

Overall Assessment of the Period

Given the novel experience of supply shocks during the 1970s it is heartening to realize that they were recognized as such almost immediately and that they caused the policy debate to be altered accordingly. Nevertheless, there was still some confusion as late as 1980 about the major effects of the oil-price increases on the macroeconomy. Specifically, it is worth exploring the argument that they influence inflation directly and also reduce aggregate demand by shifting spending power to the government and foreigners. Let equation (2.2) be rewritten as the aggregate-supply curve:

$$\pi = \pi^e + \alpha(y - y^*) + s_\pi, \tag{2.7}$$

where s_π is the supply shock's direct influence on the inflation rate via firms' decisions on mark-ups. Because it is unpredictable, π^e does not incorporate this event. Now, a simple aggregate-demand equation can be written as

$$y = \beta_f g + \beta_m(\mu - \pi) - s_d, \tag{2.8}$$

where g is the fiscal-policy variable or other exogenous expenditures in the economy, $(\mu - \pi)$ represents the growth rate of real money balances, β_f and β_m are fiscal and monetary multipliers and s_d is the effect of the supply shock on aggregate demand. Equations (2.7) and (2.8) can be solved for the two endogenous variables:

$$\pi = \frac{1}{1 + \alpha\beta_m}\left(\alpha\beta_f g + \alpha\beta_m\mu + \pi^e - \alpha s_d - \alpha y^* + s_\pi\right)$$

and

$$y = \frac{1}{1 + \alpha\beta_m}\left(\beta_f g + \beta_m\mu - \beta_m\pi^e - s_d + \alpha\beta_m y^* - \beta_m s_\pi\right).$$

The supply shock makes s_π and s_d positive; however, its influence on the inflation rate is ambiguous, depending on the value of α. If $\alpha > 1$, then the inflation rate would be predicted to fall, instead of rising substantially as it did in 1974-75 and again in 1979-80. It would therefore appear to be more appropriate to capture the oil-price increase as a positive s_π alone or to reinforce it by a temporary reduction in y^*, which would cause π to rise and y to fall.

These determinants of π and y also point to the dilemma for aggregate-demand policies. If the aim is to stabilize the inflation rate, a reduction in g or μ is required (e.g., $d\mu = dy^*/\beta_m -$

$s_\pi/\alpha\beta_m < 0$); on the other hand, an attempt to maintain y at the previous y^* requires expansionary policies (e.g., $d\mu = s_\pi - \alpha dy^* > 0$). Furthermore, if the reduction in y^* is not soon recognized, the policies will be more expansionary than is consistent with long-run equilibrium.

Chart 2-6 shows the policy stance for these years. It is notable that the two years, 1974 and 1979, have virtually the same location and both have contractionary monetary and fiscal policies applied. In both cases, the unemployment and inflation situation gets even worse in subsequent years, but the policy stance is still basically contractionary in 1975 and again in 1980. 1976-78, the years of recovery from the first oil-price increase, have contractionary fiscal policy offset in two of the years by expansionary monetary policy. As a result, there is no clear evidence of the priorities that the government had in the 1970s, but in view of the awkward dilemma faced by the authorities when unemployment and inflation rates are rising, one should not expect a clear choice.

Blinder (1981) was very critical of the emphasis placed on reducing the inflationary effects of the oil-price increases but not on the recessionary effects. His criticism is especially directed to the Federal Reserve in 1974-75. He writes:

> There was ... an economic catastrophe in progress in late 1974 and early 1975, and no reading of the data will lead to the conclusion that the Fed took a vigorous antirecessionary stand. Furthermore, there can be no doubt that a preoccupation with inflation was the reason for this ... Many economists have advanced the view that an appropriate policy response to the oil shock would have been a step increase in the *money stock* large enough to finance the higher oil prices (p. 192).

Blinder, who was one of the first economists to suggest that oil-price increases be treated as supply shocks, does not make clear whether their impact is only through s_π in equation (2.3) or whether y^* was also affected adversely, but his policy advice is consistent with the former only. Given the importance that this issue has in making policy decisions, it remains surprising that the Council of Economic Advisers throughout the 1970s still only had a rudimentary approach to potential output, using constant growth rates through previous peaks as their estimate of this crucial variable.

It is this naiveté more than any other failure that stands out as a lost opportunity to learn about the macroeconomic environment at a time of great stress.

2.4.4   The Return of a Stable Phillips Curve: 1981-90

In retrospect, 1981 was a watershed year; after that, inflation became the primary target and unemployment rates of close to 10% were tolerated to achieve a semblance of stable prices. As Table 2-1 shows, the predictions made in the 1980 and 1981 *ERP*s by the previous administration are much too pessimistic as far as the projected inflation rate is concerned, but too optimistic with regard to the unemployment rate, suggesting that the trade-off combination of the two variables was to be much different now. Nevertheless, by about 1985, the Phillips-curve relationship had re-established itself, as can be seen from the inflation-unemployment combinations for 1985-90 in Chart 2-6.

The Reagan-Bush Administrations

In reviewing the legacy of the past, President Reagan in his first *Report* in 1982, blamed the "... stagflation" of the past 15 years on the "substantial increase in the Federal Government's role in the economy." (p. 21). Only "Part of the decline in U.S. economic performance was clearly attributable to developments ... such as the oil-price increases of the 1970s... Most of the increase in Federal spending over the past 15 years has been in the form of transfer payments, which tend to reduce employment of the poor and of older workers. A combination of increases in some tax rates and inflation raised marginal tax rates on real wages and capital income. The rapid growth in regulatory activity ... has significantly increased production costs." (p. 22). Reliance on fighting inflation was to be placed on monetary policy by producing low rates of growth of monetary aggregates. "Concerns have been expressed that the Federal Reserve's targets for money growth are not compatible with the vigorous upturn in economic activity envisaged later in 1982... We believe that such fears ... are unjustified in light of current policies and the Administration's determination to carry them through." (p. 25). "A critical element in this outlook is the assumption that inflationary expectations will, in fact, continue to recede." (p. 26).

In dealing with the rationale for government intervention in market activity, the *Report* justifies macroeconomic intervention on the basis of risk aversion which means that a steady stream of income is preferable to a stream that has the same expected value but higher variability, but the *Report* also argues that, "... many fluctuations in income which seem to be caused by private sector actions are actually caused by attempts to outguess the government." (p. 35). "The Administration believes that 'fine tuning' of the economy — attempting to offset every fluctuation — is not possible." (p. 36). The administration was trying to obtain needed credibility in its anti-inflation battle by sounding decisive. "The decision to end inflation over a period of several years will be sustained by this Administration, even though short-run costs will be suffered before long-term benefits begin to accrue." (p. 47). The *Report* also criticizes previous administrations for trying to exploit a long-run trade-off between unemployment and inflation and then using wage and price controls when inflation became too high (pp. 48-50). Despite this warning, the temptation to promise a rosy future is too great to resist: "Significant progress toward the interim goals for unemployment and inflation is also anticipated within this period [1982-87]." (p. 214).

In a chapter dealing with unemployment, the 1983 *Report* states that, "Econometric studies of historical data suggest that when unemployment is close to 6 percent, the rate of inflation tends to accelerate" (p. 37), without detailing this econometric evidence nor making reference to the previous estimate of 4.9% used as the natural rate during the later 1970s. It then lists a number of factors that may have contributed to a rising natural rate, including increased wage rigidity, but "The reasons for this change are not well understood." (p. 39). "The preceding analysis suggests that it would be imprudent to use macroeconomic policies to reduce the unemployment rate below its threshold level of 6 to 7 percent." (p. 41).

"The Administration believes that the four-point program it has pursued — reducing the growth of Federal outlays, taxes, regulation, and the money supply — constitutes the best approach for attaining and maintaining the economic goals set forth in the Full Employment and Balanced Growth Act of 1978 ... A major cause of our present economic ills was the inclination in the past to pursue one economic goal single-mindedly, without adequate attention to the longer run consequences for other economic objectives. This Administration remains determined to avoid the errors of past policies." (pp. 143-4). Nevertheless, by 1985, the Reagan administration intended to pursue price stability single-mindedly despite the lessons of the past. In the *ERP* for that year, there is a declaration that, "... accepting some inflation has the great disadvantage of promoting distrust of the government's commitment to maintain control over inflation. As a political matter, an inflation target other than zero is not entirely credible." (p. 48). The goal of price stability and its benefits were outlined a year earlier: "This assumption [about macroeconomic targets for the next five years] reflects the view that the goal of stability of the general price level is appropriate because inflation not only is costly and inequitable in and of itself but is also disruptive of economic growth and employment stability ... [but] such a result will not be 'forced' by deliberate actions to choke off economic growth whenever there is any sign of a rise in inflation." (1984, p. 199)

Since inflation is now the only macroeconomic problem, monetary policy becomes the primary instrument. "The rate of growth of money should be reduced until the rate is consistent with price stability." (1984, p. 24) This assumes a stable *LM* curve, despite recent institutional changes that made velocity unpredictable.

Although fiscal policy is no longer meant to be countercyclical, concern about getting control over budget deficit is a new focus of attention. "Despite the dramatic progress in reducing spending on domestic programs governmental outlays are still projected to equal 23 percent of GNP in 1989, about 3 percentage points higher than in 1970." (1984, p. 31). Most of the fault lies with inadequate planning for future expenditures, especially for entitlement programs. According to the 1984 *Report*, an entitlement program initially does not estimate correctly the number of eligible participants because of "adaptive behavior" nor the cost since providers of the service have an incentive to increase the resources devoted to the program when government covers all the costs. Medicare is offered as an example: it started in 1966 as a minor program, but by 1984 consumed 2% of GNP (p. 27). In the 1985 *Report*, initial estimated cost of medicare was reported to be $2.8 billion and expected to rise to $8.2 billion in 1983; instead it was $57.4 billion in 1983 (p. 129).

The 1985 *ERP* reviews the problems of the 1970s and concludes: "Many observers attributed the rise in inflation in 1973 and again in 1979 to the two oil price shocks. That view is fundamentally incorrect, although it is certainly true that the oil price shocks did provide further upward boosts to inflation in environments that were already marked by substantial inflationary pressures. The pattern of rising inflation was established before both of the oil price shocks. These shocks would have had much less impact on inflation had they occurred in an environment of market confidence in underlying price stability." (p. 49). The evidence for this assertion is mixed: the inflation rate in 1972 was lower than in either 1970 or 1971, but it had been rising through 1976-78; the first shock occurred during excess supply in the labor market, the second during excess demand. The *Report* also produces new arguments for abstaining from countercyclical fiscal policy, pertaining to both tax and expenditure changes: "If taxpayers expect income tax changes to be temporary ... then the tax changes are likely to have relatively little effect on consumption behavior ... A problem with increasing government purchases for countercyclical purposes is that such increases run directly counter to the long-run goal of constraining government expenditure to reduce waste and promote growth. It often proves difficult to reverse spending increases — even those adopted initially as temporary." (p. 58). This theme is reinforced by the 1986 *ERP*: "Several factors contribute to government spending growth. One basic force explaining such growth is that the benefits of individual spending programs are typically concentrated among a relatively small number of beneficiaries whereas the costs of individual programs are widely dispersed among millions of taxpayers. The beneficiaries of government spending programs, including private suppliers of inputs to such spending and government employees who administer such programs, have incentives to support and muster forces for lobbying efforts that may influence the final outcome of the legislation." (pp. 62-3). Nevertheless, "The Gramm-Rudman-Hollings Act provides for a mechanism for reducing spending and the deficit and is designed to produce a balanced budget by 1991 ..." (p. 63).

In approaching the "optimal path" for disinflation, the 1986 *Report* says, "The economic costs — lost jobs and output — associated with reducing inflation occurs [sic] when private behavior that is adapted to an inflationary environment confronts a disinflationary monetary policy." (p. 35). "Credible, pre-announced policies that are consistent with the stated goal of lower inflation can facilitate the downward adjustment of inflation expectations ... A gradual move to disinflationary monetary policy allows time for the public to recognize and believe in the new policy and adjust inflation expectations and behavior accordingly." (p. 36). It then accuses the Federal Reserve of being too drastic in its contractionary stance in 1981 and is forced to admit that monetary targeting is not as simple as textbook presentations of the subject. "Uncertainty about M1 velocity behavior in recent years has made the formulation of monetary policy more difficult ... There is ... no reason to believe that velocity behavior will not return to a reliable pattern ... Moreover, the variables commonly suggested as alternatives to M1 ... have well-known drawbacks as targets for policy." (p. 65). Shortly afterwards M1 is abandoned as a target. In 1987, the *Report* announces, "It appears that inclusion of interest-bearing deposits in M1 has increased [sic] the interest-elasticity of the demand for money."[8] (p. 53). "Until a more reliable relationship between M1 and nominal income growth is reestablished ... the implications of this rapid M1 growth [during 1986] remain uncertain." (p. 55). By 1988, the administration admits that, "... neither a target nor a monitoring range for M1 was announced" (p. 33) because M1 velocity dropped dramatically in 1985-86. "The two most likely explanations ... are deregulation and the sharpest disinflation since the late 1940s." (p. 34). Also, in response to the stock market crash of October 17, 1987, "The Federal Reserve reacted promptly, indicating by word and deed that ample liquidity would be provided to help the financial system and the economy weather the stresses associated with the market break." (p. 43).

This *Report* also returns to developments on the unemployment front: "... further reductions in the unemployment rate can be sustained without the damaging effects of accelerated wage and price inflation." (p. 57). It discusses the causes of frictional unemployment (pp. 80-1) and states, "The factors that have caused frictional unemployment to increase since the early 1970s explain only a fraction of the total increase in unemployment rates since that time ... unemployment rates have risen for all demographic

---

[8] If interest-earning assets are included in a monetary aggregate it becomes *less* interest sensitive.

groups." (p. 81). It then makes the startling argument that the Phillips curve is essentially horizontal: "Recent data provide little evidence of a tradeoff between inflation and unemployment... During this 6-year period [1981-87], the inflation rate has been essentially constant [at about 4%], while the unemployment rate has fallen almost 5 full percentage points — from 10.6 percent at its peak in November 1982 to 5.7 percent in December 1987." (p. 83). There is "... no inherent barrier that prevents the unemployment rate from falling below 5 percent" (p. 84), but no revision to previous estimates of the natural rate is announced at this time.

The 1989 *ERP* takes up once more the theme of discretionary policy changes as stabilization instruments. "Government can make, and has made, two major mistakes in promoting these goals [contained in the Employment Acts of 1946 and 1978]. Policy can be so passive that it is procyclical, exacerbating cyclical downturns. By contrast, policy can be so active that it increases instability and uncertainty." (p. 24). The Great Depression was an example of the first type and the 1970s saw mistakes of the second type, but the *Report* does not say how it will avoid either mistake in the future except to announce: "Desiring not to repeat the failures of short-term discretionary policy in the 1970s, the Administration abandoned discretionary fiscal policy. In its place the Administration has used fiscal policy as a tool for restoring incentives and efficiency, both in the private sector and in the government ... It has encouraged the monetary authorities to pursue the goal of noninflationary growth." (pp. 55-6). "Government expenditure and tax policies are determined through the political process, which inevitably means that attempts to adjust aggregate demand to stabilize the economy are constrained." (p. 74). "Lags between the proposal of a discretionary change in fiscal policy and its enactment vary considerably." (p. 75). "During the postwar period the Federal Reserve System and some administrations have attempted to coordinate monetary and fiscal policies to stabilize the economy. Despite the good intentions of policymakers, sometimes monetary policy has acted to frustrate the goals of discretionary fiscal policy, and the combination of the two policies has destabilized the economy." (pp. 76-7).

Although 1990 is the occasion of President Bush's first *Report* it is a seamless continuation of the Reagan administration's policies and thus his two *ERP*s will be appended here. Bush is also committed to avoiding countercyclical fiscal policy: "... agreement is now widespread on the detrimental effects of a short-sighted discretionary approach to macroeconomic policy ... research and experience have demonstrated the great advantage of establishing credible commitment to a policy plan." (p. 22). Instead of discretionary policy, there is now to be "... systematic policy [which] might be very simple and specific, such as a promise not to raise marginal tax rates or a law that sets a target for the budget deficit for several years into the future ... a systematic policy has significant advantages over a discretionary policy if it places some discipline or general guidelines on future changes in the policy instruments, and if policymakers commit to this discipline." (p. 65). This applies especially to the long-term goal of deficit reduction. "Since the mid-1980s, fiscal policy in the United States has been guided by the Gramm-Rudman-Hollings law, which has served as a fairly systematic rule for budget policy." (p. 66). *When viewed from a broad perspective, GRH has provided valuable control over Federal spending.* To some, the failure to match the targets exactly is an indictment of GRH. But this is a narrow view." (p. 70, italics in original).

Also, monetary targeting has received further setbacks. "Substantial movements in the velocities of the monetary aggregates in recent years has made rigid monetary targeting inappropriate. Given this situation, but recognizing the disadvantages of short-sighted, discretionary policy discussed earlier in this chapter, the Federal Reserve has not regressed to an undisciplined, ad hoc approach to policy." (p. 84). "The Federal Reserve's ability to react flexibly to unforeseen adverse shifts in financial market conditions is especially useful." (p. 85); "... as long as there are no signs of *permanent* shifts of M2 velocity, the Federal Reserve would do well to commit to eventually maintaining *long-run* growth of M2 consistent with expansion of the economy's potential to produce ..." (p. 86, italics in original). But it recognizes that commitment to a policy is not enough. "Credibility probably depends more importantly on a track record of following the stated principles of policy." (p. 88).

Because the economic boom of the late 1980s is continuing without strong inflationary pressures, the *Report* for 1990 is forced to address the slope of the Phillips curve once more. "There is no inconsistency in projecting continued low unemployment and declining rates of inflation. The idea that there is a simple, stable, and permanent tradeoff between inflation and unemployment does not accord with modern macroeconomic theory, which emphasizes the importance of expectations, or with historical experience." (p. 59). But unemployment is also expected to decline, so this is not consistent with movements down a vertical, long-run Phillips curve as inflationary expectations decline. Instead, after discussing features of the U.S. labor market that might have reduced the natural rate of unemployment in recent years the *Report* concludes, "... *the average rate of unemployment in 1989 — 5.3 percent — may not be far above the nonaccelerating inflation rate of unemployment.*" (p. 184, italics in the original). However, no empirical evidence other than that cited is offered to substantiate this claim and no reference is made to the Reagan estimate of the natural rate at 6-7% in 1983. However, Adams and Coe (1989) estimate the natural rate to be about 5.6% for 1989.

In 1990, the American economy was once again hit by an oil-price increase, but it was so temporary that it did not have the same inflationary consequences as the two shocks in the 1970s; nevertheless, the 1991 *Report* is quite worried about such events and devotes a whole chapter to this topic. It asserts that the major effects of oil-price increases is inflation and reduced demand for goods and services, an explanation that was made in the wake of the 1970s episode by Ford and Carter but repudiated later by Reagan. However, it does add "supply effects" to the previous list: "An oil price shock may temporarily reduce the economy's capacity to supply goods and services until producers' plant and equipment and workers' skills realign to higher oil prices." (p. 87). In the face of such shocks, the administration believes that "systematic policies" are still the best option. "Under a systematic policy, money and credit growth rates might change in the wake of an oil price shock or other major disturbances to ameliorate the adverse effects on unemployment and output. Once the price shock has passed through the economy, the policy would readjust monetary and credit policy instruments in a way that would continue to guide the economy toward its longer run goals." (p. 91).

Overall Assessment of the Period

The performance of the U.S. macroeconomy improved from 1981 to 1990, with a consistently falling inflation rate and a substantially, although only temporarily, lower unemployment rate. These features are shown in Chart 2-6. What is also evident, is that predictions for these two variables were not generally more optimistic than events warranted. Table 2-2 continues the reporting of the predictions — or "Administration Assumptions" as they became to be called — required by the Humphrey-Hawkins legislation and is similar in interpretation to Table 2-1. In these nine *Reports*, there are 39 predictions for unemployment and inflation rates: for the former, 26 predictions are higher than the actual rate and for the latter, 22 predictions are larger than actually experienced. Also the "pessimistic" predictions are concentrated: all six estimates for unemployment made in the 1983 *Report* were too low; on the other hand, predictions made in all years for the inflation rate in 1987-90 were consistently too low.

Stein (1988, p. 236) refers to "Reaganomics" as the "economics of joy" in which one of the assertions is that, "There is no necessary connection between inflation and unemployment, even in the short run, and inflation can be reduced without a transitional period of increased unemployment." Supply-side economics was to be the all-encompassing answer. For example, "... people were unemployed because high tax rates made it unprofitable for them to work, or because high welfare benefits made it profitable for them not to work ... This argument, however, mixed up the long-run effects of changing tax rates and benefits, which might be favorable, with the effects of disinflation, which would dominate in the short run." (p. 252). Furthermore, "If people in the private sector believed that the government would really stop the inflation the expectations acquired during previous inflationary period would disappear. Inflation could then be reduced with little or no increase in unemployment ... But few economists believed that after fifteen years in which promises of government had been repeatedly broken a new government could immediately establish complete credibility for a promise to end inflation." (p. 252).

Perhaps credibility was lacking, but inflation and unemployment rates can both decline even if the Phillips curve relationship continues to hold. As long as there is excess supply in the labor market,

Table 2-2. *Projected Unemployment and Inflation Rates in* Economic Report of the President *for 1982-90* [†]

Year of ERP	1982	1983	1984	1985	1986	1987	1988	1989	1990
unemployment rate, percent									
1982	8.9	7.9	7.1	6.4	5.8	5.3			
1983		10.7	9.9	8.9	8.1	7.3	6.5		
1984			7.8	7.6	7.3	6.8	6.1	5.7	
1985				7.0	6.9	6.6	6.3	6.1	5.8
1986					6.7	6.5	6.3	6.1	5.8
1987						6.7	6.3	6.0	5.8
1988							5.8	5.6	5.4
1989								5.2	5.1
1990									5.4
actual*	9.5	9.5	7.4	7.1	6.9	6.1	5.4	5.2	5.4
natural#	7.1	6.9	6.6	6.4	6.4	6.2	6.0	5.6	
inflation rate (CPI), percent									
1982	6.6	5.1	4.7	4.6	4.6	4.4			
1983		4.9	4.6	4.6	4.6	4.5	4.4		
1984			4.4	4.6	4.5	4.2	3.9	3.6	
1985				4.1	4.3	4.2	3.9	3.6	3.3
1986					3.5	4.1	3.7	3.3	2.8
1987						3.0	3.6	3.6	3.2
1988							4.3	4.1	3.6
1989								3.8	3.7
1990									4.1
actual††	6.2	3.2	4.3	3.6	1.9	3.6	4.1	4.8	5.4

[†] Sources: 1982, Table 8-9; 1983, Table 6-10; 1984, Table 6-11; 1985, Table 1-5; 1986, Table 1-7; 1987, Table 1-5; 1988, Table 1-3; 1989, Table 7-3; 1990, Table 2-4. * From 1991 *ERP*, Table B-39. # From Adams and Coe (1989). †† From 1991 *ERP*, Table B-62.

the negative slope of the Phillips curve dictates that the inflation rate will move lower year by year if expectations of future inflation do not counteract this tendency. Moreover, if the natural rate of unemployment is itself falling, then excess supply in the labor market can be maintained even as the actual rate falls. Table 2-2 also reports the natural rate of unemployment calculated by Adams and Coe (1989) for 1982-89, since the Gordon data are constant at 6% for this period. As is obvious, both the natural rate and the actual rate decline, but the former remains below the latter until 1987. After that, the excess demand in the labor market should start to put upward pressure on inflation, a prediction that is borne out by the evidence as the inflation rate hits a low of 1.9% in 1986 and then rises steadily to 5.4% in 1990. Therefore, given the severe recession of 1982 which broke the back of high inflation and the fortuitous reversal of the previous twenty-year rise in the natural rate of unemployment, the Reagan administration was able to project a fairly lengthy period of recovery, without violating the Phillips curve, but not by eliminating it as it claimed. Then, in 1987, the "economics of joy" was once again replaced by the trade-off between lower unemployment and higher inflation, as the labor market shifted from excess supply to excess demand.

For the period 1981-90, Chart 2-6 shows the relevant combinations of the inflation rate and the extent of excess supply or excess demand in the labor market; also fiscal and monetary policy changes are indicated next to each year's observation. Of particular note is the virtually horizontal movement from right to left during 1983-90. However, the policy response to these developments is probably no better than in previous eras. While the expansionary policy stance is quite appropriate for 1983-86, the continuation of these policies in 1988-90 must be criticized. If the administration had seized the opportunity of a reduced need for additional aggregate demand in 1988-90 by curtailing budget deficits, the subsequent response to the 1991 recession might have been more helpful.

2.5   Concluding Remarks

It is difficult to summarize this 43-year period in terms of the macroeconomic performance and policy environment that prevailed in the United States in the postwar period. However, the lengthy presentation of the evidence for both the actual performance of the economy and the legislative and policy intentions in reacting to that performance allows one to reach a mixed and perhaps tentative conclusion: (1) the cyclical pattern of economic activity was mild compared to the 1930s and the shocks that gave rise to the cycles came mostly from the demand side of the economy, except for the two supply shocks in the 1970s; and (2) the policy response to the demand shocks could have been better, even without much benefit from hindsight. The argument for this potential improvement in macroeconomic policy will conclude this chapter. The point of assembling the empirical evidence for 1948-90 in this chapter has been to support the hypothesis that a Phillips curve adequately describes the behavior of inflation and unemployment rates in the postwar period, the two variables of greatest concern to government. Of course, expectations begin to play a role in the later years and "dummy variables" are needed to explain the supply shocks of the 1970s, but it remains true that a negatively-sloped relationship between π and $(u - u^*)$ is robust. However, we know this only in retrospect and must not blame policy makers for believing from time to time that this relationship had changed and required new initiatives such as wage and price controls to deal with novel situations. Instead, the criticism is that policy makers did not attempt to reach the equilibrium position in the labor market indicated by $u = u^*$, which would have meant accepting and tolerating the "core inflation rate" implied by the value of the constant term in the Phillips-curve regression. Specifically, most administrations promised both some amorphous notion of "full employment" *and* lower inflation. Because the Phillips curve was rather flat, policy had an invariably expansionary bias, because the gains in employment were larger than the initial losses from not meeting the inflation goal. But sooner or later, this bias in the policy stance led to higher core inflation with only temporary reductions of u below u^*. Then, at a time when inflation became uncomfortably high, it was given first priority and policy was invariably contractionary even if there was a high unemployment rate.

A simple numerical example will make the point. Let $L = u^2 + \pi^2$ be the loss function experienced by the government. Compared to equation (1.2) in Chapter 1, it is assumed that $\alpha_1 = \alpha_2 = 1$ (i.e., both goals have equal importance) and that $\bar{u} = \bar{\pi} = 0$ as argued above. Also, let the slope of the Phillips curve be -0.7 as estimated in equation (2.3), but any reasonable numerical value would show the same result. The starting point is $u = u^* = 4\%$ and $\pi = 2$; therefore, $L = 20$. Now if the government follows expansionary policy to reduce the unemployment rate to 3%, $\pi = 2 - .7(3 - 4) = 2.7\%$ according to equation (1.1) and $L = 16.3$, which is an improvement, even though the inflation rate is higher. If the government followed contractionary policy by letting the unemployment rate rise to 5%, $\pi = 2 - .7(5 - 4) = 1.3\%$ and $L = 26.7$, which is worse than the starting point. This comparison indicates that expansionary policy is favored from a position of relatively low inflation and equilibrium in the labor market. If, however, the starting point is $u = 6\%$ and $\pi = 10\%$, with $L = 136$ after a supply shock, letting u rise to 7% while $\pi = 10 - .7(7 - 4) = 7.9\%$, allows L to fall to 111.4, but a reduction in u to 5% with $\pi = 10 - .7(5 - 4) = 9.3\%$ would cause L to fall to 111.5. In this situation, there is a slight bias in favor of contractionary policy.

To prevent misunderstanding, it is not being argued that policy could have maintained $u = u^*$ at all times; we must allow policy makers time to recognize the effects of shocks and produce a reasonable response. Instead, the criticism is against wrong-headed policies being applied in years when excess demand or excess supply in the labor market is already evident. The years of labor-market excess demand in which at least one of the two instruments is expansionary includes (from Charts 2-5 and 2-6): 1948, 1951, 1952, 1953, 1957, 1964, 1966, 1967, 1970, 1972, 1988, 1989, and 1990. There are also a number of years with the opposite problem, namely contractionary policies applied when the labor market experiences excess supply: 1950, 1954, 1959, 1960, 1962, 1963, 1975, 1976, 1977, 1978, 1980, 1981, 1984, 1986, and 1987. Therefore, in a total of 26 years, the nature of the problem should have been known, yet the direction of at least one of the two policy instruments was procyclical in these circumstances. Even if we allow for the fact that our measures of the fiscal and monetary stance may be in error some of the time and that even *ex post* calculations of excess demand and supply in the labor market can be mistaken, there are simply too many years in which the policy prescriptions were ill advised and possibly intensified the cyclical nature of the macroeconomy.

The crucial piece of information that was missing in the policy decisions of the postwar era seemed to be the evolution of the natural rate of unemployment. Why did policy makers not have some working estimate of this variable from time to time that might have prevented — or at least minimized — these policy errors? Why did the Council of Economic Advisers not report annually on their evaluation of the factors that might have influenced the natural rate? Although Phelps (1967) and Friedman (1968) introduced this concept halfway through the 1948-90 period, there were earlier notions of "target" unemployment rates that were at least indirectly linked to equilibrium in the labor market. For example, Okun's Law was published in 1962. It had an explicit reference to an equilibrium unemployment rate: "The full employment goal must be understood as striving for maximum production without inflationary pressure; or more precisely, as aiming for a point of balance between more output and greater stability, with appropriate regard for the social valuation of these two objectives" (1970, p. 133). He then argued that 4 percent unemployment represented this equilibrium in the labor market but was careful to note that, "Economists have never developed a clear criterion of tolerable price behavior or any quantitative balancing of conflicting objectives which could be invoked either to support or attack the target of a 4 percent rate." (p. 133). Unfortunately, Okun obscured the directions for future empirical research by suggesting that the value of the natural rate of unemployment was a public-choice problem instead of a labor mismatch problem. In any case, is it likely that this 4-percent target rate was subsequently accepted as a "rule-of-thumb" for policy decisions without further analysis? Is it possible that ignorance of this critical value was the sole cause of mismanagement of macropolicy in the next three decades? It would be implausible to argue that the Council of Economic Advisers did not have the theoretical foundations and the econometric resources to get some reliable estimate of the rate of unemployment that was consistent with equilibrium in the labor market in the 1960s and later. Walter Heller (1967) who was the Chairman of the Council of Economic Advisers during the Kennedy-Johnson administration wrote: "Careful analyses of the statistical record within CEA convinced us that the structural-unemployment thesis was more fancy than fact, since the structural component of unemployment had *not* risen; that the 4-percent unemployment target was not only attainable but should be viewed as an interim target, later to be reset at a lower level (after manpower programs had increased labor skills and mobility); ... the alleged hard core of unemployment lies not at 5 or 6 percent, but even deeper than 4 percent — how deep still remains to be ascertained." (pp. 63-4, emphasis in original). The theoretical argument behind these assertions remains unexceptionable, but the lack of documentation for the quantitative evidence is worrisome.

Instead of blissful ignorance, the explanation is that the Council knew that the natural rate was probably rising, but it was politically unacceptable to admit this publicly, as Stein's previous quotation indicates (see p. 66), concerning the Nixon Council's effort to reveal a rise of only 0.5%. From time to time, there were revisions to the natural rate, but as the evidence from the previous section shows, these are never buttressed by quantitative evaluations and econometric evidence. Also, these revisions are usually announced only as a means of embarrassing previous administrations for earlier inept policy decisions.

Why would a popularly elected government be afraid of stating publicly that in its informed opinion the "achievable" rate of unemployment has risen from 4% to 5% because of demographic or labor-market developments? Given the number of people who have a stake in inflationary developments against the number of people who are affected directly or indirectly by unemployment, the voter trade-off between reducing unemployment and allowing inflation to rise should be very large. However, in a competitive political market place, if one party can promise to lower both unemployment and inflation, it seems impossible for the other party to survive if it makes a less extravagant claim. We do not understand this possible inconsistency between unattainable promises and actual performance, but Chapter 4 will explore in more detail the welfare economics of labor-market developments and will try to predict whether voting majorities can be assembled to favor some particular self-interested outcome.

3

The Market for Labor Services
and the Macroeconomy

It is not an exaggeration to say that interactions between buyers
and sellers in the labor market are more complicated than in either
the goods market or the money market. The reason for this is an
intricate and ill-defined division of property rights to a job. Unlike
a loaf of bread or a dollar bill, where mere possession gives the
owner virtually unlimited rights to dispose of the item in question,
employment gives ambiguous property rights to both the employer
and the employee. The employer does not *own* the individual who
happens to work for the firm, nor does the employee *own* the job
that he happens to have. The principal cause of the inability to
stipulate inviolate property rights to a job is that there is too much
at stake, in the sense that the side holding these rights could abuse
them. For example, if workers received the property rights exclusively, they presumably could not be fired, even if they were incom-
petent, lazy, or both. On the other hand, if firms could pay their
workers whatever they wanted *ex post*, they would have difficulty
keeping their most productive workers, who would prefer to work
for themselves, rather than put up with a capricious employer. As
a result, since these property rights to a job cannot be allocated
on the basis of some uniformly accepted conditions, they must be
negotiated between workers and their employers. These negotiations give rise to fixed costs for both parties and to minimize them
they enter into long-term agreements where these property rights
are allocated. Worker-employer relationships are often included in
contracts, either explicit union agreements that can be enforced in
the courts or implicit "hand-shake" arrangements that are binding
only to the extent that tradition and a sense of "fair play" make
them so. In many instances, contracts represent a sharing of the

property rights in the labor market: workers get a wage rate that is guaranteed for the life of the contract and firms are given the opportunity to adjust unilaterally the hours of work and the number of workers that they employ. When contracts are unalterable for some period of time, it is conceivable that transactions can take place in a state of disequilibrium in the labor market, without at the same time requiring involuntary exchange.

The purpose of this chapter is to review our understanding of labor-market transactions both in equilibrium and in disequilibrium. It will be important to show that unemployment exists in both states: the "natural" rate in equilibrium and "excess demand" or "excess supply" unemployment added to the natural rate in disequilibrium. To understand the operation of the labor market, the following sequence will be followed: (1) present the behavior of worker-consumers in deciding their work-leisure choice and derive the supply curve of labor; (2) show how firms make decisions about the demand for labor; (3) introduce the factors that give rise to unemployment in equilibrium; (4) show how equilibrium is determined; and (5) consider the need for and characteristics of disequilibrium transactions.

Before proceeding with these tasks, the nature and extent of unemployment in the U.S. economy is presented in Chart 3-1, which plots both the actual and natural rates of unemployment. The natural rate is not directly observed and can only be estimated from an assumed equilibrium in the labor market. The natural-rate time series from Gordon (1993) for 1948-90 and from Adams and Coe (1989) for 1965-89 are shown. Of the two, Gordon's estimates are virtually constant at about 5.5%; Adams and Coe, on the other hand, allow demographic and other factors to influence the natural rate of unemployment, which rises throughout the 1970s and then falls in the 1980s. These differences highlight the fact that empirical evidence on the natural rate of unemployment, despite its importance to macroeconomic policy, is not a settled issue.[1]

Excess demand in the labor market exists when the actual rate falls below the natural rate as it did during 1966-70 and again after 1986 or 1987. On the other hand, excess supply occurs when the

---

[1] For a recent assessment of the empirical evidence see Topel (1993). He argues that the demand for low-skill jobs has decreased significantly, despite a fall in their wages.

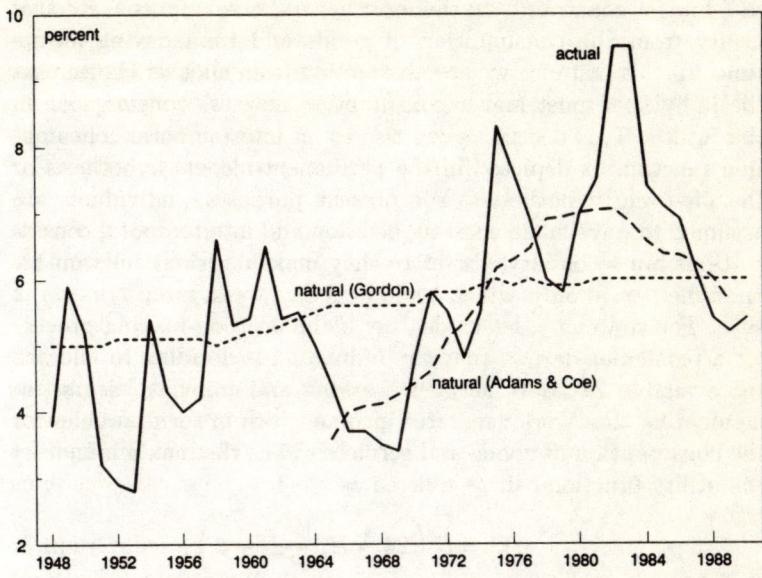

Chart 3-1. Actual and natural rates of unemployment, 1948-90.
Sources: *ERP*, 1991, Gordon (1993), and Adams and Coe (1989).

actual rate is above the natural rate as in 1982-86. It is important
to note that such situations can prevail for a number of years and
the rationale for this lengthy disequilibrium must be part of any
theory of labor market transactions.

3.1 The Supply of Labor

To derive the labor-supply curve we need to find the relationship
between the wage rate and hours of work that individuals are prepared to offer. Since the labor-supply curve applies to the economy
as a whole, we must first deal with the individual's decision to supply hours of work and then aggregate over all persons in the labor
force.

3.1.1 The Choice of Optimal Hours

Each individual is assumed to maximize a utility function subject to a budget constraint. In the most general case, a person receives utility from the consumption of goods and from having leisure time. In this instance we are abstracting from another choice that the individual must make: consumption now *vs.* consumption in the future. This decision gives rise to an intertemporal consumption function as depicted in the permanent-income hypothesis or the life-cycle hypothesis. For present purposes, individuals are assumed to have made a saving decision and intertemporal considerations are secondary; therefore they make decisions relevant for one time period only, which could be a day, week, month or even a year. For simplicity, let us deal with the decision-making process for a particular day, so that the individual is deciding to allocate the available 24 hours between working and enjoying leisure, remembering that work generates income which in turn provides for the consumption of goods and services. Thus the maximization of the utility function can be written as,

$$\underset{H}{\text{Max}} \quad U = U\left(24 - H, \frac{W}{P}H + I\right), \qquad (3.1)$$

where H represents the number of hours worked and becomes the variable that the individual manipulates in the utility-maximization process, $(W/P)H + I$ are the resources available for the consumption of goods and services during the period, with W/P as the real wage per hour, or the purchasing power of one hour of labor and I representing nonearned income such as dividend or interest payments, an allowance from one's parents, lottery winnings or any other source of income that is unrelated to work. The utility function has the following characteristics: (a) positive marginal utilities of both leisure and goods so that U_1 and U_2, the derivatives of the utility function with respect to each of the two arguments, are strictly positive; and (b) an absence of either leisure or goods leads to a zero level of utility, so that $U(0, C) = U(24, 0) = 0$.

The utility-maximizing choice is made when,

$$\frac{U_1}{U_2}\left(H, \frac{W}{P}, I\right) = \frac{W}{P}. \qquad (3.2)$$

Even though all individuals face the same real wage, the hours that they would want to work will vary according to tastes and the size of nonwage income. Moreover, it is uncertain that the response of every person to a higher real wage will be to offer more hours of work; it all depends on the income effect of the higher wage. If the reduction in hours offered from the income effect is smaller than the increase in hours worked from the substitution effect, the net result is an increase in hours supplied when the wage rate rises and such a person would have a positively-sloped supply curve. However, if the income effect has a large negative impact on hours offered it will overpower the positive influence of the substitution effect and hours supplied by the individual will fall and the supply curve is negatively sloped. It is also quite possible to have a person increase hours of work in response to wage increases when the wage is quite low and then reduce hours worked if the wage rate rises from some higher level. This gives rise to a "backward bending" supply curve. As a result we are left with a great deal of uncertainty about the shape and position of the aggregate supply curve of labor, which is the horizontal summation of the individual supply curves.

Nevertheless, the situation is not nearly as hopeless when we consider that the choice made by individuals about the hours that they wish to work is made in a somewhat more constrained framework. One of the features of the labor market that is universally observed is that firms dictate the hours of work that they expect from their employees. In other words, a job description includes hours of work which are not usually subject to unilateral alteration by the prospective worker. This observation does not deny the existence of part-time work or of job-sharing nor does it mean that everyone in the economy must work eight hours a day, five days a week. In fact there is great variety in the job market as far as the work schedule is concerned, with some jobs requiring shift work, others imposing longer hours per day but fewer days per week and so on. The important feature is that the individual person must take these requirements as given; the only major exception are self-employed professionals, who are really acting like a one-person firm maximizing profits rather than utility. Let us simplify this limitation of choice to mean that a job requires $\bar{H}$ hours per day; nothing more or less will do. Therefore, the person makes an all-or-nothing decision. He or she makes a choice between not working at all or working $\bar{H}$ hours. This will lead to a second-best-optimum for the worker, but it is a necessary sacrifice in order for the labor market to operate efficiently. Just imagine the chaos if workers, especially those in jobs requiring much co-ordination with others, could vary their hours of work day by day or week by week

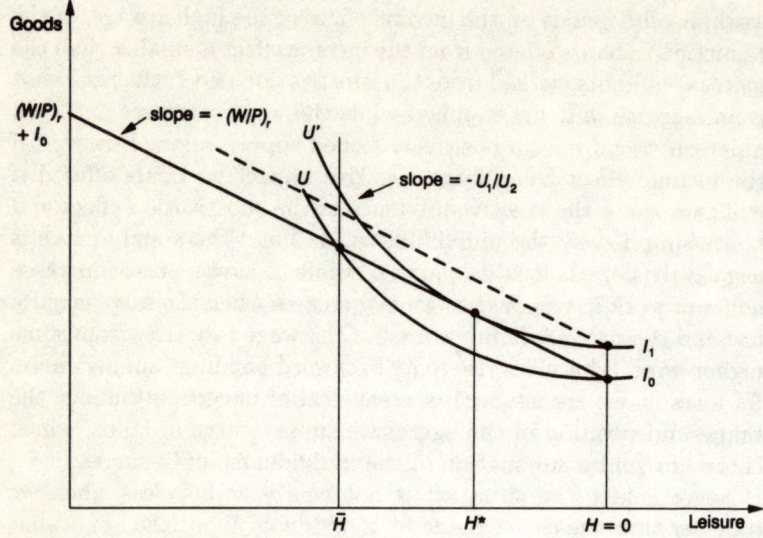

Fig. 3-1.   Determining the reservation wage.

depending on what might have happened to their nonwage income, or their marginal utility of leisure or of goods consumption. In any case, those individuals who value leisure highly will tend to look for part-time employment, while those who place a great deal of emphasis on goods consumption will not mind taking a job that involves a lot of overtime hours.

3.1.2   The Choice to Participate in the Labor Market

In this constrained environment an individual essentially makes a decision to be in the labor force or not because he or she either works $\bar{H}$ hours or not at all. As a first step we need to find the wage rate that makes the individual indifferent between these two choices. That wage rate is called the reservation wage. If the actual wage rate is above the reservation wage she will want to work $\bar{H}$ hours; if it is below the reservation wage she will be at $H = 0$. To find the reservation wage we equate the utilities from these two possible situations, namely

$$U\left(24 - \bar{H}, \left[\frac{W}{P}\right]_r \bar{H} + I_0\right) = U(24, I_0), \qquad (3.3)$$

and find the real wage rate, $(W/P)_r$, that achieves this result. Fig. 3-1 shows this process diagrammatically. An initial indifference curve, U, is drawn through the point at which $H = 0$ and the person spends I_0 on consumption. This indifference curve will also pass through the constraint $\bar{H}$. These two points are then connected with a budget line that has a slope of $-(W/P)_r$, which becomes the reservation wage.

The inferiority of this outcome is seen by the fact that at the wage rate $(W/P)_r$, this person would want to work H^* hours which will always be between $\bar{H}$ and $H = 0$. At H^* her utility would rise to U', suggesting that the "costs" of constraining everyone to work prespecified hours is measured by the utility lost of moving from U' back to U. If the wage rate were to rise above $(W/P)_r$, the budget line would be steeper and this person would now definitely choose to work since a higher indifference curve could be reached. However, as the wage rate continues to rise the individual still only works $\bar{H}$ hours. This supply curve is shown in Fig. 3-2(a) as a reversed 'L' starting at $(W/P)_0$. Another individual who perhaps has a stronger taste for leisure will have a higher reservation wage, say $(W/P)_1$ in part (b) of Fig. 3-2. His supply curve will also be of the same shape but starting higher on the wage axis. To obtain the aggregate supply curve, we merely add hours horizontally to create the step-shaped "curve" in Fig. 3-2(c). For the economy as a whole, these steps become very small; hence the dashed upward-sloping line, marked N^s, represents the number of persons who want to work $\bar{H}$ hours at any given wage rate and becomes the aggregate labor-supply curve. As is easily verified, the supply curve will always be positively sloped because as the wage rate is increased, someone's reservation wage will be surpassed and that person will add her $\bar{H}$ hours to the previous supply of hours. Only when all persons have passed their reservation wage and have entered the labor force will the supply curve become vertical.

Because this treatment involves a second-best equilibrium, it is prudent to analyze the result in some detail by performing comparative-statics exercises. First, consider what would happen if $I_0 = 0$. Unless we have a very strange preference system, every person would choose to work, no matter how low the wage rate is. Opting to take all leisure, this person would not be able to consume any goods whatsoever. The mere thought of starvation would probably force him to accept the first job that paid any positive

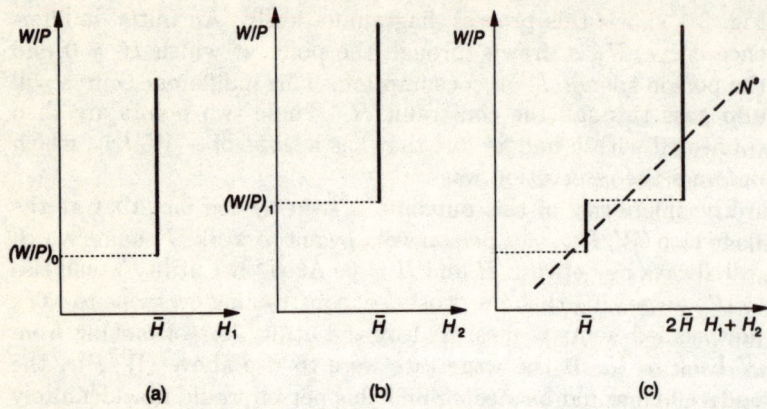

Fig. 3-2.   Aggregating two individual labor-supply decisions.

wage. In that case, the aggregate labor-supply curve is vertical
as all persons in the economy offer their services at any wage rate.
Thus nonwage income for some individuals is a necessary condition
to obtain a positive slope to the labor-supply curve.

   Second, consider the effect on the labor-market participation
decision of the average person when $\bar{H}$ is increased. If the real
wage is not changed, the person will now favor complete leisure
since utility will be reduced. Differentiating the utility function in
equation (3.3), holding I_0 constant and setting the result to zero
allows us to obtain an indifference curve; therefore,

$$\frac{d(W/P)}{d\bar{H}} = \frac{U_1 - (W/P)U_2}{\bar{H}U_2} > 0,$$

because the marginal utility of leisure, U_1, exceeds the marginal
compensation for sacrificing leisure, $(W/P)U_2$ at $\bar{H}$. As a result, a
higher reservation wage will be demanded when firms increase the
number of hours that they expect from their employees. In turn,
wage income will increase for two reasons: (1) more hours at work
and (2) at a higher wage. By the same token, part-time jobs which
involve fewer hours per day than full-time jobs will tend to attract
people with lower reservation wages.

   Finally, consider the effect on the reservation wage when nonwage income rises. Differentiating the equal-utility function of

equation (3.3), holding $\bar{H}$ constant, produces:

$$d\left(\frac{W}{P}\right)_r = \frac{U_2^{H=0} - U_2^{\bar{H}}}{\bar{H} U_2^{\bar{H}}} dI.$$

Whether the reservation wage, $(W/P)_r$, and nonwage income, I, are positively related depends on whether the marginal utility of goods consumption at the total-leisure choice exceeds the marginal utility of goods consumption at the work-$\bar{H}$-hours choice. It is likely that $U_2^{H=0} > U_2^{\bar{H}}$ because there is more goods consumption at $U_2^{\bar{H}}$ and, normally, the marginal utility of anything declines as the amount available increases. In that case, an increase in nonwage income will cause the person to require a higher real wage to maintain indifference between complete leisure and offering $\bar{H}$ hours of work.

3.1.3   The Supply of Overtime Hours

There are numerous circumstances in which a firm will ask its employees to work longer hours than $\bar{H}$, but usually it is prepared to pay an overtime premium. At this stage, it is of some interest to determine whether workers are willing to supply these extra hours, which will be denoted by $\tilde{H}$. The choice again involves the determination of a reservation wage, this time specified by an equal-utility condition for working standard hours and working the additional overtime hours:

$$\left(24 - \bar{H} - \tilde{H}, \left[\frac{W}{P}\right]_p \tilde{H} + I_1\right) = U(24 - \bar{H}, I_1), \qquad (3.3')$$

where $I_1 = I_0 + (W/P)\bar{H}$ and $(W/P)_p$ is the overtime wage at which the person is indifferent between the extra income from working overtime hours and the greater leisure involved in standard hours. If the actual overtime premium is greater than $(W/P)_p$, the person will want to work the extra $\tilde{H}$ hours, but if the overtime wage offered to the worker is less than $(W/P)_p$, the person would have to be coerced into overtime activity. Involuntary overtime may in fact be prevalent, since many union contracts specify the conditions under which overtime work will be *required* of existing workers. However, it is clear that if the overtime premium is large enough, everyone will have an incentive to work these additional hours. Hence, "time-and-a half for overtime" is an arbitrary choice for the overtime premium; sometimes it is too high and sometimes it is too low to obtain the required number of extra hours.

3.1.4   Properties of the Labor-Supply Curve

The positively-sloped curve in Fig. 3-2(c) is the aggregate labor-supply curve. It is captured by the following equation:

$$N^s = N^s \left(\frac{W}{P}, I, \bar{H}, \frac{U_1}{U_2} \right), \tag{3.4}$$

$$\frac{\partial N^s}{\partial (W/P)} > 0, \quad \frac{\partial N^s}{\partial I} > 0, \quad \frac{\partial N^s}{\partial \bar{H}} < 0, \quad \frac{\partial N^s}{\partial (U_1/U_2)} < 0.$$

It has a number of features that are worth emphasizing at this stage.

1 Although it appears that the horizontal axis in Fig. 3-2(c) is in hours, the fact that everyone works $\bar{H}$ hours, means that the supply curve relates the hourly wage to the number of people who want to work these standard hours, namely N^s. It therefore represents an aggregation of the participation decision by each individual. There are however some complications arising from the assumption of "standard hours". If in fact there are submarkets with different levels of $\bar{H}$ and different reservation wages, then the supply of total hours will not depend only on additional participants. If a person enters the part-time job market with a low reservation wage and then shifts to full-time work when the actual wage rises above the higher reservation applicable for that market, then hours supplied to the market will increase without an additional worker.

2 The supply curve is always upward sloping since it is not possible for a person to withdraw from the labor market after his or her reservation wage has been exceeded.

3 Despite the fact that each person is making a suboptimal choice between not working at all and working $\bar{H}$ hours, positions on the labor-supply curve are superior in a welfare sense to those positions off the curve. To the left of the supply curve at any given real wage, there are a number of people who want to work but are not employed and are therefore involuntarily unemployed. On the other hand, a position to the right of the supply curve would require involuntary exchange.

4 The supply of labor is composed of heterogeneous individuals, even though the participation decision has been derived from a utility-maximizing "representative agent". Remembering that the supply curve is generated by having more and more people pass their reservation wage, those with very low reservation wages and early entry into the labor market enjoy rents at any wage above their reservation wage. These people earn rents because their welfare rises with the real wage but without any adjustment of their behavior. Hence, it is possible to order sequentially all individuals in the labor market by the amount of rent they receive from employment; those with the lowest reservation wage receive the largest rents.

3.2   The Demand for Labor

While supply decisions in the labor market are made by individual worker-consumers, demand decisions are made by firms and their management. The major choice made by a productive enterprise is the input-output relationship: given a certain goal for output over a specific time frame, what factors of production should the firm use and how much of each? The ultimate aim of the firm is to maximize its profits, which represents the difference between its revenue generated by sales of output and costs dictated by payments to its factors of production.

3.2.1   Profit-maximizing Choices for a Firm's Inputs

This maximization process can be written as:

$$\underset{N}{\text{Max}} \quad \Pi = Y(N\bar{H}, K) - \frac{W}{P}N\bar{H} - \frac{R}{P}K, \qquad (3.5)$$

where Π are profits in real terms (i.e., adjusted for price changes), $Y(\cdot)$ is the production function for output, a composite commodity for the entire economy, $N\bar{H}$ stands for the total hours worked by the firm's labor force and K represents the capital stock used in the production process. Consistent with the assumption made in the discussion of labor supply, each person works $\bar{H}$ hours per day for W/P per hour in real terms or $\bar{H}W/P$ per day. Capital, on the other hand, is a stock of equipment and structures such as machinery, warehouses and computers, available to the firm, for which it pays a user cost per unit of time, R/P, as if it were leasing its capital from a firm specializing in this function. Some of the properties of the production function are: (a) marginal products of each factor are positive, $Y_N, Y_K > 0$; (b) marginal products decline as more of the factor is used, $Y_{NN}, Y_{KK} < 0$; and (c) marginal products increase when more of the co-operating factor is available, $Y_{NK}, Y_{KN} > 0$.

The firm is assumed to have chosen K and $\bar{H}$ by a prior optimization process and these variables will not change, although we will later analyze the effect of exogenous changes in K and in the demand for overtime hours. The stock of capital is taken to be constant for the relevant time period because of the lengthy gestation period for investment expenditures. In this setting, the optimal number of workers is given by the equilibrium condition:

$$\bar{H}Y_N(N\bar{H}, K) = \frac{W}{P}\bar{H}. \qquad (3.6)$$

Now we can investigate the effects of exogenous events on the demand for workers. First, consider an increase in the real wage, with both hours and capital held constant. When a firm has to pay its workers a higher wage it will do so only if the marginal product of each person rises. The only method by which the firm can achieve this is to reduce the labor input; hence, W/P and N are inversely related and the demand curve for workers is downward sloping, (i.e., $dN/d(W/P) = 1/\bar{H}Y_{NN} < 0$).

Second, assume the firm has an additional amount of capital. In this event, the firm will hire more workers because their marginal product at the original labor input is now automatically raised and needs to be reduced to the level of the prevailing wage. This is seen as a rightward shift of the demand curve (i.e., $dN/dK = -Y_{NK}/\bar{H}Y_{NN} > 0$). In the process, output will rise, because of both the initial increase in the capital stock and the subsequent hiring of new workers.

Finally, let us investigate the effect of increasing the hours per day that each person is expected to work. The effect of this experiment on the optimal number of workers depends on the parameter Y_{NH}. If workers become less productive the longer they stay on the job, then $Y_{NH} < 0$ and the firm will have to find a way of raising the marginal product of workers back to its original level and it does so by reducing the number of workers that it employs. On the other hand, if $Y_{NH} > 0$, as it might be when individuals are initially working only a few hours a day and become more productive as they find their "rhythm", then the firm will want more workers and the demand curve would shift to the right, as it did when the capital stock was increased, allowing output to rise for two reasons: (a) more hours and (b) more workers.

3.2.2 The Demand for Workers by Monopolists

The profit-maximizing behavior of a perfectly competitive firm involves holding the price of the commodity it sells constant because at that price it can sell as much output as desired. However, a firm in an imperfectly competitive environment, especially a monopolist, would find that it can sell more only at a lower price. A monopolist will equate the marginal product of an additional worker, $\bar{H}Y_N$, times its value to the producer, namely the marginal revenue available from the extra sales, $P + Y(dP/dY)$, to the nominal wage, W. Because the demand curve facing a monopolist is downward sloping, instead of horizontal, marginal revenue is always less than price by $Y(dP/dY)$, where dP/dY is the slope of the demand curve. If the nominal wage were to fall, both a perfect competitor and a monopolist will increase the number of workers but the latter less than the former since the extra output produced by the additional workers depresses the monopoly price and a new profit-maximizing position is reached sooner. Thus the demand curve for workers by the monopolist is steeper than would be the case if the product market were perfectly competitive; however it is still negatively sloped.

3.2.3 The Demand for Overtime Hours

Although "standard hours" equal to $\bar{H}$ have been assumed, it is useful to determine how firms decide on their demand for overtime hours based on contractual obligations to pay a fixed premium such as time-and-a-half for each hour of overtime. The firm equates the cost of an overtime hour to the cost of a new employee, divided by $\bar{H}$. Unless there are fixed costs (e.g., hiring and training costs, fringe benefits) in addition to the hourly wage paid to the new employee, the firm would *never* use overtime hours because the new worker is always a cheaper source of extra hours. However, such additional costs cannot be ruled out, especially if the fringe benefits are unrelated to the hours worked by an employee. In general, a firm would hire the new worker if the fixed costs, amortized over the period they expect the employee to remain with them, are lower than the extra cost per hour of overtime. From that perspective, it is easy to see that in situations where the extra hours are not expected to become a permanent feature of the production process, the firm would rather use overtime hours than incur these fixed costs, but if the expansion is likely to last for some time, they will hire new workers instead. In the initial stages of an economic upturn, it is not unusual to find that overtime hours increase more than new workers; later the number of employees will rise and overtime will stabilize or even fall. At the margin, firms would be indifferent between the two methods of increasing the labor input and we would find that the overtime premium is equal to the fixed costs of new employees divided by the total hours they are expected to remain with the firm.

3.2.4 Employment and the Demand for Labor

Although labor is being treated as a relatively homogeneous factor of production, it is in fact composed of a large variety of submarkets, divided regionally or by skill. In that environment, a firm may want to hire a person with particular characteristics, but may not find a qualified person immediately. While it is searching for this person the firm has a vacancy. By definition, total demand for labor equals actual employment plus vacancies. Even if we allow time to pass, it is unlikely that vacancies will disappear entirely since some existing workers will quit or retire in every time period, making it necessary for the firm to find their replacement. We can therefore think of equilibrium vacancies that are proportional to employment. The exact proportion will depend on a number of factors. The more heterogeneous is the labor market, the more time it takes the firm to find the right employee and the larger are vacancies relative to employment. The greater is the labor turnover through quits, the higher is the ratio of vacancies to employment. To determine the factors that influence vacancies, we assume that a firm minimizes a quadratic cost function,

$$C = \alpha_1(N - N_{-1} + Q)^2 + \alpha_2 V^2, \qquad (3.7)$$

where α_1 measures adjustment costs and α_2 represents disequilib-

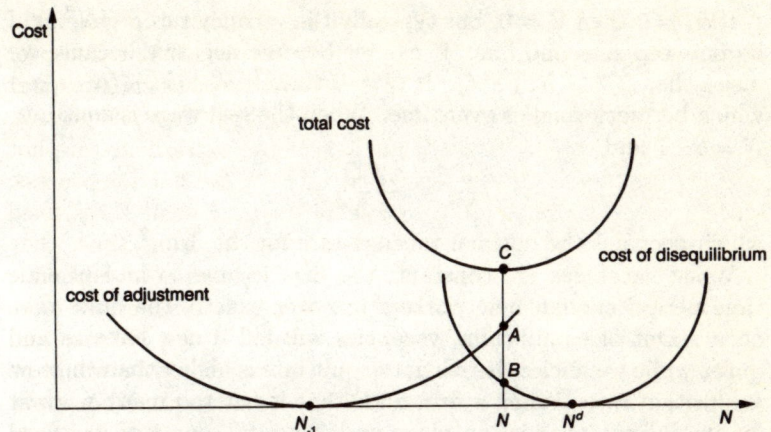

Fig. 3-3. Adjustment and disequilibrium costs of employment.

rium costs, with $V \equiv N^d - N$ measuring the number of vacancies and Q is the number of quits per period of time. Minimizing this cost function involves setting $\partial C / \partial N = 0$. This produces

$$V = \frac{\alpha_1(N^d - N_{-1} + Q)}{\alpha_1 + \alpha_2}.$$

Firms operating in the labor market face an adjustment-cost curve centered on N_{-1} and a disequilibrium-cost curve centered on N^d in Fig. 3-3. The curvature of these cost functions is dictated by the value of α_1 and α_2, respectively. The total-cost curve in the diagram represents the vertical summation of the two individual cost curves. The firm will minimize total costs to reach its preferred employment level which is N, based on adjustment costs equal to NA and disequilibrium costs of NB, for a total of NC. It will, in these circumstances, hire new workers equal to $N - N_{-1}$ and have an optimal number of vacancies, shown by the distance between N^d and N. However, because of turnover in the labor market the firm will not actually reach N, but instead $N - Q$ after it has experienced its normal number of quits in the period. Therefore, at the beginning of the next period, another adjustment-cost curve is centered on $N - Q$ and the firm again hires more workers. Nevertheless, as long as there are periodic quits, the firm will never reach N^d.

If $\alpha_1 = 0$ then $V = 0$, but typically the vacancy rate, V/N^d, will lie between zero and one. V cannot become negative because we insist that $N^d > N_{-1} + Q$. If $Q = 0$ then $V = \alpha_1 V_{-1}/(\alpha_1 + \alpha_2)$ which becomes smaller over time. When the real wage is constant, $N = N_{-1}$ and

$$\frac{V}{N^d} = \frac{\alpha_1}{\alpha_2} \frac{Q}{N^d} = v$$

which becomes the optimal vacancy rate for the firm.[2]

When vacancies are constant, the firm is able to hire in each time period enough new workers to cover exactly the quits that occur. Out of equilibrium, vacancies will fall if new hires exceed quits, while vacancies rise when the quit rate is higher than the new acquisition rate. When a firm finds that it has too many workers for its current production plans and "lays off" some of its existing workers, it reduces both its demand and actual employment, with vacancies remaining constant. The co-existence of lay-offs and vacancies would seem to be inconsistent with each other since it implies that the firm is simultaneously trying to hire some workers while firing others. This inconsistency is removed however, when it is realized that vacancies are likely to be for different types of workers (e.g., computer operators) than for those jobs being eliminated (e.g., unskilled workers).

While vacancies depend on the two parameters, α_1 and α_2, they will also vary systematically with the business cycle. During a recession, when N^d is low, it is usually the case that Q falls as well. The opposite movements in N^d and Q are expected during a boom. Therefore, to obtain the Beveridge-curve relationship that stipulates a low vacancy rate during a recession, it would be necessary for the changes in Q to outweigh the changes in N^d or for α_1 to fall and α_2 to rise during a recession. Blanchard and Diamond (1989) found that during the period 1952-88, the vacancy rate rose during the boom period and fell in recessions.[3]

---

[2] It is, of course, possible to combine the optimization of all inputs and vacancies simultaneously by including the cost function of equation (3.7) in the profit function of equation (3.6), but then there would be no distinction between the demand for labor and employment of workers by the firm.

[3] See their Figure 8. They relied on an adjusted help-wanted index from CITIBASE (i.e., LHELX) to measure vacancies.

3.2.5 Properties of the Labor-Demand Curve

The demand curve for workers is summarized by the following equation:

$$N^d = N^d\left(\frac{W}{P}, \bar{H}, K\right), \qquad (3.8)$$

$$\frac{\partial N^d}{\partial (W/P)} < 0, \ \frac{\partial N^d}{\partial \bar{H}} = ?, \ \frac{\partial N^d}{\partial K} > 0.$$

There are a number of characteristics of this relationship that need to be stressed.

1 The demand curve represents points of equality between the marginal product of labor and the real wage; the negative slope is derived from the assumption of diminishing returns to a factor of production.

2 The demand curve will shift upward whenever there is an exogenous increase in the marginal product of labor.

3 Actual employment is always less than a firm's demand for labor and the difference is represented by vacancies. These vacancies cannot be eliminated in a heterogeneous labor market since firms experience quits all the time.

4 Currently employed workers are also heterogeneous with respect to the "security" of their employment. Workers are rarely "laid-off" or dismissed randomly; instead, seniority is an important determinant of security. Secure workers will be sure of continued employment if the demand curve for labor shifts to the left or if the real wage rises, whereas insecure workers are the first to go in these circumstances. At any given wage, the most secure workers can be positioned closest to the vertical axis on the labor-use curve.

3.3 Equilibrium in the Labor Market

Having laid the groundwork by deriving the supply and demand relationships in the labor market from optimizing procedures by consumer-workers and by firms, we are now ready to discuss the operation of the labor market when supply and demand interact with each other.

3.3.1 Characteristics of Equilibrium

The supply and demand relationships are drawn in Fig. 3-4, with

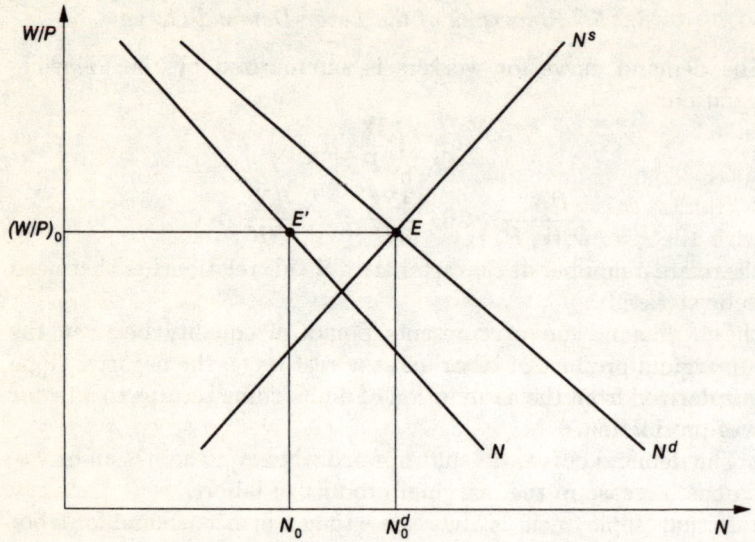

Fig. 3-4. Equilibrium in the labor market.

the supply curve positively sloped as it was derived in equation (3.4), and the demand curve negatively sloped as in equation (3.8). Various events could shift one or the other curve. For example, an increase in the capital stock would be captured by an increase in the vertical intercept of the demand curve and would cause the demand curve for labor to shift to the right. As another example, an increase in nonwage income will probably cause the reservation wage of the receiving individuals to rise and force the supply curve upward, as represented by an increase in the vertical intercept of the supply curve.

Equilibrium in the labor market is depicted in Fig. 3-4 at E, where the supply and demand curves intersect. However, we need to obtain another piece of information from this analysis, namely the level of actual employment at equilibrium. From the previous discussion, we asserted that vacancies equaled a given proportion of employment, so that employment is also a given proportion of total demand. Thus the employment curve is to the left of N^d, with the horizontal difference between the two curves measuring the number of vacancies. This new N curve, called the labor-use curve, is steeper than N^d because at high wages, demand is low and so are vacancies, whereas at low wages both demand and vacancies are higher.

3.3.2   The Natural Rate of Unemployment

At the equilibrium point, E, while the demand for labor is equal to N_0^d units, the satisfied demand or actual employment is only N_0, with the remaining $N_0^d N_0$ representing the number of vacancies that firms have. At the wage rate $(W/P)_0$, they are able to hire new workers that just equal those they lose through quits. Also, these vacancies equal the number of labor-market participants who are unemployed. The point E' is to the left of the supply curve, suggesting that some individuals who have passed their reservation wage at $(W/P)_0$ are unable to find jobs at that wage rate. They are involuntarily unemployed. Milton Friedman has labelled this as the natural rate of unemployment. It is the unemployment rate consistent with equilibrium in the labor market. It would be observed at the point where the number of vacancies equals the number of unemployed. This is a "square-pegs-round-holes" problem, with the unemployed being the square pegs that do not fit into an equal number of round-hole vacancies. If the labor market were completely homogeneous, the problem would disappear as all pegs would become round or all holes become square. In that sense, geographic immobility or skill mismatches are the cause of heterogeneity in the labor market and the more serious they are, the larger is the natural rate of unemployment and the larger is the distance between the N^d and N curves in Fig. 3-4. Furthermore, the natural rate of unemployment is not fixed for all time. It has varied a great deal in the past twenty years. In the United States, as shown by the Adams and Coe estimates in Chart 3-1, the natural rate rose in the 1960s and 1970s as women and young people, who have a difficult time finding an initial job, increased in importance in the labor force and raised the natural rate. Also, increased generosity of unemployment insurance benefits is said to have caused some individuals to pretend that they were in the labor force in order to obtain these benefits. This also raised the natural rate during that time period. Since the 1970s, these trends seem to have reversed themselves and the natural rate is considered to have fallen.

It is tempting to re-interpret equilibrium in the labor market as the intersection of the N^s and N curves in Fig. 3-4 because at the wage rate $(W/P)_0$ not all workers are employed and those that are unemployed would bid down the wage; hence $(W/P)_0$, it is argued, cannot be sustained. While the existence of unemployment surely puts downward pressure on real wages, it must be remembered that existing vacancies put upward pressure on wages. At E, where vacancies and unemployed workers are equal, these pressures cancel each other and leave the real wage constant, a requirement for equilibrium in a market.

3.4 Disequilibrium and Unemployment

Having dealt with the characteristics of equilibrium, we can now move on to situations in which the labor market is in disequilibrium. Remembering that the labor market relies heavily on contracts, both explicit union contracts and implicit "hand-shake" agreements, which fix the wage for some period of time into the future, it is quite possible for the labor market to make transactions in a state of disequilibrium. Although a great deal of effort has been expended on rationalizing disequilibrium transactions by welfare-maximizing agents, it will be shown in the next chapter that for the large majority of labor-market participants there really is no disequilibrium even when the market as a whole exhibits excess supply or demand. It is therefore in their interest to continue to make transactions and they will do so. No matter what, firms demand $\bar{H}$ hours from each continuing employee who has already made a decision to accept work with those hours. The only thing that changes in disequilibrium is the amount of rent received by each worker as the real wage deviates from its equilibrium value.

What is the nature of these transactions and are they voluntary exchanges? To answer these questions, it is necessary to appeal to an institutional arrangement in the labor market, namely that firms unilaterally decide on the number of workers that they employ. Although a number of union contracts specify manning requirements and seniority rights, typically these firms have the right to lay-off workers if they deem this to be the most appropriate way of shedding excess labor costs, as long as they comply with any advance-notice requirements or other obligations imposed by existing contracts or government regulations. It is also worth noting that reducing the number of workers is much more prevalent than cutting hours per worker if the firm has decided it needs fewer total hours of the labor input.

In this setting, actual employment will always be on the N curve because that is what firms would choose to do once they know the real wage rate. Consider a real wage above $(W/P)_0$, which is too high for equilibrium in Fig. 3-4. Actual employment at N_0, would mean that the marginal product of workers is below the real wage and firms could generate more profits if they reduce the number of workers, with those that remain having a higher marginal product. Only on the N curve does the firm have the profit-maximizing number of workers for a given real wage. Next, consider a real wage which is now below the equilibrium real wage. Here, the firm will want actual employment to be greater than N_0, but since the labor market is now experiencing excess demand, with $N^s < N^d$, can the firms always obtain the number of workers they want without relying on involuntary exchange? The answer is yes as long as the wage rate does not fall below the intersection of the N and N^s curves. Because actual employment is still less than those willing to work, firms are able to dictate their complement of workers.

From this discussion we can conclude that excess-supply situations which prevail at wages above $(W/P)_0$ give rise to the number of workers who are unemployed exceeding the number of vacancies; hence the actual unemployment rate is higher than the natural rate of unemployment. In equilibrium, the number of square pegs is equal to the number of round holes, but here there are some round holes that are empty. Excess demand prevails at wages below $(W/P)_0$ and vacancies are now less than the number of workers who are unemployed; by the same token, the actual unemployment rate is now less than the natural rate but still positive. In these situations, square pegs have been forced into some round holes with the resulting mismatch reducing the marginal product of workers, but at the lower wage rate firms can tolerate this outcome.

3.4.1 Wage Determination

Although there is only one real wage consistent with equilibrium in the labor market, wage determination is usually in nominal terms and can take place in a period of disequilibrium. As a consequence, nominal wages may rise just to keep pace with price inflation in a steady-state equilibrium, or they may rise more or less than the rate of inflation in order to re-establish equilibrium.

The real wage is a ratio of a nominal wage rate to the price of a basket of goods. From the worker's perspective it represents the purchasing power of an hour's work, while the producer views it as the real cost of employing a worker for one hour. Since wage rates are set in nominal or in dollar terms, the real wage can remain in equilibrium if the nominal wage and the price of the basket of goods move in the same direction and in the same proportion. Hence, it is quite possible to have significant nominal wage increases and still maintain a constant real wage as long as prices of goods are rising at the same rate. If we let ω stand for the percentage increase in the wage per period of time (e.g., one year) and π is the rate of price inflation for the same period, then $\omega = \pi$ keeps the real wage constant. On the other hand $\omega > \pi$ will force the real wage to rise by the difference between ω and π.

Consider an initial situation where $\omega = \pi$ and then let workers raise ω above π in the belief that they have some monopoly power in the labor market. When $\omega > \pi$, and the real wage is rising, firms will reduce their labor input. The result is higher unemployment, which in turn will put downward pressure on the real wage so that ultimately ω will have to fall again, temporarily below π, to re-establish the original real wage. Alternatively, if ω cannot be forced down by the existence of excess-supply unemployment, π will rise to meet it. Either way, an inequality between ω and π would mean continuous movement along the employment curve, N, in one direction or the other which cannot be sustained in the face of the growing disequilibrium that it would entail.

3.4.2 Derivation of the Aggregate-Supply Curve

The aggregate-supply relationship is derived from the labor market and shows how output responds to changes in the rate of inflation. The reason that the labor market plays such a pivotal role here is to be found in the production function which links labor inputs and output of goods and services. If the inflation rate were to increase, firms would find that the real wage begins to fall in the face of contracts that hold nominal wage increases to previously negotiated rates. Profit-maximizing behavior dictates that firms should expand output and hire more workers. They will receive the right signal through unintended inventory depletions which occur because of extra demand that created the inflationary pressures in the first place. Firms are able to obtain the extra workers despite the excess-demand situation that might prevail because there are still some unemployed workers available to be hired. They are not exactly the match that the firm seeks, but when the real wage has been lowered, firms are willing to use less productive workers.

The equation for the labor-use curve is given by

$$n = n^d - v = \beta_2 - \beta_3(w - p) - v, \tag{3.9}$$

where n and n^d are natural logs of the actual number of employees and desired workers, respectively, while $(w - p) \equiv \ln(W/P)$. The production function can be written in log-linear form:

$$y = \beta_4 + \beta_5 n, \tag{3.10}$$

where y is the natural log of the output of goods and services and β_5 is interpreted as the output elasticity of the labor input. By taking first differences of equations (3.9) and (3.10), we obtain

$$y = y_{-1} + \beta_5\beta_3(\omega - \pi), \tag{3.11}$$

since $\omega \equiv \Delta w$ and $\pi \equiv \Delta p$. By assuming that $\omega = \pi^e$, $y^* = y_{-1}$ and inverting equation (3.11), we obtain the aggregate-supply curve used in Chapter 2:

$$\pi = \pi^e + \alpha(y - y^*). \tag{3.12}$$

The fact that inflation and output are predicted to move together means that the aggregate-supply curve is positively sloped as long as nominal wage growth is fixed. Ultimately, the disequilibrium in the labor market will cause wages to adjust, forcing the aggregate-supply curve to shift upwards or downwards over time. Since there is only one equilibrium level of employment, there can only be one level of output associated with that number of workers and the rate of inflation is immaterial to that level of output, often called natural rate output, since it is consistent with the natural rate of unemployment. Hence, the long-run aggregate-supply curve is vertical.

3.5 Stabilization Policy and the Labor Market

Stabilization policy operates in either the goods market when fiscal policy is used or in the money market when monetary policy is implemented. Yet the ultimate aim is often to influence the labor market and the unemployment rate. In other words, macroeconomic policy uses aggregate demand to find the appropriate position on the aggregate-supply curve. Repeating equation (2.8) from Chapter 2 as the short-cut version of an aggregate-demand curve,

$$y = \beta_f g + \beta_m(\mu - \pi), \qquad (3.13)$$

where β_f and β_m are fiscal and monetary multipliers, g is the fiscal-policy variable and $(\mu - \pi)$ is the growth rate of real money balances.[4]

Solving equations (3.12) and (3.13) produces:

$$\pi = \frac{1}{1 + \alpha\beta_m}(\alpha\beta_g g + \alpha\beta_m \mu + \pi^e - \alpha y^*)$$

and

$$y = \frac{1}{1 + \alpha\beta_m}(\beta_g g + \beta_m \mu - \beta_m \pi^e + \alpha\beta_m y^*).$$

Changes in stabilization-policy instruments not only affect π and y but through them the level of employment and the rate of unemployment. To increase employment, equation (3.10) dictates that output must increase, but equation (3.9) stipulates that the inflation rate must rise to allow the real wage to fall. Since both of these equations are incorporated into the aggregate-supply equation the results will be consistent with these requirements.

Therefore, either expansionary fiscal policy (i.e., $dg > 0$) or expansionary monetary policy (i.e., $d\mu > 0$) force y and π to rise. In turn, the greater output requires an increase in the labor input, or alternatively, the higher inflation lowers the real wage and increases the employment level. This is the traditional way of thinking about stabilization policy, but another possibility is to allow the government to operate in the labor market directly by its own hiring. This would increase the parameter β_2 in the labor-use equation (3.9) and lead to greater employment as well. Unlike the indirect effect of an increase in government expenditures on goods and services, direct hiring will have a permanent effect on employment and output, but not on the unemployment rate which

---

[4] The aggregate-demand curve can be derived from a combination of the *LM* and *IS* equations. See Prachowny (1985, Ch. 2) for more details.

will always be equal to v in equilibrium. If it were possible for the government to hire selectively those workers who are the "square pegs" that do not fit into the "round holes" of private businesses, then even the natural rate of unemployment could be reduced.[5] In terms of the labor-market diagram of Fig. 3-4, general government hiring would shift both the N^d and N curves to the right by equal amounts, but government hiring of "square pegs" would shift the N curve closer to the N^d curve.

The effects of stabilization policy can be summarized by looking at the unemployment rate, which is determined by

$$u = n^s - n = \beta_0 + \beta_1(w - p) - \beta_2 + \beta_3(w - p) - v \qquad (3.14)$$

and the equilibrium real wage, which is reached when $n^s = n^d$:

$$w - p = \frac{\beta_2 - \beta_0}{\beta_1 + \beta_3}. \qquad (3.15)$$

By relying on expansionary policy in the goods or money markets, the government increases p faster than w and causes the unemployment rate to fall until nominal-wage increases catch up; since $(w - p)$ is unaltered in the long run, this type of policy can have no permanent effect on u. By direct hiring, it raises β_2 in both equations (3.14) and (3.15), leaving u unchanged, although both n^s and n are now higher. Finally, hiring the "unemployable" persons who are contained in v reduces u by an equal amount.

3.6 Types of Unemployment

It is useful to categorize different types of unemployment. First, the natural rate of unemployment which equals the vacancy rate, v, can be thought of either as *frictional* or as *structural* unemployment. Although unemployment in equilibrium continues because

---

[5] During the early 1970s, the federal government passed a number of pieces of legislation to provide public employment, the most important of which was the Emergency Employment Act of 1971. These programs transferred funds to state and local governments in the form of grants which allowed for subsidies of about $10,000 for every public service job created. Some of these programs were restricted to the poor and long-term unemployed. (See Wiseman (1976) for an evaluation.) Another possible application of this policy was attempted by the Carter administration when it proposed to give public service jobs to those who were structurally unemployed. (See *ERP*, 1979, pp. 120-1.)

of the natural turnover in the labor market, these quits would be translated into jobs immediately if there were no structural mismatches in the labor market, which in turn give rise to adjustment costs. Next, *cyclical* unemployment is equal to $u-v$, which is larger than v when there is excess supply in the labor market and smaller than v when there is excess demand. Keynes distinguished between unemployment caused by deficient demand for goods and *classical* unemployment caused by a real wage that was too high to clear the labor market, with the former being, in his mind, the appropriate explanation for the Great Depression. However, this is a taxonomy without meaning. If demand for goods falls, the inflation rate will also fall below the previously determined increase in nominal wages and the real wage rises. Firms will respond by reducing the number of employees and output will be reduced. Whether we ascribe the resulting unemployment to having insufficient aggregate demand or too high a real wage makes no substantial difference. The real wage is a ratio of two nominal variables and blaming the numerator instead of the denominator (or *vice versa*) for failing to bring about an optimal ratio is by itself not helpful. What Keynes (1936, Ch. 19) had in mind was that a reduction in money wages would reduce aggregate demand through a fall in consumption, but there are many possible counterarguments: (1) even if real wages fall, total wage income could rise if the elasticity of demand exceeds one; (2) even if wage income falls, the disposable income of nonwage earners could rise and they also make many consumption decisions; and (3) it is not obvious that the functional distribution of disposable income is an important determinant of consumption expenditures.

3.7   The Empirical Relevance of the Model

The crucial implication of the labor-market model developed in this chapter is that employment will be dictated by a downward-sloping labor-use curve, both in equilibrium and in disequilibrium. Thus, there should be a negative relationship between employment and real wages. To test this hypothesis, equation (3.9) is adopted as a starting point. The following adjustments are made: (a) it is estimated in first-difference form; (b) in the absence of up-to-date data on the capital stock, particularly human capital, output changes will be used as the scale variable; (c) the natural rate has been omitted since its first difference would be virtually zero; and (d) a constant term, that would have captured such things as disembodied technical change, was not significantly different from zero. The resulting specification conforms to the suggested estimation equation (48) in Hamermesh (1986) for a CES production function. Variables are defined as follows: n is the natural log of total civilian employment, in thousands of persons (*ERP*, 1991, Table B-33); y is the natural log of GNP in billions of 1982 dollars (Table B-2); and $(w - p)$ is the natural log of average weekly earnings in private nonagricultural industries in 1982 dollars (Table B-44). The equation was estimated with annual data for 1954-90 after a Chow test indicated a structural break in the mid 1950s when estimated for 1948-90. The results, employing TSLS, are as follows:

$$\Delta n = \underset{(.054)}{0.641} \ \Delta y - \underset{(.098)}{0.354} \ \Delta(w - p) \quad \begin{array}{l} \bar{R}^2 = 0.616, \\ F = 6.922 \end{array} \quad (3.16)$$

with bracketed terms being standard errors.[6] These robust results are obtained despite the substantial changes in the composition of employment over this time period, despite the fact that total compensation has probably increased faster than weekly wages, and despite the supply shocks of the 1970s that temporarily shifted the labor-use curve downward. The parameter estimates can be given further quantitative evaluation. At an initial level of employment, a 1% increase in output with a constant wage would cause firms to reduce the marginal product of workers by hiring more of them. The end result is an increase in n by 0.064, which in 1990 would have meant an employment level of 118,539 thousand instead of the actual 117,914 thousand. Hamermesh (1986, p. 448) interprets the coefficient on output as a measure of the returns to scale. Since the coefficient is significantly different from one, constant returns to scale can be rejected. Turning to the coefficient on the wage rate, a decline in the weekly real wage by 1% would have lead to an employment level of 122,088 thousand in 1990. The coeffi-

---

[6] The instruments in this regression were the following variables: a trend, its square, the growth rate of M1, Gordon's natural rate, a dummy variable for oil-price shocks in 1974 and 1979 and government employment. A further Chow test for a structural break between 1974 and 1975 produced an $F = 0.597$ and a test for first-order serial correlation using Pindyck and Rubinfeld (1991, eq. 6.28) generated a t value of -0.028.

cient is an estimate of the elasticity of substitution between labor and capital, according to Hamermesh (1986, p. 453) who reports previous estimates in the range 0.15 to 0.5.

In their pioneering empirical work in this area, both Dunlop (1938) and Tarshis (1939) failed to find a strong negative relationship in prewar employment and real wage data. More recent efforts with postwar data have not been any more successful. This has lead Lucas (1981, p. 226) to state: "Observed real wages ... do [not] exhibit consistent pro- or countercyclical tendencies. This suggests that any attempt to assign systematic real wage movements a central role in an explanation of business cycles is doomed to failure." It should be noted that most previous studies have concentrated on hours of work and hourly wages, whereas the variables used here are number of employees and the weekly wage. Furthermore, the estimated demand equation performs very well in the difficult period of 1982-90. It predicts the negative change in 1982 and the largest error is only -0.8% in 1988.

What is particularly encouraging about these empirical results is that the demand for labor included in n contains a growing proportion of government employment that is unlikely to respond to wage changes as would the number of employees in a profit-maximizing firm in the private sector. In 1950, government employment was 13.3% of total employees on nonagricultural payrolls, but by 1990 this ratio had risen to 16.6% (*ERP*, 1991, Table B-43). In fact, government employment in 1990 was almost as large as employment in the manufacturing sector. Therefore, if we re-estimate the labor-use equation for the private sector alone, the relationship between n and $(w - p)$ should be even stronger. The new variables are: n^p is the natural log of total employees on nonagricultural payrolls minus government employees (Table B-43)[7] and y^p is real GNP minus government sector GNP (Table B-9). In all other respects, the estimation is the same as above. The new results are:

$$\Delta n^p = 0.729 \ \Delta y^p - 0.490 \ \Delta(w - p) \quad \bar{R}^2 = 0.641.$$
$$\quad \ (.077) \qquad \quad (.147) \qquad \qquad F = 11.257 \quad (3.17)$$

Both coefficients are now larger than previously, but otherwise the

---

[7] These employment data differ from those in Table B-33 used previously which include proprietors, self-employed persons, domestic servants, and unpaid family workers.

results are quite comparable; the larger coefficient attached to the real wage verifies that private-sector firms are more responsive to wage changes than all employers taken together.

The factors influencing government employment are difficult to summarize. State and local governments have approximately five times as many employees as does the federal government, without having the same stabilization role. While there have been a few years in which federal government employment has fallen (e.g., 1981), state and local governments seem always to be hiring more workers. Is there any evidence of countercyclical employment practices in the government sector? The "best" explanation of government employment was provided by the following first-order serial correlation regression:

$$
\begin{aligned}
\Delta n^g = {} & 0.019 + 0.547 \ \Delta y^g + 0.001 \ (u - u^*) \\
& (.006) \quad (.141) \qquad\ (.001) \\
& + 0.711 \ \epsilon_{-1}, \quad \bar{R}^2 = 0.663, \ D.W. = 1.70, \\
& \ (.124) \qquad\ F = 24.593
\end{aligned}
\tag{3.18}
$$

where n^g and y^g represent the natural logs of government employment (Table B-43) and output (Table B-9) and $u - u^*$ is the difference between the actual and natural rates of unemployment, the latter taken from Gordon (1993). In this regression, the unemployment gap replaces the real wage as a determinant of employment because governments are not profit maximizers; instead they are supposed to be countercyclical in their behavior. The lack of a *significantly* positive coefficient for $u - u^*$ indicates that employment by government does not respond systematically to changes in the unemployment rate; instead it is geared to their output plus an exogenous growth rate of about 1.9% per annum.

3.8 Conclusions about Labor-Market Characteristics

Transactions in the labor market have greater implications for individual welfare than transactions in any other market. Not only are career choices and decisions about employers of life-long importance, but involuntary unemployment or the lack of sufficient labor-market transactions have been the source of macroeconomic intervention by governments since the Great Depression of the 1930s. The analysis of the labor-market behavior developed in this chapter has brought out one important conclusion for welfare evaluations that will be attempted in the next chapter: the heterogeneity of individuals who sell their services in that market. Workers differ in two important respects: (1) they have different reservation wages and thus derive different levels of rent from their work effort and (2) they have greater or lesser security in their employment. Therefore, those individuals who have low reservation wages but high security will have a greater level of welfare than those with higher reservation wages and low security, even though they do the same job and work the same number of hours. These differences in welfare lead to divergent opinions about optimal macroeconomic policies, as Chapter 4 will try to establish.

4

The Welfare Economics of Macropolicy

Welfare economics is concerned with comparing two or more situations and making systematic decisions about the potential improvements in well-being available by moving from one position to another. An unambiguous improvement is possible only if some people are made better off and no one is made worse off. In other words, there must be some "winners", but no "losers". This is called a Pareto improvement. It has the advantage of avoiding interpersonal comparisons in which it would be necessary to conclude that person A's welfare gain is somehow more important than person B's welfare loss. Very few changes in an economy have this characteristic; there will almost always be some identifiable losers. It is still possible to favor a move if the losers can be compensated by the winners, but such compensation schemes are difficult to implement and virtually impossible to enforce in real-world circumstances. As a result, welfare comparisons usually lead to bitter debates concerning the pros and cons of new initiatives and ultimately to unresolvable conflicts over "property rights to the *status quo*". It is in the labor market that these struggles are most fierce and we must investigate the characteristics of the participants in this market to understand how the welfare of specific groups changes with macroeconomic policies.

4.1   Welfare Analysis in the Labor Market

To start the analysis we need to identify three groups in an economy: (1) the owners of firms, (2) those individuals who currently have a job, and (3) those persons who have decided to participate in the labor market but are currently unemployed. Firms will be treated as identical, making the "representative" firm's welfare the appropriate measure of its approval or disapproval of any proposed change.[1] However, individuals who supply labor differ in two respects: (1) their reservation wage and (2) the likelihood of losing their job based on the "security" of their employment. The first characteristic determines the amount of rent a worker receives from employment; the lower is the reservation wage relative to the actual wage the larger is the rent component of wage income. Although certain factors such as nonwage income can help to determine a person's reservation wage, it remains virtually unobservable and most labor-force participants probably would not reveal their reservation wage if asked by a poll taker, for example. Security of employment, on the other hand, is likely to be determined to a large extent by seniority with a firm. Most explicit union contracts in the United States have lay-off clauses based on "last-in-first-out". Even in nonunion settings, firms often lay-off the least experienced workers. More recently however, particularly in the 1982 and 1991 recessions, whole plants have closed their doors and even the most senior workers have lost their jobs, although they usually get severance packages that are geared to years of employment.

Because the contract nature of the labor market suggests the possibility of transactions at other-than-equilibrium wages and because, even in equilibrium there are unemployed workers,[2] it is necessary to analyze the welfare implications of all possible price-quantity combinations in that market. For that purpose we need the labor-market diagram of Fig. 3-4, which is here reproduced as Fig. 4-1. It should be remembered that the horizontal axis represents the number of workers who are all working a fixed number of hours, $\bar{H}$. The demand curve, N^d is downward sloping as firms will want to increase their labor input (i.e., the number of workers) when the wage falls. This feature relies only on a requirement that the marginal product of workers declines as their employ-

---

[1] Firms differ in a number of characteristics, but it is possible for owners of shares to these firms to diversify and everyone could, at least potentially, have the same portfolio.

[2] Despite the awkwardness of the phrase, "unemployed workers" is better terminology than "participants in the labor market who are involuntarily unemployed".

ment increases. The supply curve, N^s, represents the number of workers who have made a choice to work $\bar{H}$ hours rather than not work at all. Since this choice depends on the reservation wage and since individuals will differ with respect to their reservation wage as the actual wage rises, more and more individuals will surpass their reservation wage and be available for employment. Hence, each point on the supply curve represents a different individual, with persons having a low reservation wage being near the lower left-hand end of the curve and those with high reservation wages being at the upper right-hand end of the curve. As was shown in Chapter 3, diversity of tastes in the work-leisure choice, in access to nonearned income and perhaps in other factors, gives rise to entry into the labor force at different wages.

4.1.1 The Preferences of Firms

If the owners of firms have a choice in the price-quantity combination of wages and number of workers, they would opt to be on their demand curve and once there, they would like the lowest possible point. In this instance, the "demand curve" is the actual-employment curve, N in Fig. 4-1, rather than the demand curve as shown by N^d in the same diagram since in Chapter 3 it was shown that there are likely to be optimal vacancies that the firm does not fill because of adjustment costs that it faces. To keep terminology as transparent as possible, we will refer to N as the labor-use curve. First, we must show that points on the labor-use curve are superior to those off the labor-use curve. From the equilibrium condition that the marginal product of labor should equal the real wage, we can find all combinations of W/P and N that maintain a given level of profits for the firm. Such an isoprofit curve is shown in Fig. 4-1 as Π_0. It has an inverted 'U'–shape with its apex on the labor-use curve since any other level of N for a given W/P would lead to lower profits than the one that is actually on the N curve. In other words, the firm would have to be allowed to pay a lower real wage if it were "forced" to use a suboptimal number of workers. This result can be shown by differentiating $W/P = Y_N(N)$ totally to obtain the slope of the isoprofit curve:

$$\frac{d(W/P)}{dN} = \frac{Y_N - W/P}{N}.$$

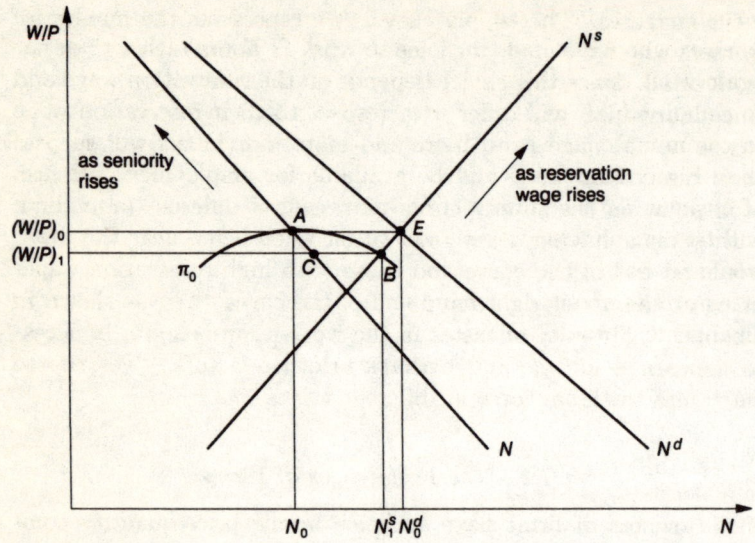

Fig. 4-1. Welfare positions in the labor market.

To the right of the demand curve, $Y_N < W/P$ and the slope of the isoprofit curve is negative; to the left, $Y_N > W/P$ and the slope is positive.

Second, a whole family of isoprofit curves could be drawn with their highest point always on the labor-use curve. As we move down and to the right along N, profits would rise since, although additional revenues and costs are equal from extra employment, the reduction in the wage costs of existing workers adds to profits. By differentiating the profit function from equation (3.5), $\Pi = Y(N, K) - (W/P)N - (R/P)K$, with respect to W/P and N, we obtain:

$$d\Pi = Y_N dN - \frac{W}{P} dN - N d\frac{W}{P},$$

where the first two elements cancel when $Y_N = W/P$ and thus $d\Pi > 0$ for $d(W/P) < 0$.

From this analysis, it is easy to see why firms want to maintain flexibility in the labor input when they are presented with a fixed real wage during a contract period. For example, if the real wage rises because W increases faster than P, firms want the freedom to lay off some workers to get back to the labor-use curve. Alternatively, if the N curve shifted down and to the left because of some exogenous decrease in the productivity of workers, they would again want the right to get rid of some workers, this time in order to get on to the new labor-use curve. In either case, if they had to commit themselves to keep N_0 workers and pay them $(W/P)_0$ as in Fig. 4-1, their profits would fall and they may in fact go out of business if they cannot cover their variable costs. Therefore, it will be difficult to insist on a new institutional arrangement that would fix both the real wage and the level of employment without attempting to compensate firms for the extra rigidity that such an arrangement would impose.

4.1.2   What do Workers Want?

All individuals want to maximize their welfare, but since they differ in at least two respects in terms of the their labor-market experience (i.e., reservation wage and employment security) it will not be surprising to find that some workers will have greater economic satisfaction than others from a particular combination of a real wage and employment level on the labor-use curve. What then are the effects of these differences on welfare? We will find that workers are distributed along the labor-use curve in Fig. 4-1 on the basis of their employment security and along the labor-supply curve on the basis of their reservation wage. Most firms when faced with the uncomfortable task of letting some workers go do not rely on some random-number system or on an arbitrary selection system such as an alphabetical order of names. Instead, they use inverse seniority or "last-in-first-out". Even if such rules were not incorporated into union contracts as they frequently are, firms would find it useful to let the least experienced and thus presumably the least productive workers go when all workers are paid the same wage. Therefore, one can think of all existing workers being distributed on the labor-use curve, with the most senior workers at the upper left and the lowest seniority workers at the lowest-to-the-right point on the labor-use curve consistent with current employment. If the wage were to rise, firms lay off the most junior workers; workers with many years of seniority would only lose their jobs if the real wage rises by a great deal or if the firm shuts down completely. Since workers retire or leave for their own reasons, continuing workers move up the seniority ladder and for that reason a worker who remains with a firm will find his exposure to lay-offs reduced over time.

In Chapter 3, the supply of workers was derived from allowing the actual wage rate to rise above the reservation wage of more and more individuals. Once a person's reservation wage is passed he or she does not alter any decision in the labor market; nevertheless, welfare is increased as a result of higher rents. In fact, for any one person, the difference between the actual wage and their reservation wage is all economic rent; therefore, the lower a person's reservation wage compared to the actual wage, the more rent they receive. By differentiating the utility function of a person who has chosen to participate in the labor market and has a job working $\bar{H}$ hours a week, we obtain $dU = U_2 \bar{H} d(W/P) > 0$ for $d(W/P) > 0$.

On the other hand, a person who has not yet entered the labor force because the reservation wage is still higher than the current wage will not benefit from a change in the wage-employment outcome. In fact, since their utility is depicted by $U_0 = U(24, I_0)$, where I_0 is nonwage income, utility remains constant. Finally, a person who is in the labor force but becomes involuntarily unemployed when the wage rises, will be worse off. From the determination of the reservation wage we know that $U_r = U_0$, where U_r is the level of utility available from working exactly at the reservation wage. Now if the wage rises and employment continues utility will also rise. If the wage rises once again but now the worker becomes laid off, utility will fall again to U_0 and this person is worse off.

These changes in welfare are shown in Fig. 4-2. Until the reservation wage is reached, utility is constant based on total leisure and goods consumption from nonwage income, I_0. After the wage passes $(W/P)_r$, the person works $\bar{H}$ hours and welfare rises until the wage becomes so high that the person becomes unemployed once more. It can be seen in part (b) of Fig. 4-2 that the increase in welfare between $(W/P)_r$ and $(W/P)_u$ is derived from a rent payment to that person because she has done nothing different in that interval. Also, it is obvious that the amount of rent depends on these two variables. A person with a lower reservation wage and a higher wage that results in unemployment will enjoy a larger amount of rent, as indicated by the dotted lines in Fig. 4-2 (b). Moreover, at a wage between $(W/P)_r$ and $(W/P)_u$, welfare is greater for the person with the wider range between these two variables.

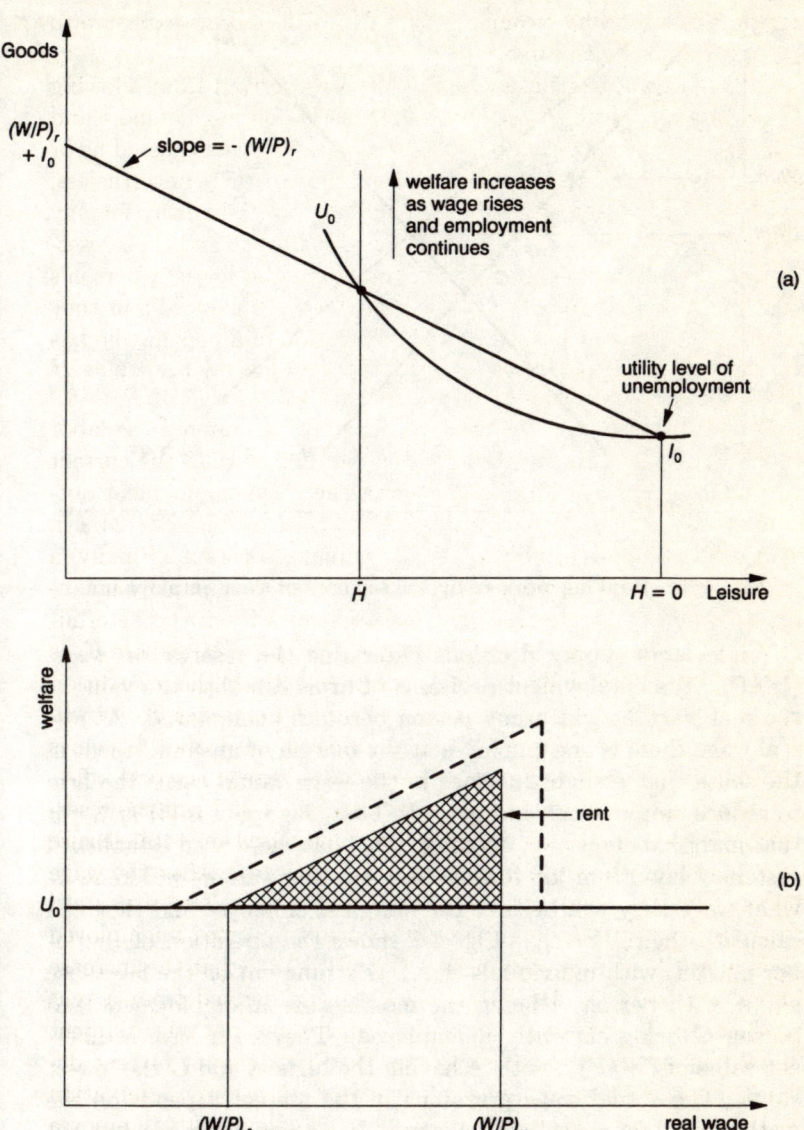

Fig. 4-2. Welfare of the employed and the unemployed.

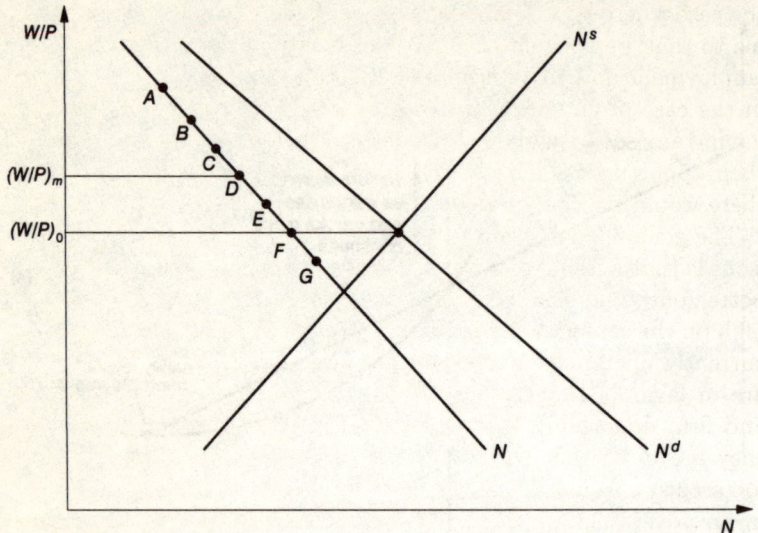

Fig. 4-3.   Ranking workers by the security of their employment.

While labor-supply decisions determine the reservation wage, $(W/P)_r$, the employment decisions of firms establish the value of the real wage at which any person becomes unemployed. At any real wage there is one employee at the margin of unemployment in the sense that a slight increase in the wage would cause the firm to reduce employment and output. That wage rate is $(W/P)_u$ for that marginal employee. To the extent that there is an established system of lay-offs or job termination, existing workers will know at what wage they will become the marginal employee and they can calculate their $(W/P)_u$. Fig. 4-3 shows the operation of the labor market, with individuals $A, \ldots, G$ strung out on the labor-use curve, with person A being the most secure in employment and person G being currently unemployed. They each have a different value of $(W/P)_u$, with A having the highest and G the lowest value. The actual wage prevailing in the market depends on the method used for wage determination. In a competitive market, the real wage will be established at $(W/P)_e$ and only person G remains unemployed. If, on the other hand, a median-voter method is used, person D is the decision-maker and he would choose a wage just below $(W/P)_m$ causing E, F, and G to be unemployed. Only in the case where lay-offs are completely random would it be impossible to rank persons on the labor-use curve by the security of their employment and to determine individual values of $(W/P)_u$. Even in the case of an entire firm closing its operations and no worker having any security of employment, individuals would still differ in their opportunities for jobs elsewhere and severance pay; therefore there would still be a range of values for $(W/P)_u$.

The general conclusion to be drawn from these welfare comparisons is that a rising real wage makes some labor-force participants better off while others become worse off. Those with a position high on the seniority list favor high real wages while those who are currently unemployed or would become so if the wage were raised are in favor of lower wages. In that sense, unemployed workers and firm management have identical goals of keeping wages low; they are in conflict with those workers who have a great deal of job security. While it is quite normal to think of workers and firms in an adversarial or even confrontational environment, it is perhaps unusual to think of workers in conflict with themselves. In recent times the distinction between "inside" and "outside" workers has come to mean that some individuals in the labor force have more power to influence events than others. In this context, inside workers could be thought of as those who gain from high wages because of their immunity to lay-offs while outside workers are those who would benefit from lower wages. The recent history of entire companies disappearing through mergers and bankruptcies makes it possible that the complete work force will lose their jobs. In these situations, there are still "inside" workers because they have market power in other job opportunities.

4.2 The Possibility of Pareto Improvements

The reason that the labor market does not satisfy the requirements of optimality at equilibrium is the existence of a positive natural rate of unemployment. In that light, it is useful to consider methods of reducing or even eliminating the natural rate and find out who gains or loses from such initiatives.

4.2.1 Optimal Subsidization

Such policy initiatives should involve *optimal intervention* to remove the distortion in the labor market, which in the presence of adjustment costs means that the firm has to pay more for every worker than the value of the marginal product of that worker. In other words, hiring and training costs are not easily recouped by the firm and it will therefore not incur these costs to the extent necessary to provide all willing workers a job in equilibrium.

Optimal intervention involves taking action in the market in which the distortion is located and should mirror the distortion itself. This would involve the government subsidizing the firm's costs of filling vacancies. From Chapter 3 we were able to conclude that when firms face adjustment costs, α_1, and disequilibrium costs, α_2, there will be an equilibrium level of vacancies, the size of which depends positively on α_1 and negatively on α_2. If governments were able to pay for these costs without introducing other distortions elsewhere, vacancies would disappear in equilibrium, or in other words, the N curve in Fig. 4-1, would shift rightward until it coincided with the N^d curve. Then unemployment could only occur during periods of excess supply. When excess demand prevails, actual employment would have to be dictated by the supply curve, N^s.

Subsidies of this type would clearly be welcomed by the firms themselves, who would lobby for their introduction. Moreover, currently unemployed workers would benefit from receiving job offers, which allow them to reach a higher utility level than exists at U_0 based on I_0. Finally, workers who have jobs would be indifferent to these subsidies, since the real wage would remain at $(W/P)_0$ in Fig. 4-1 at the intersection of the N^s and N^d (now also the N) curves. As a result this is a Pareto improvement when two of the groups operating in the labor market benefit and the third group is not made worse off.

In this abstract setting, optimal intervention in the form of government subsidies to cover firms' adjustment costs has much appeal, but for practical reasons it is not likely to be a useful solution. This pessimistic appraisal arises from a situation of moral hazard, in which a firm has the ability to choose between events, only one of which is rewarded. In this instance, firms would have an incentive to label everything as "adjustment costs" in order to maximize their subsidy. If there were an objective test of what constitutes adjustment costs, firms would not face moral hazard, but in practice it would be virtually impossible for government bureaucrats to enforce rules against illegitimate activity in this area. A subsidy paid to the firm for each worker on their payroll, while easier to administer, would not be optimal either since employment costs and adjustment costs may only be loosely connected.

Moreover, these subsidies would have to be financed by a new tax, which would have to be of a "lump-sum" nature in order to make it nondistortionary. But most taxes are themselves the source of distortions. For example, if the government decided to levy a wage tax to generate the necessary revenue for the subsidy, then wages paid by firms would have to rise but wages received by workers would fall as the tax drives a wedge between them, and employment might in fact decrease as firms substitute towards a cheaper factor of production. Such a situation would clearly not benefit either firms or existing workers.

An alternative policy would be to reduce the search costs faced by firms by making the labor force more homogeneous, that is to reduce or eliminate the "square-pegs-round-holes" problem. This would involve policies that promote the mobility of workers, either geographically or between skills. Nevertheless, despite many attempts at skill-training schemes, there is little evidence that they have reduced the natural rate of unemployment. In fact, some recent governmental policies such as more generous unemployment benefits that are designed to make it easier for workers to search for jobs or to improve their qualifications have in fact raised the natural rate in the 1960s and 1970s by increasing the incidence of voluntary quits. What is more, such labor-mobility programs cost a great deal of money and would again require a tax that would generate its own distortions.

In the same vein, government hiring of those who are unemployed at the natural rate has the same advantages and drawbacks as the subsidy scheme discussed earlier. Government could offer the going wage to anyone who would take a job. Presumably, only those who are "naturally" unemployed would accept the offer. Those with jobs in private industry would not be affected, nor would the owners of firms; thus a Pareto improvement is possible. However, it is crucial that the wage offered is the equilibrium wage, $(W/P)_0$ in Fig. 4-1. If the going wage were at a position of excess demand, then governments would hire not only those who are trapped in the natural rate of unemployment, but also those between the supply and demand curves, namely those individuals who were lured into the job market and those who have lost their jobs because of the temporarily high wage. Moreover, funding for this hiring would again require distortionary taxes since the government would probably make a loss in its production, when the workforce is likely to have low productivity and therefore, $Y_N < W/P$.

If the natural rate could be eliminated by optimal intervention, it would lead to disequilibrium transactions that are different from those when a positive natural rate exists. Instead of being always on the labor-use curve, now excess demand would mean transactions limited by the demand curve in excess-supply situations and by the supply curve in excess-demand situations. From the previous discussion we know that if the real wage rises to create excess supply, existing workers are better off, while owners of firms and those who become unemployed are worse off. In excess-demand situations, actual employment would fall along the supply curve as the wage also falls. Those who continue to hold jobs are worse off because of the lower wage; those who become unemployed appear to be doing so willingly, but compared to their previous position, they are worse off. The effect on firms is ambiguous since both wages and employment are lower. By differentiating the profit function, we obtain $d\Pi = (Y_N - W/P)dN - Nd(W/P) = ?$ when $Y_N > W/P$ to the left of the demand curve and $dN < 0$, $d(W/P) < 0$.

Since disequilibrium transactions will not be considered abnormal by all participants in the labor market, how will they respond to the possibility of having to make these transactions on the supply curve when the natural rate has been eliminated? The choice is between points C and B in Fig. 4-1, the former being the relevant position with a natural rate and the latter without one. At C profits are higher than at B, therefore, firms favor the existence of a natural rate. Workers who continue to work are indifferent between C and B, while those who are involuntarily unemployed prefer B to C. From that perspective, eliminating the natural rate is not a Pareto improvement if participants are aware of the need for transactions in excess-demand conditions.

4.2.2   *Alternative Labor Market Institutions*

If it proves difficult or inadvisable to rely on subsidies or direct government hiring to eliminate the adverse consequences of a positive natural rate of unemployment, might one consider altering some of the institutional arrangements in the labor market that would improve its operation? One suggestion is to change the rules for lay-offs: instead of seniority, firms would use a random-number system. In these circumstances, since all workers would face the same probability of lay-offs, the distinction between inside workers and outside workers would be reduced and all workers would face the possibility of being at U_0 in Fig. 4-2. However, such a change in the rules applicable to the labor market would have to involve some democratic decision-making process whereby the median voter makes the crucial decision which is then binding on everyone else. Since the current arrangement based on seniority favors the vast majority of workers, "inside" workers who are never laid off would prevent the adoption of the random-number system since it deprives them of their current privileged status. Moreover, this system of lay-offs would not contribute to the reduction of the natural rate of unemployment.

Another suggestion that would spread the burden of unemployment more equally than the current system would be to allow hours per worker to vary as demand for labor rises or falls. In this case, when firms require extra labor, they would ask all their current workers to work overtime, whereas reductions in the labor input would involve shorter hours for everyone. Again, the very egalitarian nature of this system would make it unacceptable to inside workers who prefer to force a small minority of workers to absorb all of the costs of disequilibrium in the labor market. As shown in Chapter 3, it is not always the case that workers wish to work overtime hours, unless the overtime premium is large enough. Also, shortening the workweek may not satisfy those workers who find $\bar{H}$ hours to be optimal. Moreover, firms would not want to be placed in a position where the number of workers is fixed and only hours per worker can be adjusted. In a normally expanding firm, extra workers would be cheaper than paying overtime (e.g., time-and-a-half) to existing workers despite the adjustment costs faced by a firm when it hires more workers. Therefore, because firms would not be allowed to take on more workers, they would object to the rigidities and overtime costs imposed by a system of variable hours. In this case, there is a viable coalition between management of firms and existing high-seniority workers against such an arrangement.

4.2.3   Macropolicy Initiatives

The previous attempts in this chapter at optimal intervention or institutional changes were addressed at the labor market itself, but it is worth investigating the possibility that macroeconomic policies which operate in the goods market (i.e., fiscal policy) or the money market (i.e., monetary policy) may be able to reach "full employment" without eliminating the natural rate. Starting from a position of equilibrium in Fig. 4-1, denoted by A in terms of the wage-employment combination, we could move along the isoprofit curve to B, by lowering wages and increasing employment without having any adverse consequences for the firms, but creating new jobs for some of those who were previously unemployed and who therefore gain from the move to B. In fact, at B, unemployment has been entirely eliminated since actual employment is now equal to the supply of workers. However, "inside" workers have become worse off because of the lower wage. Thus a Pareto improvement is not possible, but one could argue that those who are secure in their jobs should be forced to make some sacrifices for the unemployed. However, even if we are prepared to accept this interpersonal comparison, there are additional arguments against this change. The difficulty is that it is impossible to sustain the wage-employment combination at B for two reasons: (1) it would maintain excess demand in the labor market, and (2) it would be virtually impossible to force firms to operate to the right of the labor-use curve.

The government could in some circumstances move the real wage down to $(W/P)_1$ by increasing the inflation rate after contracts have been agreed through expansionary monetary or fiscal policies, but sooner or later the pressures of excess demand will cause new contracts to incorporate a higher expected inflation and the real wage will rise again towards $(W/P)_0$. It can now be seen that the sacrifice required by existing workers to make room for some of the unemployed workers would be to accept the reduction in the real wage to $(W/P)_1$. However, it is difficult to imagine how that would be enforced, especially in a fragmented market for labor where many different contracts are "signed" at different times. It would require some kind of governmentally-imposed wage controls, not for short periods of time as they have been used in extraordinary inflationary situations in the past, but permanently.

Even if it were possible to keep the real wage at $(W/P)_1$, it is also necessary to ensure that firms comply with the requirement that employment expand to N_1^d. Since this is on the same isoprofit curve as A, it would seem that firms are indifferent between these two points. Nevertheless, firms now have an incentive to reduce employment to C which has more profits than Π_0. It could pretend that the labor-use curve has shifted to the left as an excuse for reducing employment, without much fear of contradiction since the location of a demand curve is difficult to establish without inside information of the firm's situation (i.e., profits).

4.3   The Welfare Effects of Stabilization Policy

While the previous section was devoted to the issue of trying to determine the benefits of deliberately changing the natural rate of unemployment, here the focus is on the question of whether the government should use its macropolicies to restore equilibrium in the labor market when some unpredictable event creates excess supply or demand in that market and the wage contract cannot be changed immediately. In some sense the issue here is the same as in the clash between Keynesians and new classical economists who have debated the usefulness of government intervention in the macroeconomy for the past two decades. In that confrontation, both sides took for granted that equilibrium in the labor market was optimal and at stake was the ability of stabilization policies to reach this equilibrium faster or with less pain. Here, in this chapter, we have already seen that with a natural rate of unemployment, equilibrium is not a *summum bonum* because some individuals will be involuntarily unemployed. The question then becomes fundamentally different: Can stabilization policy improve on the *status quo ante*?

In Fig. 4-4, an initial equilibrium is shown at E, with a real wage of $(W/P)_0$. At this point expected and actual inflation coincide or nominal wage increases just match the current rate of inflation. Now consider an unexpected event that raises the actual inflation rate above the contractually agreed increase in nominal wages. This event will cause the real wage to decline to $(W/P)_1$ and employment will expand from N_0 to N_1. From our previous analysis of the welfare effects on specific groups we can predict that: (1) firms are better off because of higher profits, (2) existing workers are worse off because of the lower wage, and (3) newly

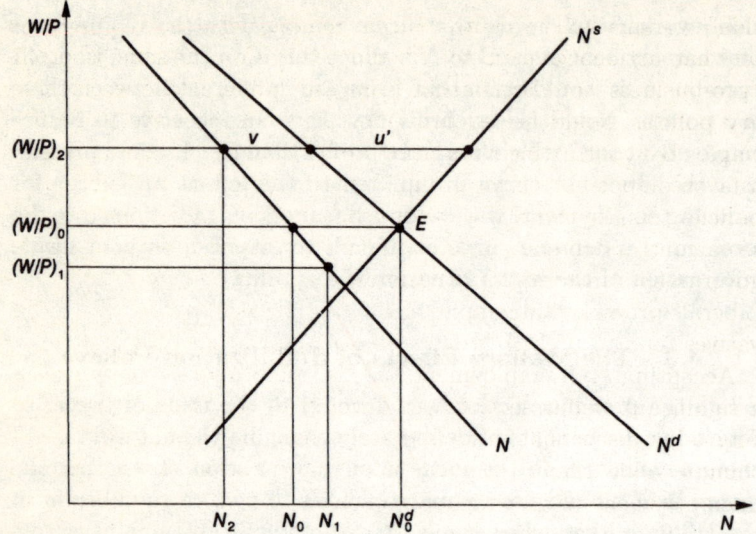

Fig. 4-4.   Welfare and excess demand or excess supply.

hired workers are better off than they were in a state of unemployment. As a consequence, there is no clear consensus that the government should use contractionary policy to return the labor market to equilibrium since some individuals would gain while others would lose.

By symmetry, if the economy were pushed to a higher wage, $(W/P)_2$, because of some contractionary event that lowered the inflation rate below the increase in nominal wages, firms would want policies implemented that restored equilibrium. They would be joined by workers who became unemployed as firms reduced their work force from N_0 to N_2, but they would be opposed by "inside" workers who enjoy the extra rents from the higher wage.

In both instances, sooner or later, market pressures will exert themselves and the labor market will return to equilibrium, but in the meantime a significant portion of labor-market participants are better off in disequilibrium than in equilibrium. Therefore, one *cannot* assert that stabilization policies designed to speed the adjustment of the labor market back to equilibrium represent a Pareto improvement. Even if we dismiss "outside" workers as a small fringe group with little political power, firms and their "inside" workers will remain in an adversarial position on the issue of what action governments should take. Only if government is "pro-business" or "anti-labor" could we predict that expansionary policies would be favored since they help to reduce the real wage. By contrast, governments that treat labor movements as a favored special-interest group would tend to use contractionary policies to raise the real wage of inside workers. These predictions seem contrary to our expectations of "conservative" and "liberal" governments in terms of commitment to intervention in markets. Liberals promise "full employment" to the electorate while conservatives tend to preach "price stability".

Accepting "full employment" as a macroeconomic goal involves a significant welfare loss for a large number in the electorate. In Fig. 4-1, we saw that inside workers would have to sacrifice something to allow the economy to move from A at the natural rate of unemployment to B which eliminated all involuntary unemployment. That sacrifice was measured as a permanent reduction in the real wage from $(W/P)_0$ to $(W/P)_1$. Unless these workers are altruistic or they have a fear that their employment is in some jeopardy, their own welfare would dictate disapproval of this wage reduction. In other words, full employment is difficult to accept as a self-interested, democratically-determined decision.

4.4 The Equity Argument

If Pareto improvements cannot be used as arguments in favor of activist stabilization policy, equity grounds are all that is left, where one simply accepts the notion that relegating 5% to 10% of the labor force to virtually permanent unemployment goes against the concept of "fairness". Despite being outnumbered in a democracy, those who are involuntarily unemployed should not be expected to accept a lower standard of living just because the labor market operates efficiently when they are out of work. If that position is adopted, then stabilization policy can be thought of as an elaborate system of transfer payments from those who are employed to those who are not.

It may be argued that self-financing unemployment insurance schemes meet that requirement already: those who are employed pay insurance premiums into a fund which in turn makes payments to those who are unemployed. In that way, it is possible to give everyone the same level of income. However, it is immediately obvious that such a scheme has the seeds of its own destruction because it is again subject to moral hazard. Since it is now possible to enjoy leisure from $H = 0$ *and* the level of goods consumption that derives from working $\bar{H}$ hours, it would be in everyone's interest to be labelled involuntarily unemployed by pretending to look for a job, but always without success. It is for that reason that most unemployment insurance systems make payments that are substantially below the current wage (i.e., the replacement ratio is less than one), to make work more attractive and unemployment less attractive.

But this still penalizes those who are genuinely unemployed through no fault of their own. By using activist stabilization policy the government can create an environment where more unemployed workers get job offers, thereby generating greater equity among all members of the labor force. From that perspective, a level of employment equal to N_1 in Fig. 4-4 is better than N_0 which in turn is better than N_2. Therefore, governments may not be attempting to return the labor market to equilibrium when they use stabilization policy measures, but instead they are trying to maximize employment, not for its own sake, but to reduce the welfare discrepancy between the employed and the unemployed. It may be the notion of "fairness" that makes "Jobs! Jobs! Jobs!" such a powerful political slogan.

It should be noted that such a policy circumvents the moral-hazard problem of unemployment insurance since individuals actually have to work in order to obtain these "benefits". Furthermore, it is worth pointing out that these equity grounds for stabilization policy impart an expansionary bias to policy decisions. Unlike the goal of equilibrium in the labor market which would require contractionary policies in the face of excess demand, "full" employment requires almost continuous expansionary policy.

4.5   Democratically Determined Wages

Transactions continue to take place in the labor market during periods of excess supply or excess demand because for the vast majority of workers who have job security there is no disequilibrium, except to the extent that they do not wish to work exactly $\bar{H}$ hours. Also, firms will not refuse to continue buying labor inputs in disequilibrium, as long as they are allowed to remain on the labor-demand curve, or more precisely, on their labor-use curve. In that setting, wages are not determined by atomistic competition, but instead, by some democratic process. One feature of labor-market transactions that we do *not* observe is unemployed workers offering their services at wages that are lower than those of currently employed workers at a firm. Instead, there is a solidarity between employed and unemployed workers that suggests a uniformity of interests despite their differences in welfare.

If there is only one "going wage" in the labor market — assuming no differences in skills or other attributes that influence marginal product — but if there are different views as to what that wage should be, it must be determined by some sort of voting process. In a union contract, this procedure would be quite explicit, but in nonunion firms, it may be impossible to generalize the wage-setting process. Nevertheless, the median-voter model seems to be a useful starting point for analyzing the determination of wages. It would appear to be in the self-interest of the median voter to restrict the demand for labor until he or she becomes the marginal worker; that result would maximize his or her utility because it creates the highest wage at which employment continues. Because this would result in an unemployment rate of just less than 50% it is not a plausible outcome, but if we make the median worker risk averse, then a wage will be chosen that makes him or her the marginal worker only if a negative shock to labor demand occurred. Therefore, the equilibrium wage would equal the wage resulting from only half the labor supply being employed minus a risk premium that the median worker would pay to ensure continued employment even in the worst of circumstances.

Let $(W/P)_2$ in Fig. 4-4 now be this equilibrium wage. Instead of observing $u = v$, where v is the natural rate of unemployment arising from the mismatch problem in the labor market and is the optimal vacancy rate for firms, a constant real wage would now require that $u = v + u'$, as shown in Fig. 4-4. Excess demand in the labor market would now exhibit $u < v + u'$ and excess supply would be depicted by $u > v + u'$. The size of u' depends on the role of the median worker according to the structure of the labor market: (a) in a competitive market, u will move to v which is exogenously determined by the size of the "square-pegs-round-holes" problem and $u' = 0$; (b) with a risk-neutral median worker, $u' = .5 - v$, which could be in the neighborhood of 45%; and (c) with a risk-averse median worker, u' will be somewhere in between the outcomes in (a) and (b).

It would be of substantial interest to determine what that risk premium is in the U.S. labor market and how it alters the unemployment rate when the labor market is in equilibrium. The starting point for the analysis is an expectations-augmented Phillips curve:

$$\omega = \pi^e + \rho - \lambda(u - v - u'), \qquad (4.1)$$

where ω is the rate of change of nominal wages, π^e is the expected inflation rate, and ρ is productivity growth that permits the real wage to rise over time. In equilibrium, $\omega = \pi^e + \rho$, which would allow us to calculate $u' = u - v$.

To obtain a quantitative evaluation of the role of the median worker, equation (4.1) is estimated, using an additional proxy variable to capture workers' predictions of their own vulnerability to lay-offs. If lay-offs were based entirely on seniority, the majority of workers would be completely secure in their employment, since the unemployment rate has never exceeded 10% in the postwar era. Only if an entire firm or plant is threatened with closure do "inside" workers have to worry about their jobs. This feature will be captured by the index of business failures, BFR, published in the *Economic Report of the President* (1991, Table B-94). When BFR rises, the median worker will demand a lower wage increase, *ceteris paribus*, because that might save his or her job. It is a relatively volatile index; in 1986, it reached a peak value of 120 per 10,000 enterprises, but by 1989, it had fallen to 65. The other variables have been defined previously, but are summarized here: ω is the percentage change in average weekly earnings in current dollars, $\pi^e = \pi_{-1}$ is the percentage change in the GNP deflator in the previous year, u is the actual rate of unemployment, and v is the natural rate of unemployment from Gordon (1993). Also, instead of a constant term, ρ, in equation (4.1) to measure average productivity growth for the entire period, $\Delta(y - n)$ is used as a variable to measure annual changes in productivity; y is the natural log of GNP in 1982 dollars and n is the natural log of total civilian employment. Finally, a dummy variable to capture the oil-price increases, D_o (1974, 1979 = 1), is included to determine whether workers were able to prevent a fall in their real wage. The estimated equation for 1954-90, using TSLS, is the following:

$$\omega = 1.000 \; \pi_{-1} + 0.749 \; \Delta(y - n) - 0.857 \; (u - v)$$
$$\quad\quad (.256) \quad\quad\quad\quad (.195)$$

$$- \; 0.011 \; BFR_{-1} + 1.269 \; D_o \quad \bar{R}^2 = 0.698,$$
$$\quad (.006) \quad\quad\quad (.915) \quad\quad F = 26.59$$

(4.2)

with standard errors in brackets.[3] Using a one-tail test, all coefficients, except for D_o, are significantly different from zero at the 95% confidence level. The coefficient for π_{-1} was set equal to one when the unrestricted coefficient was found not to be significantly different from one. Compared to previous estimates of the *price* Phillips curve, the coefficient for $(u - v)$ in this *wage* Phillips curve is now absolutely larger than in Chapter 2, where estimates of -0.7 and -0.5 were obtained. Finally, the coefficient for productivity growth indicates that about 75% of the increase in output per worker goes to increase real wages; since capital has not been held constant, this productivity growth is not a measure of the change in the marginal product of labor and a coefficient of less than one indicates that as both capital and labor increase their productivity, the gains are shared approximately in the ratio of their contribution to output.

The variable BFR was lagged because it is not published until well into the following year and could not be known contemporaneously. A major drop in this index from 120 to 65, as between 1986 and 1989, would not have a substantial effect on wage increases; they would rise by 0.605 percentage points in the following year. We can also calculate the effect of this additional variable on the unemployment rate in equilibrium. If $\omega = \pi^e$, and assuming a mean value of $BFR = 58.189$, while $\Delta(y - n) = D_o = 0$, then $u' = v + .011/.857 \times 58.189 = v + .747$, indicating a very small increase in the equilibrium unemployment rate. By adding and subtracting a standard error to the coefficient estimate for BFR_{-1}, the range for the additional unemployment becomes 0.339 to 1.154; at most, median-voter behavior increases the unemployment rate

---

[3] The instruments are the same as for the labor-demand regression in Chapter 3, with the addition of π_{-1} and BFR_{-1}. An LM test for first-order serial correlation produced a $t = 1.085$. A Chow test for a structural break between 1974 and 1975 produced $F = 0.040$ and a test for omitting both BFR_{-1} and D_o generated $F = 1.673$.

in equilibrium by about 1%. The conclusion to be reached from this result is that the median worker is either extremely risk averse or does not have a powerful influence on wage determination.[4]

One possible explanation for these minuscule effects of the median worker on the real wage is that current measures of the natural rate of unemployment include both v and u', since there is no reliable way of separating these two variables. If that is the case, then additional variables to capture the risk-averse behavior of the median worker will not have a significant influence on the wage. In Gordon's data for the natural rate this is unlikely because that time series is virtually constant as seen in Chart 3-1. However, the Adams and Coe data for the natural rate could include u' indirectly as Chart 3-1 shows a rising natural rate during the period in which business failures were also increasing.

Nevertheless, since the unemployment rate is nowhere near 50%, it remains a major puzzle why unemployment is such an overwhelming concern to so many people. Opinion polls indicate that unemployment ranks with inflation as the chief source of economic anxiety among voters; politicians promise to "create" jobs when seeking election; and legislation is passed that makes full employment a mandated target. It would be unthinkable for a political party to have a plank in its platform that featured deliberately higher unemployment, yet Chapter 2 documents the upward trend in the unemployment rate and the lack of a coherent and persistent policy to increase employment opportunities.[5]

There are a number of ways of reconciling the desire of the av-

---

[4] Other estimates of equation (4.1) used an index of consumer confidence for the risk-aversion variable and/or the natural rate from Adams and Coe (1989) without obtaining larger quantitative effects on the equilibrium unemployment rate. An earlier study, Prachowny (1987a), covering 1957-83, used Tobin's q variable from *ERP* (1983, Table B-88) as the proxy for risk aversion. The increase in the equilibrium unemployment rate was also very small, about 0.25 percentage points.

[5] A historical study of Congressional races between 1896 and 1964 by Kramer and Lepper (1972, pp. 264-66) found that the inflation rate and the change in the unemployment rate were not significant explanatory variables of the voting patterns. Nevertheless, if we apply the point estimates of the coefficients for these variables in their equation (3), we obtain an "indifference curve" with a trade-off of a one-percent increase in unemployment against a 0.143 percentage-point increase in inflation, suggesting that the latter is much more important in the minds of voters.

erage worker to raise his wage and his wish to have governments provide employment opportunities for those who are involuntarily unemployed. First, the Phillips curve provides a positive relationship between added employment and the real wage, but only in the short run. According to equation (4.1), any policy that leads to lower unemployment, will also lead to an increase in nominal wage growth; given an expected inflation, the *ex ante* real wage will rise. Thus it is in the average worker's interest to have excess demand in the labor market. From the estimates above, a reduction in the unemployment rate by one percent will raise the real weekly wage by somewhat less than one percent in the first year. Of course, this view of the Phillips curve obscures the need for the real wage to fall in subsequent periods in order to re-establish equilibrium in the labor market. This would require the inflation rate to rise above the growth rate of nominal wages for some time and this adjustment is a loss of welfare to the average worker. Therefore, a short-run Phillips curve approach to welfare considerations in the labor market provides only a short-run reconciliation between the interests of employed and unemployed workers.

Second, the average worker may have the view that expansionary policy would involve additional government demand for workers. Traditional stabilization policy operates in either the goods market or the money market and changes the real wage by altering the inflation rate after wage contracts have been made. Then private firms are influenced to hire more workers when the real wage falls. Therefore, real wages and employment move in opposite directions and there is a conflict between the welfare of the worker with a job and the person looking for work. But, if the government hired workers directly, it would shift the demand curve and the labour-use curve outward. Employment and real wages would rise; both groups are better off. Nevertheless, the natural rate is not eliminated by governments adding demand for average workers, unlike the case considered previously, where the government restricted its hiring to those who were "naturally" unemployed.

Third, workers can see a direct link between their employment security and government demand for the output of their industry. While a general reduction in government expenditures will increase the real wage through lower inflation and make secure workers better off, a reduction in government demand in a particular sector of the economy will reduce employment security in that sector and may even reduce wages. Since the democratic process is ill suited to the *allocation* of a given reduction in overall government expenditures, it is safest to resist the reduction in the first place. This issue of allocating reductions in government demand will be analyzed empirically in Chapter 5.

None of these reconciliations is entirely satisfactory because they all rely to some extent on a lack of complete understanding by the average worker of the operation of the labor market or the consequences of policy changes. As a result, it is worthwhile to explore in greater detail the behavior of the median voter concerning issues connected with stabilization policy.

4.6   Democratically Determined Macropolicy

Macropolicy is not typically decided by referendum or townhall meeting, but since the politicians and bureaucrats who are involved in stabilization-policy decisions are responsible, directly or indirectly, to the electorate, the median voter plays a crucial role in determining whether macropolicy will be expansionary or contractionary in any set of circumstances.

To make the policy choice meaningful, there must be a belief by the median voter that governments can select a particular point on the labor-use curve in Fig. 4-1. If the choice were restricted to equilibrium employment at A in Fig. 4-1, then there are no policy choices to be made: the economy has the natural rate of unemployment and any inflation rate that it wants, but the real wage is constant and the welfare of employed and unemployed workers is fixed. Therefore, a public-choice decision about macropolicy must allow governments any point on the labor-use curve as an acceptable outcome. From that perspective, a democratically determined macropolicy involves a democratically chosen real wage. What real wage would put the median voter at his or her maximum welfare? From Fig. 4-2, a real wage just below $(W/P)_u$, the wage that causes the person to become unemployed, would satisfy that requirement because it maximizes the rent available from work effort. Although the size of the rent component in the real wage also depends on the reservation wage, it remains true that this rent reaches its maximum at $(W/P)_u$.

To find the median voter among all workers requires that individually they must all be able to know their $(W/P)_u$ so that they can be ranked from high to low $(W/P)_u$ and the median person chosen. Therefore, the ranking must be based on a single characteristic, such as seniority, which means that the person with median seniority is the median voter. With his or her vote as the deciding factor, policies would be adopted that resulted in a wage rate high enough to cause unemployment in the region of 50%. It was argued in the previous section that risk-averse behavior on the part of the median voter would decrease the optimal wage for this person, but the empirical evidence for risk aversion was difficult to find. Nevertheless, it is worth trying to explain the evident self restraint of the individualistic median voter or, in other words, the apparent desire for low unemployment by those who would gain from having a wage rate that is higher than is consistent with that requirement.

An additional feature of the labor market that is needed for such an explanation is that the median voter in the determination of the wage is in the middle of an array of *currently employed* workers. That is, unemployed workers are disfranchised. As pointed out earlier, this involves the inability of unemployed workers to offer their services to employers at wages that are lower than those prevailing for employed workers. In other words, in their search for employment, the unemployed can make themselves as attractive to employers as they wish but the accepted rules of behavior prevent them from suggesting a lower wage as a means of securing a job offer. An alternative view is to think of unemployed workers being allowed to seek newly created jobs but not being allowed to compete for existing jobs.

In that setting, the median voter depends on the current state of the economy, or more precisely on the current unemployment rate. Starting at the natural rate of unemployment in equilibrium, a self-indulgent median voter could chose a real wage that results in a large increase in the unemployment rate to approximately 50%. The median voter now becomes a person who is in the middle of the array of remaining workers. He or she would have much greater seniority or security of employment and the real wage would rise again, causing the original median voter to become unemployed. The original median voter is fully aware of this potential outcome and therefore does not push the real wage to the individualistic optimum in the first place.

Moreover and perhaps even more importantly, the original median voter is aware of the possibility that the disfranchisement of unemployed workers could be challenged when there is massive unemployment. In other words, the median voter is risk averse, not in terms of adverse shocks to the demand for labor from which he is protected by seniority, but in terms of not wanting to change the rules of conduct in the labor market that put him or her in a privileged position. When the unemployment rate is relatively low, there is an unwritten and unspoken law of solidarity between employed and unemployed workers that requires the latter to refrain from competing with the former. If the unemployment rate became larger, the unemployed workers would begin to question the benefits of labor solidarity and start to undermine the existing wage. It is probably impossible to predict the unemployment rate at which such a shift in regimes would take place. All that is being argued here is that as the number of unemployed workers becomes larger, they will become less afraid of breaking the bond with employed workers. Also, the more predictable is unemployment through seniority rules or other forms of tenure, the more obvious will be the disparate interests of the employed and unemployed workers and the solidarity between them will be weakened. Therefore, "secure" workers will recognize the tension between fostering solidarity with "insecure" workers that preserves their privileged position in the labor market and maximizing that privilege.

Once that tension is recognized, it is not surprising to find that secure workers are concerned and worried about rising unemployment in a recession and that politicians are urged "to do something". For secure workers, the political promise of job creation blunts the urge for insecure workers to compete with them, while the fulfillment of such promises usually works to the disadvantage of the majority of all workers. In Chapter 2, a recurring theme in U.S. postwar macropolicy was the great concern expressed about the ill effects of unemployment together with the virtually complete absence of a sustained effort to eliminate unemployment. The various issues of the *Economic Report of the President* contain many statements criticizing previous administrations for neglecting employment policies and many promises to deal with this problem in the future, but only rare instances of firm commitments on this front. Such a potential inconsistency between promise and performance can be made into a consistent pattern of political behavior if politicians are trying to hold out hope of new jobs to the unemployed and the protection of current wages to secure workers. If unemployed workers think that labor demand will soon expand they are less likely to start competing for a fixed number of jobs and will maintain solidarity with secure workers.[6]

There remains a most important unanswered question: Why do the unemployed workers not recognize the underlying conflict between themselves and secure workers and begin to compete for the limited pool of jobs? After all, workers in many firms or industries that were previously unionized and had a centralized system for approving wage contracts, have changed the rules of determining wages when enough of them believed that they could achieve more without a union. There are two possible explanations. First, the distinction between secure and insecure workers is not as sharp as has been suggested so far. There will always be some random element to lay-offs and job termination and therefore no identifiable group could be completely confident that it has job security. In that case, the observed concern about unemployment by a majority of workers is really a self-interested stance. In other words, the solidarity between employed and unemployed workers arises simply because they are the same persons but at different times. Second, even if an identifiable minority of workers was perpetually relegated to marginal jobs or unemployment, they would find it difficult to change the current rules. They would have to organize into a bloc because any one individual would be afraid to challenge the rules while employers are unlikely to know how to cope with this new type of behavior. But such organization takes resources that the unemployed do not have or could easily be matched by the forces that want the *status quo*. If, on the other hand, unemployment rose substantially and permanently because the median voter had become more greedy, the balance would shift toward the unemployed finding the resources for organizing and benefiting from it.

4.7 Conclusions

Much of the debate in macroeconomic theory has concerned itself with the ability of stabilization policy to improve the performance

---

[6] In private correspondence, Professor Robert Solow has expressed the view that, "It has never been permissible in U.S. politics to say explicitly that creating or allowing unemployment is an anti-inflation policy."

of the macroeconomy. However, the standard of performance seems to be that equilibrium in the labor market is automatically desirable. Robert Barro's (1979, p. 56) often quoted assertion on this point is worth repeating: "Supply not equal to demand as a basis for quantity determination in non-market-clearing models is not on the same analytical level as supply equals demand. The latter mechanism implies that — at least in a direct sense — the private market manages to exhaust trades that are to the perceived mutual advantage of the exchanging parties." That proposition would hold if all individuals in the market were identical. In the labor market, individuals differ in at least two respects: their reservation wage and their seniority, both of which have highly predictable effects on their employment opportunities and the rents that they receive from them. This causes some individuals to try to raise the wage beyond its equilibrium value while others want to depress it to stimulate job offers for themselves. There is no guarantee that these two forces will offset each other to produce equilibrium. Only by trying to make the labor market more egalitarian would equilibrium be in everyone's interests, but such rule changes would be opposed by those who benefit from the current system and since they are in the majority it would be difficult to obtain democratically approved institutional reform.

If macroeconomic performance is measured by the standards of Pareto improvements, then the *status quo* has precedence and stabilization policy initiatives are to be considered undesirable, leaving market forces to cope with disequilibrium situations until they are rectified. Activist macropolicy can only be justified by appeal to equity considerations, where it is acknowledged that involuntarily unemployed persons must be helped, without at the same time giving a "free ride" to those who enjoy the leisure that they have.

5

Public Expenditures
and the Private Interest

As the Cold War and the attendant arms race fade into history, U.S. federal government expenditures on defense are expected to fall significantly, producing what is called a "peace dividend". But it is already apparent that the defense build-up of the early 1980s was an easy political accomplishment compared to the "downsizing" that is required in the early 1990s. How has this asymmetrical approach to spending on defense as a public good arisen? An anecdotal answer is provided by a news report in *The Economist* (June 13, 1992, p. 28):

> [Senator John] Warner [of Virginia] ... has been squeezed from a key seat on the powerful armed-services committee, which will limit his power to influence the military debate in the future. The squeezer is Strom Thurmond [of South Carolina] ... who is first in Senate seniority, [and] has pulled rank to bump Mr Warner as the ranking minority member of the committee in order to save South Carolina from defence cuts. This leaves Mr Warner worse-placed than he was to argue against defence cuts in Virginia, which ranks first in the nation in defence spending per head.

The proposition that will be put forward in this chapter is that public expenditures are not aimed at public goods, but instead are an elaborate and often adversarial system of satisfying individual welfare requirements of voters. In other words, individual preferences for government activity differ for a wide variety of reasons and we must find those of the median voter, the person who, in a democracy, makes the political decision to expand or to contract government expenditures for goods and services. This decision may or may not coincide with the economic interests of the nation as a whole, as represented by the "average" person. What is at issue here is the potential conflict between the political power of the median voter and the economic interest of the average person. Fiscal policy, being a public-choice decision, must satisfy the median voter even if it sacrifices the welfare of the average individual.

In this environment, it will be argued that expanding government demand for goods and services has greater political appeal than contracting that demand. During a business cycle the pressures on the government to follow countercyclical spending patterns will be stronger in a recession than during a boom period, with the end result that total expenditures will spiral upwards even if public goods do not become a stronger element in the welfare calculations of the citizens of the country. This bias in favor of enlarging government expenditures does not inevitably lead to larger fiscal deficits because it is always possible to raise taxes to keep receipts and outlays roughly equal, but Chapter 6 will provide arguments in favor of another bias: deficits are politically more palatable than surpluses.

5.1   Government Demand and Industry Welfare

Government activity affects different individuals in different ways, depending on personal characteristics such as tastes and the size and source of income. One can think of the following links between individual characteristics and views about the appropriate level and financing of government activity: (1) tastes dictate the extent to which a person receives benefits from the provision of public goods; (2) the size of income determines, in large part, the amount of taxes one has to pay; and (3) a person's income usually has some "attachment" to an industry and the welfare of those in that industry depends on government purchasing the output produced there. As a rough guide, one could predict that a person who enjoys public goods, who has a low income that is derived from working in a public-sector industry would want to continue or enlarge government demand for that activity, while those with the opposite characteristics would have a contrary view. During a business cycle, symmetrical fiscal policy requires that the median voter shifts from one favoring higher public expenditures in a recession to someone else who wants lower government demand in a boom period. Unfortunately, asymmetrical fiscal policy leads to ever-larger government expenditures primarily because the median voter will usually accept nothing less than the *status quo* at any point in the business cycle.

Of the three factors that determine an individual's preference for government activity, it will be argued that the third is the crucial one. While it cannot be asserted that tastes for public goods are everywhere equal or that the tax burden is uniformly shared by everyone, the emphasis here will be on the government as provider of employment and income as the major source of differences among individuals.

How does government activity affect those that work in an industry? In a standard general-equilibrium model with mobile factors of production, welfare does not depend on location, but instead, according to the Stolper-Samuelson theorem, on factor intensities and abundances. However, Mussa (1974) and others have pointed out that as long as there are factors of production that are fixed in the short run or that are specific to an industry, the size of the industry directly influences the welfare of the factors that work there. Moreover, one should not draw too sharp a distinction between fixed and variable factors. While labor is normally characterized as the variable factor in a Marshallian short run, workers tend to think of themselves as being "attached" to a firm or industry because they cannot move costlessly to alternative employment without losing seniority rights, pension benefits or payments for firm-specific skills. Here then is a case where all factors in an industry have a uniform opinion about a course of action, unlike the Stolper-Samuelson theorem in which capital and labor oppose each other.

In situations where welfare is determined by one's attachment to an industry, the conflict that appears is not between factors but between industries, depending on specific industry characteristics relative to the average for the economy as a whole. Individual opinion on the appropriate stance for fiscal policy is not geared to their assessment of the state of the business cycle but instead on their industry's reliance on government demand for the sale of their output. For the economy as a whole, a reduction in government demand will be replaced by the "crowding in" of investment expenditures, so that in the long run total aggregate demand remains unchanged. Therefore, in the labor market, the real wage is constant after the policy change and for "secure" workers welfare is the same as before. However, for individual industries, the real wage may be higher or lower depending on what happens to the demand for labor. In Chapter 3, an equilibrium real wage was determined by equation (3.15), which is rewritten here to apply to the ith industry:

$$(w - p)_i = \frac{\beta_{i_2} - \beta_0}{\beta_1 + \beta_3}, \tag{5.1}$$

where $(w - p)_i$ is the natural log of the real wage in the ith industry and the βs are the parameters of the demand and supply functions, equal across all industries, except for β_2, the shift parameter in the demand function which is specific to an industry. The utility of a secure worker in the ith industry depends only on the real wage in that industry.

Government demand has a number of possible effects on the welfare of a worker. Contractionary policy will reduce temporarily the growth rate of p below w for all workers in all industries and thus make them all better off in the short run. In the long run, however, the real wage is determined only by factors on the right-hand side of equation (5.1). In that case, a reduction in government demand for the output of a particular industry that is not matched by an increase in demand from other sources (i.e., "crowding in"), will lead to a lower β_{i_2} for that industry and to a lower $(w - p)_i$. Not only are secure workers worse off when the real wage falls but also insecure workers, who are on the margin of being laid off, will be concerned that reduced government demand will lead to a lower employment level. Finally, owners of the capital stock will see their returns decrease as output falls if a component of that return is rent. There will, of course, be other industries where the crowding-in process is strong enough for β_{i_2} and $(w - p)_i$ to rise in the face of reduced overall government demand; for such industries all fixed factors are better off. Therefore, industries that sell more of their output to the government than the average industry will oppose contractionary fiscal policy, while those who work for industries in which government demand is less than the average will be in favor of such a move.

It may be argued that wage differentials between industries could not appear if the supply of workers is completely elastic to any one industry. This would involve $\beta_1 \to \infty$ and $(w - p)_i$ would remain constant when β_{i_2} changes, but labor is being treated as a virtually fixed factor so that it is more likely that $\beta_1 = 0$, which accentuates the wage change. Thus, the welfare of factors of production "attached" to a particular industry are concerned about the level of output in that industry and their assessment of the benefits of contractionary fiscal policy depends not on the state of the business cycle but on their evaluation of the private-interest effects on their industry. In a democratic setting, the median voter will make this decision and it would be of great interest to find the characteristics of this median worker in the U.S. economy to determine whether he or she is the cause of spiraling public expenditures.

5.2 The Welfare of Producing Agents

Economic welfare is presumably related to the consumption of goods and services, but in this chapter the emphasis has been on production as the source of wellbeing. Before embarking on an empirical evaluation of this proposition for the U.S. economy, the analytical foundations of the link between output changes and welfare effects will be explored.

Consider the option, discussed in this chapter, of reducing the budget deficit by a reduction in expenditures on public goods, G_2, the private good being G_1, which would expand, as "crowding in" takes place. In Fig. 5-1, the initial situation is shown by point E, where the economy produces $0G_1$ of the private good and $0G_2$ of the public good. There are also two types of individuals: those who work in the government sector and produce G_2, called B and those who work in the private sector and are called A. Given the relative price of the two goods as established by the tangency at E, we can draw the individual budget constraints with the same slope: G_1X_A for A individuals because their only source of income is the value of G_1 output and G_2X_B for those who produce G_2. Because G_2 is a public good, it must be paid for by taxes collected from the two types of individuals; otherwise, voluntary contributions would be too small because of the free-rider problem. Another alternative is, of course, to allow deficit spending by collecting taxes less than $0G_2$. In this case, it is arbitrarily assumed that each group pays for one half of the cost of G_2. Therefore, B individuals will have E_B as the expenditure point on their budget line, having paid $0t$ in taxes and the rest for G_1. Of course, the consumption point is at C_B

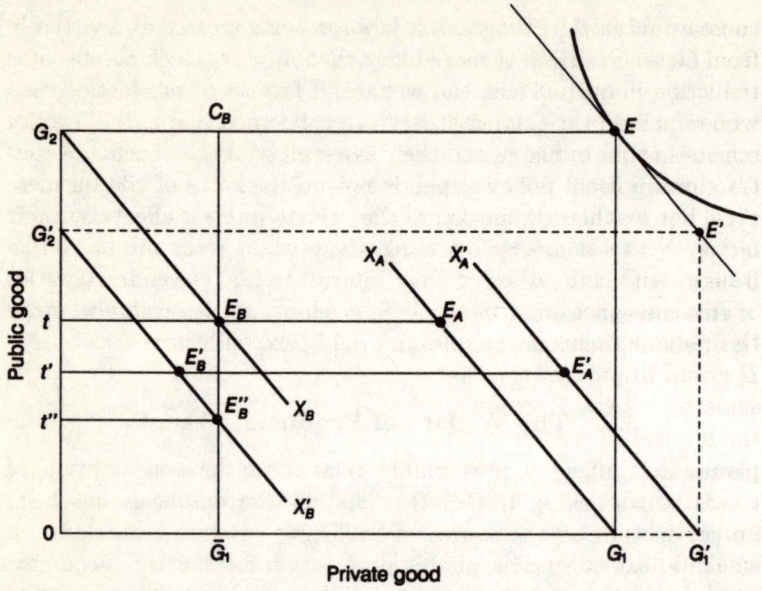

Fig. 5-1.   Welfare of two producing agents.

because all of the public good can be consumed by both groups. Individuals of type A will be at E_A, using the lower left origin, 0; alternatively, they would have $G_1 \bar{G}_1$ of G_1 and the full amount of G_2 to consume. No interpersonal comparison is implied by giving A individuals more G_1 than B individuals; there could be more As than Bs and they would have to share the shown amount.

The aim of the exercise is to show that a collective decision to reduce the output of G_2 will make B type individuals worse off, even if this move is a welfare-improving change for the economy as a whole. Assume that the collective indifference map shifts so that a new tangency is found at E' in Fig. 5-1. To prevent terms-of-trade effects, it is further assumed that the production possibility curve is linear with a constant marginal rate of transformation. The new budget lines facing the two groups will retain the same slope, but will shift inward to $G_2'X_B'$ for B individuals and outward to $G_1'X_A'$ for the other group. If tax collections are still equalized at t', the first group must move to E_B' and the second group will be at E_A'. Taken as a group, B individuals will be worse off, although it is not possible to look at their per-capita welfare since there would now be fewer of them as some resources are transferred from G_2 to G_1. However, as long as income contains some rent, the reduction in output will lead to lower welfare for those individuals who remain in the G_2 industry. It would be possible to use transfer schemes to make the B group just as well off as before in terms of G_1 consumption, for example, by reducing their tax payments to t''. That would still leave the other group with more G_1, namely $\bar{G}_1 G_1'$. Nevertheless, such transfers are considered impractical and fraught with difficulties of their own.

From another viewpoint, we can think of the distance tt' as the maximum lobbying resources that would be devoted by the B group to prevent the change from E to E' taking place. By the same token, the A group would be prepared to spend as much as the horizontal distance between E_A and E_A' to get the change implemented. Although, group A has more to gain than group B has to lose, the lobbying battle should not necessarily be won by the A group. Olson (1965) has argued that lobbying is more effective by small tightly-controlled groups because the successful effects can be shared in predictable ways. Because the government industry is more concentrated than the private industry, group B may be able to marshall larger lobbying resources than group A which has more diffused aims than to keep government expenditures from shrinking. In other words, because lobbying involves transactions costs, only those groups who anticipate a gain in excess of these transactions costs will make the effort to lobby for their preferred outcome. Individually, members of group A may find that the net gains from lobbying are negative, while those in group B will predict positive gains after transactions costs have been subtracted. It is on this basis that the prediction is made that a small group with potentially large losses can overpower a large group with individually small gains even if the sum of the gains is greater than the sum of the losses.

5.3   A Measure of Industry Welfare Changes

In a long-run macroeconomic setting, a reduction in government demand for goods and services, with taxes and income held constant, will lead to a reduction in the budget deficit and an increase in private investment expenditures that are "crowded in" through lower interest rates. In fact, long-run equilibrium requires that the reduction in government demand be equal to the increase in investment demand. For each industry however, the change in the composition of total demand will involve a reallocation process that may lead to larger, smaller or unchanged demand for output. Consider the following experiment. The government is assumed to reduce its demand for goods and services from each industry in the same proportion in which it allocates its total budget to that industry and investors increase their demand in the same proportion in which they allocate their budget. The net effect on each industry depends on this reallocation process which can be summarized by the following formula:

$$\Phi_i = \frac{I_i/I - F_i/F}{Y_i} T, \tag{5.2}$$

where I_i = gross private investment expenditures on output of the ith industry, with $\Sigma I_i = I$, F_i = government expenditures on output of the ith industry, with $\Sigma F_i = F$, Y_i = value of output of the ith industry and T = amount by which the government reduces its expenditures. Hence Φ_i can be thought of as the loss or gain of the value of output of the ith industry as a proportion of its total output.

Let us consider some properties of this ratio. It can vary between $-T/Y_i$ when $I_i = 0$ and $F_i = F$ and T/Y_i when $I_i = I$ and $F_i = 0$. These extreme cases would arise if one group spent its entire budget on the output of one industry and simultaneously the other group spent nothing. The important dividing line is $\Phi_i = 0$, where $I_i/I = F_i/F$, with this industry being indifferent between expansion or contraction of government purchases. It should be noted that the size of T has no influence on whether Φ_i is positive or negative, but only determines the absolute size of Φ_i. However, it is also possible to consider cases where $T < 0$, which involves increases in government demand and "crowding out" of investment and changes the sign of all Φ_i's. Finally, $\Sigma \Phi_i Y_i = 0$, which implies that the weighted sum of the Φ_i's must be zero since the economy as a whole neither gains nor loses from the transfer.

Since Φ_i measures the loss or gain of output for each of the industries in an economy, it also ranks the welfare loss or gain for those factors of production attached to that industry. As a result, those with negative Φ_i's can be expected to oppose while those with positive Φ_i's will approve a reduction in deficit spending. Those with $\Phi_i = 0$ will be indifferent and they can be identified with the "average" person because this person measures the unchanged national welfare. As long as democratic forces are allowed to operate and as long as individuals vote only on the basis of this issue, the median voter, who may have a positive or negative Φ_i, makes this important decision. If the median voter has $\Phi_i > 0$ he or she will vote for deficit reduction, whereas if the median voter experiences $\Phi_i < 0$, a negative vote can be expected. If the distribution of Φ_i's is symmetrical about the mean, the interests of the median voter and the "average" person will coincide since both will have $\Phi_i = 0$. However, nonsymmetrical distributions will result in the aforementioned conflict between these two representative individuals.

It is probably unreasonable to assume that all individuals in the economy have an equal interest in the outcome of this referendum, even if their Φ_i is not zero. Since voting or lobbying legislators uses up resources, those whose gain or loss is smaller than the "transactions costs" of voting will not take an interest in the outcome and this creates a new median voter. Whether this person will favor deficit reduction or not depends on whether more "pro" votes have been eliminated by these costs than "anti" votes. The more heavily concentrated are the losses and the more evenly spread are the gains, the more likely that the median voter will be one who experiences a loss and therefore vote against reducing the budget deficit.

Beyond these general predictions it is not possible to identify the outcome of such public-choice decisions. For that reason, it is very important to try to obtain empirical evidence on median voters and their characteristics in particular circumstances. In the next section, an attempt is made to find the median voter among the approximately 90 million workers in the United States.

5.4 A Case Study of Federal Government Purchases

In order to identify the median voter on the issue of deficit reduction, it is necessary to measure individual industry gains and losses from the transfer of purchasing power from the government to investors and to find the person who is in the middle of the ranked losses and gains. In this study, the 1982 U.S. input-output accounts, the most recent available at this time, will be used to measure the gains and losses for each of the 85 industries in the U.S. economy. In considering this transfer, only federal government purchases of goods and services will be affected. State and local governments, which together bought $382 billion in 1982, are not under the same pressure to reduce expenditures since they have been operating with collective budget surpluses in the $30 to $50 billion range since 1977. Even within the category of federal government expenditures, transfers and grants-in-aid are not to be reduced, because it is not possible, with available data for 1982, to allocate the effects of curtailing these expenditures on the output of each of the 85 industries.[1] These budget items are also large: in 1982, they represented $395 billion or 52.8% of total federal expenditures. They can have important effects on specific industries, as shown in a study employing the 1972 input-output tables. For example, each dollar of such payments increased the output of the medical industry by 12 cents.[2] This suggests that some industries, although not direct beneficiaries of federal government demand, receive indirect benefits through financing of expenditures by other groups. However, even if data on these allocations existed for 1982, there is a good reason for not including them in budget cuts: many transfers and grants-in-aid are mandated by law and cannot be reduced unilaterally. Therefore, expenditures on goods and services are the only major discretionary component of the total federal budget.

5.4.1   Effects on Individual Industries

In 1982, the federal government spent $272,699 million on the output of 85 industries, composed of $193,828 million on national defense and $78,871 million on nondefense items. It will be arbitrarily assumed that this total amount is to be reduced by 10%. Therefore, in equation (5.2), T will be set equal to $27,269.9 million. The expenditures on individual commodities are listed in the first column of Table 5-1. These data allow us to calculate

---

[1] Transfers are payments for which services have not been rendered. Grants-in-aid are federal payments to state and local governments for transportation, urban renewal, aid to education, and research grants to state universities.

[2] See Stern (1975), Table 5, p. 6.

$F_i/272,699$, the distribution of this total. Next, total investment expenditures, composed of gross private fixed investment ($519,966 million) and changes in business inventories ($-$23,055 million) for a total of $496,911 million, are allocated among the 85 industries and shown in the second column of Table 5-1.[3] Since F_i and I_i are expenditures on commodities and not on the output of the same-named industries and to take account of the indirect purchases through the input-output structure of the economy, these calculations of $(I_i/I - F_i/F)$ have to be multiplied by the "industry-by-commodity total requirements coefficient", listed in the third column of Table 5-1.[4] To normalize these net changes, they are divided by total industry output and expressed as percentages.

The second last column of Table 5-1 shows the result of these calculations of the Φ's, together with the rank of each industry from largest loss to largest gain.[5] Not surprisingly, the military-hardware industries, (13) and (60), rank first and third respectively since they receive large amounts of government expenditures and their output is not sold as investments. The government industry, (82), which ranks second, includes the civil service and the military, which relies exclusively on government demand. It would be thought that Φ for this industry would be much higher; however, the federal government purchases only $116,615 million of the output of this industry, while state and local governments purchase $220,755 million. It would have been possible to divide this category into its two components, but then its importance, in terms of employment, would have been reduced proportionately. Among the largest gainers from the reduction in deficit spending are the "farm and garden machinery" industry, (44), "special industry machinery and equipment" industry, (48), and the "new construction" industry, (11), all of which receive relatively little government demand compared to investment expenditures.[6] The

---

[3] For some industries F_i or I_i may be negative, indicating positive net sales, instead of net purchases.

[4] Industries that produce very little of the commodity associated with that industry have small coefficients. Also, industries that sell a lot of their output as inputs to other industries will have large coefficients.

[5] Industries (80) and (81) have been omitted since they produce no output.

[6] The largest gainer is industry (85), "inventory valuation adjustment", but it is only a book-keeping entry to change from book value to replacement cost of all goods in inventory and is disregarded hereafter.

Table 5-1. *Industry Effects of Reducing Federal Government Expenditures, 1982*

No.	Name of commodity or industry	Fed. govt. purchase of commodity (million $)	Investor purchase of commodity (million $)	Industry-by-commodity total requirements coefficient	Total industry output (mil. $)	Industry loss or gain (percent of output) (rank)	Industry employment, 1977 ('000)
1	Livestock & livestock products	7	-625	1.34261	80333	-.058494(35)	443.2
2	Other agricultural products	8041	-909	1.05124	95720	-.937884(04)	893.8
3	Forestry & fishery products	-408	21	.84738	6094	.583355(63)	62.4
4	Agricultural, forestry & fishery services	93	0	.95898	13245	-.067335(32)	391.2
5	Iron & ferroalloy ores mining	-118	364	.97555	1708	1.814928(73)	24.0
6	Nonferrous metal ores mining	2	807	1.10470	3520	1.383612(70)	55.8
7	Coal mining	296	49	1.15496	28642	-.108516(26)	240.7
8	Crude petroleum & natural gas	406	899	1.04635	149599	.006110(49)	144.3
9	Stone & clay mining & quarrying	-2	2	.96048	6056	.004913(48)	91.8
10	Chemical & fertilizer mineral mining	2	-41	.81852	3089	-.064921(34)	23.9
11	New construction	10308	259377	1.00049	319130	4.139372(82)	3835.7
12	Repair & maintenance construction	4461	10709	1.01330	119661	.119906(56)	1919.2
13	Ordnance & accessories	12037	915	.94727	17808	-6.135796(01)	187.3
14	Food & kindred products	1993	865	1.25584	277396	-.068737(31)	1605.8
15	Tobacco manufactures	0	364	1.20477	19655	.122444(57)	67.0
16	Broad & narrow fabrics, yarn & thread mills	102	-592	1.40216	30221	-.198060(14)	559.6
17	Miscellaneous textile goods & floor coverings	17	1350	.99787	10621	.680089(64)	124.3
18	Apparel	523	-143	1.25700	54031	-.139930(20)	1410.3
19	Miscellaneous fabricated textile products	102	-51	.86600	10104	-.111411(25)	185.9
20	Lumber & wood products, except containers	34	-1025	1.43957	40432	-.212385(13)	641.8

21 Wood containers	6	-8	.92116	598	-.160052(17)	17.8
22 Household furniture	43	719	.98299	12672	.272726(61)	313.5
23 Other furniture & fixtures	85	8388	.97191	10991	3.995378(79)	152.0
24 Paper & allied products, except containers	226	418	1.17793	59776	.000669(47)	450.2
25 Paperboard containers & boxes	53	-96	1.03492	18807	-.058156(37)	203.3
26 Printing & publishing	670	105	1.09686	86803	-.077381(29)	1114.5
27 Chemicals & selected chemical products	1336	140	1.01481	77749	-.164352(15)	463.8
28 Plastics & synthetic materials	14	-523	.87368	28123	-.093515(27)	203.4
29 Drugs, cleaning & toilet preparations	721	381	1.05688	48150	-.112363(24)	283.6
30 Paints & allied products	4	-48	.97862	8532	-.034802(40)	61.5
31 Petroleum refining & related industries	7297	-2310	1.07099	206706	-.443756(10)	201.2
32 Rubber & miscellaneous plastics products	715	-182	.99924	54707	-.148840(19)	730.4
33 Leather tanning & finishing	2	-19	1.05279	1732	-.075537(30)	23.7
34 Footwear & other leather products	42	136	1.01822	7367	.045106(51)	233.0
35 Glass & glass products	63	-11	1.05093	12427	-.058383(36)	198.9
36 Stone & clay products	91	-64	1.09954	32119	-.043176(39)	448.1
37 Primary iron & steel manufacturing	126	-3526	1.20160	59033	-.419516(11)	830.3
38 Primary nonferrous metals manufacturing	786	-1296	1.51320	47099	-.481031(09)	358.3
39 Metals containers	72	-3	1.07960	12006	-.066224(33)	78.4
40 Heating, plumbing & fab. struct. met. products	841	3189	.99934	36997	.245557(59)	476.8
41 Screw machine products & stampings	173	-263	.94599	21474	-.139793(21)	347.3
42 Other fabricated metal products	591	1761	.93300	36145	.096905(54)	542.7
43 Engines & turbines	615	1628	.93336	12217	.212714(58)	131.1
44 Farm & garden machinery	34	8905	1.03850	12598	4.000476(80)	162.6
45 Construction & mining machinery	248	8801	1.01401	23736	1.957398(74)	257.5
46 Materials handling machinery & equipment	195	3765	.95058	6581	2.702802(77)	84.1
47 Metalworking machinery & equipment	252	11252	.93753	17247	3.219667(78)	297.1

Table 5-1 continued. *Industry Effects of Reducing Federal Government Expenditures, 1982*

No.	Name of commodity or industry	Fed. govt. purchase of commodity (million $)	Investor purchase of commodity (million $)	Industry-by-commodity total requirements coefficient	Total industry output (mil. $)	Industry loss or gain (percent of output) (rank)	Industry employment, 1977 ('000)
48	Special industry machinery & equipment	105	10181	.93644	12470	4.116893(81)	184.7
49	General industrial machinery & equipment	729	7808	.99514	23243	1.522462(72)	314.1
50	Miscellaneous machinery, except electrical	898	-138	1.01545	14950	-.661389(05)	226.1
51	Office, computing & accounting machines	2443	21384	1.15867	40697	2.645576(76)	284.9
52	Service industry machines	103	3896	1.02823	15480	1.351763(69)	192.6
53	Electrical industrial equipment & apparatus	1443	8173	.99953	26733	1.137477(66)	406.1
54	Household appliances	61	1412	.96284	12120	.567130(62)	165.5
55	Electric lighting & wiring equipment	45	222	.94270	11818	.061287(52)	164.4
56	Radio, TV & communication equipment	13147	23883	.99450	53333	-.007512(44)	628.6
57	Electronic components & accessories	1815	338	1.12588	32793	-.559458(07)	378.0
58	Miscellaneous electrical machinery & supplies	290	3064	1.00289	11880	1.174671(67)	165.8
59	Motor vehicles & equipment	1038	35879	1.27701	111241	2.141186(75)	924.6
60	Aircraft & parts	21783	9743	1.18676	58439	-3.337800(03)	460.7
61	Other transportation equipment	6006	8591	1.01474	26565	-.493278(08)	420.5
62	Scientific & controlling instruments	931	8233	.94767	22638	1.501660(71)	320.8
63	Optical, ophthalmic & photographic equipment	1385	7543	.97849	21253	1.268179(68)	182.4
64	Miscellaneous manufacturing	159	4306	1.01134	27993	.796298(65)	455.2
65	Transportation & warehousing	5844	2528	1.14186	196419	-.259083(12)	2681.3
66	Communications, except radio & TV	2259	4705	1.02194	96111	.034350(50)	896.9
67	Radio & TV broadcasting	0	0	1.00965	15715	.000000(45)	168.8

68 Private electric, gas, water & sanitary services	2506	0	1.17560	221389	-.133071(23)	591.3
69 Wholesale & retail trade	3848	34811	1.02148	577029	.270066(60)	14629.3
70 Finance & insurance	1667	0	1.29349	242008	-.089098(28)	3643.2
71 Real estate & rental	914	9535	1.05868	473823	.096494(53)	761.2
72 Hotels; personal & repair services (except auto)	1043	0	1.01921	70103	-.151639(18)	2234.2
73 Business & professional services, except medical	18688	4361	.95574	268217	-.580632(06)	4060.7
74 Eating & drinking establishments	826	0	1.00320	143209	-.057863(38)	4384.5
75 Automobile repair & services	78	6	1.00322	61079	-.012271(43)	680.2
76 Amusements	462	-90	1.15717	43517	-.135985(22)	674.7
77 Health, educ. & social services & nonprofit org.	4980	0	1.01517	307654	-.164326(16)	8236.8
78 Federal government enterprises	105	0	1.00566	33303	-.031707(41)	804.6
79 State & local government enterprises	70	0	1.02724	44347	-.016215(42)	566.5
80 Noncomparable imports*	7721	120	1.00000	0	NA	0.0
81 Scrap, used & secondhand goods*	125	-15858	1.00000	0	NA	0.0
82 Government industry*	116615	0	1.00000	337370	-3.45691(02)	16576.7
83 Rest of world industry*	-562	0	1.00000	49088	.114488(55)	-20.0
84 Household industry*	0	0	1.00000	7596	.000000(45)	1936.0
85 Inventory valuation adjustment*	0	-11299	1.00000	-11299	5.487884(83)	0.0
Total	272699	496911		5939773		90955.0

Source: "Benchmark Input-Output Accounts for the U.S. Economy, 1982," *Survey of Current Business*, July 1991, Table 2, Columns (92) + (93); Columns (96) + (97); Table 5, diagonal element; Table 2, Row T; "Employment and Employee Compensation in the 1977 Input-Output Accounts," *Survey of Current Business*, Nov. 1985, Table 3, last column.
* No industry-by-commodity total requirements coefficient is given for these industries, but since commodities and industries are the same and since these industries do not use inputs from elsewhere, coefficients of one are appropriate.

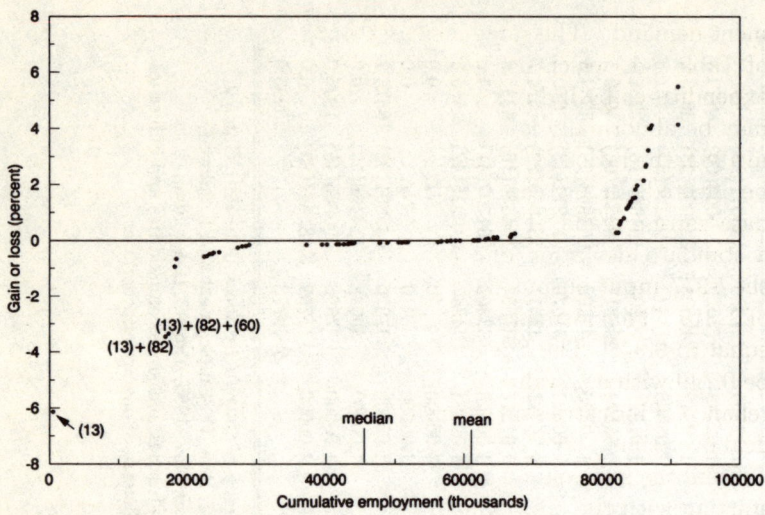

Chart 5-1.   The voting profile among U.S. workers, 1982.

average person works either in industry (67), "radio and TV broadcasting" or in (84) "household industry" which have $\Phi = 0$ since neither the government nor investors purchase any of their output. These industries are jointly ranked 45th.

5.4.2   Finding the Median Voter

To determine the median voter, it is necessary to identify the person who is in the middle of an appropriately ranked array. Since it is impossible to identify individual owners of factors of production other than labor in any one industry, this study will concentrate on workers as voters. The last column in Table 5-1, allocates the total workforce in 1977 of approximately 91 million among the 85 industries. The year 1977 was chosen in preference to 1982 for these data because the latter was a recession year during which the investment industries were hit especially hard by the prevailing high interest rates. Also, 1982 employment was affected by the military build-up initiated by the Reagan administration. Taken together these factors would bias the employment distribution among the 85 industries in 1982 in favor of industries that rely heavily on government demand.[7] The same bias may apply in the first two columns of Table 5-1, which list government expenditures and investment expenditures by industry; although total investment expenditures may be abnormally low and government demand abnormally high in 1982, the ratios F_i/F and I_i/I in equation (5.2) are not likely to be affected. In any case, comparisons using the 1977 input-output data can be made. The mean value of Φ for 1982 was 0.350 with a standard deviation of 1.566, while the mean value of Φ using the 1977 input-output data was 0.267 with a standard deviation of 1.319. The correlation between these Φs for 1982 and 1977 is equal to 0.948. The Spearman rank correlation was calculated to be 0.749 with a t-value of 10.167. This evidence suggests that the reliance of industries on government demand does not vary a great deal over time.

From the last column in Table 5-1 a cumulative total is obtained starting with the employment level in the highest-loss industry to the employment level in the largest-gain industry. The result is shown in Chart 5-1. At the bottom left-hand corner, industry (13) with its 187 thousand workers is pinpointed. Then we add the 16.6 million in industry (82) to obtain the point above and to the right of the first. This procedure is followed until all 91 million workers have been added together, tracing a curve which is initially concave from below and then convex for the remainder of its length. By definition, the median voter is the 45,478 thousandth person in this cumulative total. He or she works in the "finance and insurance" industry, (70), where a loss of .09% of output can be expected. The average (i.e., mean) worker, who neither gains nor loses, is approximately the 61,333 thousandth worker in this ranking.

Because the median voter has a Φ that is negative, one should expect a public-choice decision that maintains or even increases the size of the budget deficit. However, this loss is so small that it is likely to be overpowered by "transactions costs" of voting or lobbying and therefore workers in this industry as well as others whose gain or loss is smaller than these transactions costs are likely to disqualify themselves from this decision. But how many and

---

[7] SIC-based employment data are available monthly from *Employment and Earnings* published by the Bureau of Labor Statistics, but the concordance between the input-output classification and SIC is difficult to perform and agricultural industries are not included in *Employment and Earnings*.

Table 5-2. *The Effect of Voting Costs on the Size of the Electorate and the Distribution of Votes*

Voting costs relative to gain or loss (percent)	Size of electorate (thousands) and (percent of potential)	Number of votes for deficit reduction (thousands) and (percent of electorate)
0.0	88,850.2(97.7)	29,453.6(33.1)
0.1	70,062.2(77.0)	26,169.1(37.4)
0.2	51,477.8(56.6)	24,202.9(47.0)
0.3	33,245.8(36.6)	8,652.2(26.0)
1.0	25,069.5(27.6)	7,844.8(31.3)
2.0	23,170.4(25.5)	5,925.7(25.6)
4.0	4,370.4(4.8)	4,183.0(95.7)
5.0	187.3(0.2)	0(0.0)

how would they have voted in the absence of these costs? There is no way of knowing the answer precisely, but Table 5-2 shows the effect of various levels of these transactions costs relative to the gains or losses, expressed as a proportion of output, on the size of the electorate and the distribution of the votes for the transfer. If there are no voting costs, all but the 2,104.8 thousand workers in industries (67) and (84) would cast a ballot in this referendum, with 59,397 thousand voting against and 29,454 thousand voting for deficit reduction. As voting or lobbying costs rise, the proportion of votes favoring deficit reduction rises briefly to 47% and then falls steadily as both sides are losing votes, but those with positive Φs are dropping out of the race in greater numbers than those with negative Φs. If voting costs rise to 4% of the value of output, there is suddenly a shift to a 96% majority in favor of deficit reduction, involving 4,183 thousand workers in industries (11), (44), and (48) overwhelming 187 thousand workers in industry (13). When costs rise to 5%, there is no one left with an active interest in the subject.

When there are substantial transactions costs for voting or lobbying, it is possible for a small group of large losers to dominate the decision concerning deficit reduction. As long as these transactions costs cannot be eliminated, we need to find a balancing group of large gainers who would be just as willing to incur these costs as the losers. The only variable that can be manipulated to create such a group is F_i/F, the allocation of federal budget cuts by industry. Consider a reduction in federal government purchases concentrated entirely in the government industry, (82), the only one able to bear this "burden", so that $F_{82}/F = 1$ and all other $F_i/F = 0$. This makes $\Phi_{82} = -8.08\%$, more than double the previous value of -3.46%, but all other Φs are now smaller negative numbers or larger positive numbers. For example, industry (69), with 14.6 million workers raises its Φ from .27% to .34% and industry (77), with 8.2 million workers, now has $\Phi = 0\%$ instead of $-.16\%$. The mean value of Φ has risen from .350 to .610, so that it would appear to be easier to create a coalition in favor of deficit reduction. However, there are still 25,339 thousand workers who have negative Φs and the median worker only has $\Phi = 0$. Moreover, there is nothing to guarantee that voting costs are parametric; instead they may be competitively established, with each side prepared to devote more resources to lobbying than the other in order to knock its opponent out of the race. Since government workers stand to lose more than any other group gains, they could raise these costs to 4.5% and eliminate the last opposition from industries (44) and (48) who have Φs just above 4%.

It must also be mentioned that if deficit reduction does not bring about complete "crowding in", the Φs will be smaller than reported in Table 5-1 as private demand does not replace government purchases and it will be even more difficult to find a working majority that will support a smaller budget deficit.

5.4.3   The Attractiveness of Government Industries

If government employment were merely a stopgap during a recession until employment opportunities in other industries expanded, there might be less lobbying for preserving these jobs. Unfortunately, industries which rely on government demand more than the average tend also to pay higher wages, even in a period of economic expansion. This makes it more difficult to make government employment move countercyclically.

To present evidence in favor of this hypothesis, employee compensation data from the 1977 input-output tables will be used to show relative wages in a boom period. Annual employee compensation varied from a high of $25,868 in industry (31) to a low of $5,902 in industry (2), after industries (80) to (85) were eliminated. The mean value was $16,036 and the standard deviation was \$4,818. Much of this variation is probably due to differences in capital intensity of the industry, skill requirements, or hours worked. Data for these variables could not be found, but labor's share in total value added did not help to explain differences in employee compensation.

To measure reliance on government purchases a new variable needs to be defined because Φ measures not only government demand but also investor demand for an industry's output. Hence,

$$\phi_i = \frac{F_i \times ICC_i}{Y_i} \tag{5.3}$$

will be used. This variable had a mean value of 0.028 with a standard deviation of 0.091 for industries (1) through (79) in the 1977 input-output tables. Its highest value was in industry (13) and its largest negative value was -0.161 in industry (3) because the government made net sales to these firms.

In a regression of the compensation variable against a constant, ϕ and also an import penetration variable for industries (1) through (79), it was found that a one-percentage point increase in ϕ increased the wage by \$150.[8] This shows that industries which rely more heavily on government purchases than the average also pay their workers higher wages.

5.5   An Alternative Explanation

The featured hypothesis in this chapter is that collective decisions to reduce government expenditures are more difficult to make than decisions to expand government demand. The argument put in favor of this hypothesis relied on the existence of private interests in government demand for goods and services and the asymmetry in transactions or lobbying costs whereby those with more concentrated economic interests could marshall more resources than those with more diverse sources of welfare.

Corden (1974) has suggested another framework for making predictions about fiscal-policy decisions. He has put forward a "conservative social welfare function" the application of which implies that "any significant absolute reductions in real incomes of any sig-

---

[8] The explanatory power of this regression was $\bar{R}^2 = .128$; all coefficients were significantly different from zero at the 95% confidence level.

nificant section of the community should be avoided... In terms of welfare weights, increases in income are given relatively low weights and decreases very high weights." (p. 107). In some ways, this is similar to the Pareto-optimality condition which forbids any person becoming worse off after a policy change. The difference between Pareto optimality and the conservative social welfare function is that the former allows for side payments to prevent a net reduction in welfare for any group. "For example, a policy that gives $100 to Smith while taking $40 from Jones ... is desirable" (p. 105), from a Pareto perspective because it could be manipulated into a $60 increase for Smith without any change for Jones. The conservative social welfare function recognizes that such transfer payments that must accompany policy changes are not only theoretically desirable but practically necessary.

The bases of the conservative social welfare function are three-fold: fairness, risk aversion, and the necessity of social peace. The concept of fairness is obvious but an arbitrary choice for policy decisions. With respect to risk aversion Corden argues that, "... the conservative social welfare function is part of a social insurance system ... [to prevent] unexpected income losses" (p. 108), but this gives rise to the moral-hazard problem which would lead to agents taking on more risky ventures than otherwise, safe in the knowledge that losses will be made good by the government. Finally, Corden suggests that policies may not be implemented that threaten the social fabric of the economy, but it is not clear that any loss of income will automatically trigger such drastic reactions. In many zero-sum situations, governments do accept income reductions to some elements of the population; therefore the term "significant section of the community" seems to be an important element of the decision-making process, but one difficult to quantify. Reliance on asymmetric transactions costs, on the other hand, allows one to predict the outcome once we know who stands to gain and to lose and how much.

5.6 Conclusion

Government activity is much less concerned about providing the right amount and mixture of public goods to consumers as it is about maintaining or providing jobs, either indirectly through the purchase of goods and services from private firms or directly through its own hiring. What these people produce is less important than that they earn an income. This fact makes countercyclical government expenditure patterns difficult to achieve. Because workers whose employment depends on government demand have no incentive to move to other jobs during a boom, especially since government employment pays better than private employment, it is extremely difficult to cut total expenditures at such times. Although there are many industries and their workers — the ones that sell capital equipment to other firms — that would gain from "crowding in" of investment expenditures to replace government spending, these groups do not have the lobbying power of the competing groups that would lose from such a move. The resulting asymmetry in government expenditures during recessions and boom periods means that governments always spend more, never less. It would still be possible to design countercyclical fiscal policy if taxes could be adjusted, but the next chapter will show that deficits are preferable to tax increases to those who can influence such decisions.

6

The Macroeconomic Policy Apparatus

The search for unequivocal goals for macroeconomic policy, especially with respect to the optimal unemployment rate, has been largely unsuccessful. Despite this lack of an underlying justification, macroeconomic policy decisions, both large and small, continue to be made in the belief that they will "improve" the performance of the economy. There are literally thousands of officials and politicians in the U.S. federal government who spend a great deal of time making, implementing, analyzing, and criticizing stabilization policies. There must be some rationale for the Joint Economic Committee, for the Bureau of Management and Budget, for the Council of Economic Advisers, for the Department of the Treasury, for the Federal Reserve Board and for many other government bodies to function as collective decision makers in the area of fiscal and monetary policies. While Chapter 2 has dealt with the lack of concordance between promise and achievement in postwar U.S. macropolicy initiatives, this chapter will concentrate on a critical examination of the stabilization-policy apparatus, to justify its existence even though macroeconomic policy goals cannot be defined or defended as Pareto improvements.

It is a long-standing tradition for economists to give policy advice and to criticize existing economic policies in all fields where governments regulate, tax or subsidize. For example, in the area of international trade, policy evaluation has been guided by the principle of optimality, whereby the authorities seek to maximize the nation's welfare. For decades, it has generally been accepted that the "optimum" tariff is the only intervention that national governments should permit themselves. Yet it is quite obvious that restrictions and distortions created by almost all governments

in international markets are inconsistent with this simple requirement. Even in the face of new policy recommendations derived
from the strategic-interactions view of international trade, both
Baldwin (1989) and Harris (1989) found it to be inconceivable that
existing trade policies are anywhere near to being optimal from a
national perspective. The only way to rationalize the multi-faceted
policies that apply to international movements of goods and services is to argue that they are implemented to appease conflicting
special-interest groups.

While the special-interest explanation of actual policies has been
available for some time, it has not been applied to stabilization
policies, in part because macroeconomic analysis has masked the
heterogeneous components in an economy by relying on the "average person" as the maximizing agent. In such a world, the private
interest and the public interest would coincide. However, the previous discussion in Chapters 3 and 4 lead to the conclusion that
participants in the labor market have different views about the optimality of "full employment" and the policies designed to reach
such a goal. It will be argued that stabilization policies should
also be subjected to special-interest scrutiny precisely because all
participants in the political process that determine these policies
have their own idea of what is optimal, with the result that outcomes cannot be measured against a single objective. Stabilization
policies were initially implemented in the wake of the Keynesian
revolution as a public-choice decision to reach a collective goal of
"full employment", but once that commitment was recognized, private interests corrupted that goal and appropriated the benefits of
the policies implemented for this collective purpose. When private behavior adapts to the existence of public-choice goals, it is
no longer obvious that the goal will be reached or that the policies are Pareto optimal; in fact, it is quite possible to end up in a
prisoner's dilemma.

6.1 Individual Support for Public Choices

Buchanan (1987) and other public-choice economists have made it
a canon of their methodology to argue that individuals not only
maximize their utility in private-sector decisions but they also maximize utility in their political decisions. He writes, "The individual who chooses between apples and oranges remains the same

person who chooses between the levers marked 'Candidate A' and 'Candidate B' in the polling booth." (p. 245). The institutional constraints that they face may differ between these two settings leading to different outcomes, but individual optimization is at the core of public-sector choices. The previous analogy is elaborated: "In the market, individuals exchange apples for oranges; in politics, individuals exchange agreed-on shares in contributions toward the costs of that which is commonly desired, from the services of the local fire station to that of the judge." (p. 246). In that framework it is acceptable for a person to ask, "What's in it for me?" in a decision about public goods; it is not necessary to force the individual to ask: "How much am I prepared to sacrifice for this common goal?" Of course, individuals are forced to pay taxes to avoid the free-rider problem of public goods, but Buchanan argues that, "Individuals acquiesce in the coercion of the state, of politics, only if the ultimate constitutional 'exchange' furthers their interests. Without some model of exchange, no coercion of the individual by the state is consistent with the individualistic value norm upon which a liberal social order is grounded." (p. 246). Nevertheless, he recognizes the utopian nature of this voluntary exchange in the political arena. He acknowledges that, "Politics as observed remains, of course, far from the idealized collective-cooperative exchange ... The political equivalent of transactions costs makes the pursuit of idealized 'efficiency' seem even more out of the bounds of reason than the analogous pursuit in markets." (p. 247).

Because of the voluntary nature of political exchange, Buchanan insists on unanimity among all participants for all collective-choice decisions, but there must be instances in which governments act coercively against some individuals. To make that consistent with the unanimity principle, Buchanan argues that, "... an individual may rationally prefer a rule that will, on particular occasions, operate to produce results that are opposed to his own interests. The individual will do so if he predicts that, on balance over the whole sequence of 'plays,' his own interests will be more effectively served by the more restrictive application of the [in-period unanimity constraint]." (p. 248). This leads to constitutions (i.e., the basic rules by which public-choice decisions are made) that require unanimity, but specific decisions presumably do not have to satisfy that requirement. In turn, to produce unanimity on constitutional decisions, potential opponents can be made to acquiesce by the threat of anarchy, which presumably produces results that are worse than those being proposed within the constitution. In other words, people with heterogeneous tastes or endowments can be made to accept collective choices which are not optimal from an individualistic point of view by allowing only those alternatives which are worse (e.g., expropriation). However, it is then impossible to predict the collective choice that will be offered. What coalitions can be formed to provide viable constitutional proposals when individuals have different preferences? What issues will gain momentum until they have overwhelming support? Which self-interested individuals will fail to provide the necessary unanimity until they are bribed? Buchanan does not provide answers to such questions. Instead he writes:

> We do not, of course, observe the process of reaching agreement on constitutional rules, and the origins of the rules that are in existence at any particular time and in any particular polity cannot satisfactorily be explained by the contractarian model. The purpose of the contractarian exercise is not explanatory in this sense ... It is, by contrast, justificatory in that it offers a basis for normative evaluation. Could the observed rules that constrain the activity of ordinary politics have emerged from agreement in constitutional contract? To the extent that this question can be affirmatively answered, we have established a legitimating linkage between the individual and the state. To the extent that the question prompts a negative response, we have a basis for normative criticism of the existing order, and a criterion for advancing proposals for constitutional reform (p. 249).

It will be argued that self-interested maximizing decisions in the public domain will lead to intergenerational transfers of welfare because future generations cannot place constraints on the maximization process of the current generation. In general, public-choice decisions are zero-sum games between two or more groups; they are not Pareto-improving choices. It is therefore not possible for all groups involved in the bargain to emerge as winners, yet the individualistic approach to public choice makes it mandatory to try. If they do try to maximize individual welfare in their collective choices, they will probably end up being worse off, because the attempt itself uses up resources. In the case of budgetary decisions, it is not possible for all participants to receive net benefits from government activity; instead some will establish a net surplus position where taxes paid will be less than the benefits from public expenditures, while others will have a net deficit because taxes exceed desirable expenditures. If these losers now lobby to improve their position they can do so only by reducing the benefits of those who previously enjoyed them, who, in turn, will retaliate with lobbying of their own. In the end, both groups are worse off in the classic case of the prisoner's dilemma. The only way for both groups to be net beneficiaries from government activity is to find some other group that is powerless to prevent the absorption of the resulting loss. The nature of this political game can now be explored.

6.2 Government Activity as Zero-sum Games

The major economic activity of government is to collect taxes and to make expenditures and transfer payments. An individualistic approach to this system involves maximizing the difference between receipts of transfer payments and other benefits (e.g., income from a job in the government sector) on the one hand and tax payments on the other. If the budget is balanced and if there are heterogeneous groups that differ in their eligibility for these benefits or their vulnerability to taxation, then there must be some group that receives net positive benefits (say, $+1$) while another group receives net negative benefits (say, -1). Each group now has to make a choice: to fight this outcome or to acquiesce. If it makes the former choice it must expend resources to lobby legislators for a more favorable outcome. Alternatively, a group could alter its activities so as to avoid taxes or to attract government benefits, but since such behavior becomes desirable only in the face of government activity, it is not a first-best optimum and thus also involves the use of resources. How much would each group sacrifice in order to improve its position? The answer is as little as possible but as much as necessary to achieve net benefits from the lobbying. The rules of the resulting "game" are simple. They are:

1 The game is zero sum.
2 Group A is the initial loser and aims for the elimination of that loss; group B is the initial winner and will aim for doubling of

that pay-off. These are strictly arbitrary assumptions for illustrative purposes because there is no constrained maximization possible.

3 Each group is prepared to pay lobbying costs equal to half the expected gain from successful lobbying. This assumption is also arbitrary.

The Pay-off Matrix

A ↓ B →	fight	acquiesce
fight	−1.5, .5	−.5, 0
acquiesce	−2, 1.5	−1, 1

Starting from the lower right-hand corner as the *status quo ante* which makes group A the loser and B the winner, each group has to decide whether to fight or to acquiesce. If group A fights and wins it will cut its losses from −1 to 0 but since it must pay for lobbying resources the net pay-off is −.5; group B would lose all of its benefit to maintain the zero-sum nature of the game. Group B also has an incentive to fight for improved benefits: by making the payoff $(-2, 2)$ before lobbying costs, it achieves $(-2, 1.5)$ after subtracting the effects of lobbying. Since both groups have an incentive to fight, it becomes the dominant strategy with the same payoff as originally, but now with both groups absorbing lobbying costs equal to one unit. Since the original position or the one in which both groups acquiesced is Pareto superior to this outcome, the game involves a prisoner's dilemma.[1] Even if group A has a first-mover advantage in this game because it is the "aggrieved party", both groups will choose to fight since B will fight no matter what A does and A is better off to fight knowing that B will do likewise.

Furthermore, even if the two groups could persuade each other and themselves to acquiesce and accept the *status quo*, those who benefit from the lobbying have an incentive to promote discord between the two groups in order to stimulate lobbying activities. Zero-sum games stimulate what are called "bureaucratic parasites", an image that suggests government agencies and politicians

---

[1] Maital and Lipnowski (1985) reach a similar conclusion in their analysis of a game between labor and business, in which government also becomes a party.

expect and encourage lobbies to make their conflicting claims for better treatment; in the process, they receive attention and favors. In the end, not much has changed, but resources are wasted in what Bhagwati (1982) has lumped together as "directly unproductive activities."

So far, the game has been played by two groups, A and B, and some interested bystanders, the bureaucrats and politicians, constrained by a contemporaneously balanced budget. In budgetary decisions, it is now much more common to let both groups A and B have net positive benefits by running a deficit. The new group of losers is the future generation which has no lobbying power or resources and cannot put counterveiling pressure on governments. Buchanan (1987) concedes that, "It is almost impossible to construct a contractual calculus in which representatives of separate generations would agree to allow majorities in a single generation to finance currently enjoyed public consumption through the issue of public debt that insures the imposition of utility losses on later generations of taxpayers." (p. 250).

If government activity is voluntary, unanimously determined, and allows individualistic welfare maximization, the only way to involve future generations in this process is to rely on Barro's (1974) argument that parents include their children's welfare in their own optimizing calculations. As evidence of this, Barro argues that Ricardian equivalence holds because if the current generation decides to make larger government expenditures without raising taxes immediately, it also saves more to leave larger bequests to their offspring who will be saddled with the higher taxes. While the ensuing debate about Ricardian equivalence has centered on the implied impotence of fiscal policy to change aggregate demand, very little has been said about the rationale for deficit spending in the first place. If an extra dollar's worth of public expenditures merely replaces a dollar's worth of private spending because they are equally valued at the margin, deficits and surpluses in the government accounts should be virtually random. It does not seem sensible to keep demanding higher government expenditures if you know that they will not make you better off as you merely substitute public goods for private goods. Instead, we convince ourselves that our group is sufficiently politically powerful to be able to obtain the benefits of current spending and escape having to pay the taxes now or in the future, but we do not admit to ourselves that this argument is irrational when it is applied to all groups.

If deficits allow groups A and B to reach a co-operative solution, why do politicians insist on collecting any taxes? Is there any constraint on the size of the deficit when future generations have no lobbying power? The answer to these questions is that precisely because of the political weakness of later generations, politicians must have a credible threat to inflict pain on the present generation in order to collect "bribes" from those current-generation groups who have lobbying abilities. Presumably politicians and officials are also maximizing their payoffs and this probably happens when lobbying activity is at its greatest. If increased net benefits were granted automatically to both A and B, and costs passed on to future generations, there would be little or no lobbying and politicians would lose much of their current power. This observation may help to explain the discrepancy between promises to reduce the deficit, which are really threats, and actual performance. As a result, there is both tension and harmony among all the groups in this game that leads to equilibrium-level lobbying and generationally "optimal" deficits. These deficits are, of course, totally unrelated to stabilization-policy requirements.

6.3 Bias in Stabilization Policies

If we could observe a clear-cut macroeconomic goal such as the attainment of the natural rate of unemployment, then policies could be judged on the basis of their performance relative to that goal. If the unemployment rate is above the natural rate, budget deficits would be sensible because the public benefits of the extra expenditures or cuts in taxes would outweigh the costs, but by the same argument, surpluses would be necessary when the labor market experiences excess demand or an unemployment rate below the natural rate. For reasons enumerated above, this type of symmetry in fiscal policy is absent. Instead, there is a bias in favor of deficits under all circumstances in order to satisfy the demands of more of the multitude of heterogeneous groups that clamor for better treatment than would be possible with a budget that was balanced over the business cycle. This asymmetry in fiscal policy could in fact be justified by a similar bias in the operation of the labor market, with excess supply dominating excess demand. In the period 1968-89, using the Adams-Coe data for the natural rate, the cumulative annual excess supply was 8.14%. With Gordon's estimate of the natural rate, the cumulative excess supply would have been 9.80%. Visually, these calculations represent the algebraic sum of the areas between the natural and actual rates of unemployment depicted in Fig. 3-1. The interpretation of this evidence is that excess supply in the labor market was longer and/or larger than excess demand over this 22-year period. As a consequence, even if fiscal policy is geared to the achievement of the natural rate in the labor market, the relatively poor performance of the labor market requires virtually perpetual deficits.

Nevertheless, there are a few instances in recent decades of boom conditions in the macroeconomy that drive the unemployment rate below the natural rate long enough to make a strong case for fiscal restraint. The period 1986-89 serves as a useful illustration of deficit spending unrelated to developments in the labor market. The evidence, taken from Charts 2-3 and 3-1, is the following :

Year	Unemp. rate	Natural rate	Cyc. adj. budget deficit
1986	6.9%	6.35%	$187.9 bill.
1987	6.1%	6.22%	$157.6 bill.
1988	5.4%	6.01%	$164.1 bill.
1989	5.2%	5.63%	$177.3 bill.

After the recession of 1982, the unemployment rate dropped steadily and by 1987 it fell below the natural rate, which Adams and Coe estimated to be declining itself. Therefore, there can be little doubt that excess demand existed in the labor market for the three years, 1987-89. The cyclically-adjusted budget deficit, although it fell by $30 billion between 1986 and 1987, remained in the region of $150-175 billion thereafter. What is the macroeconomic justification for any budget deficits in a period when aggregate demand should be reduced? The Reagan administration, it will be remembered from the discussion in Chapter 2, had eschewed countercyclical fiscal policy. The *Economic Report of the President* for 1989 announced: "Desiring not to repeat the failures of short-term discretionary policy in the 1970s, the Administration abandoned discretionary fiscal policy. In its place the Administration has used fiscal policy as a tool for restoring incentives and efficiency, both in the private sector and in the government and giving incentives for the private sector to plan for the future." (pp. 55-56). However, no attempt is made to show how budget deficits of this order will contribute to efficiency and incentives. In retrospect, the continuing deficits were the product of three mutually inconsistent policies and events: (1) reduction in income-tax rates to change incentives, (2) increased defense expenditures to protect "vital" national interests, and (3) an inability to persuade Congress to reduce nondefense expenditures.

If a government takes the position that stabilization policy cannot be effective and no longer tries to make countercyclical budgetary decisions, it does not have the liberty to set the budget at any arbitrary position that it wants. Instead, to ensure consistency over time, the budget of a noninterventionist government should be set to zero and left there. By running deficits that do not provide any benefits to future generations, the government is showing a preference for the current generation. Given the short time horizon of governments and the argument presented in the previous section, this is not surprising, but the Reagan administration also pre-empted any future administration's ability to revert back to an activist role in macroeconomic policy by bequeathing a larger debt-servicing problem and restricting the discretionary component of government expenditures. Countercyclical spending to overcome the recession which started in 1990 might have had a higher priority in the Bush administration had it not been constrained by the need to keep the deficit from becoming larger.

To show this eroding base of discretionary expenditures, let us define bd as the budget deficit as a ratio of income:

$$bd = (g - \tau) + i(1 - \tau)b_{-1}, \qquad (6.1)$$

where $(g - \tau)$ is the primary deficit ratio arising from expenditures, g, exceeding the tax rate, τ, while $i(1 - \tau)$ are net-of-tax interest payments on the public debt, b_{-1}. Any constant positive value for bd will cause b_{-1} to rise over time because $b = b_{-1} + bd$. As time passes, to prevent bd from rising, g will have to fall or τ will have to rise.[2] In the process, debt servicing becomes a larger proportion of total expenditures defined as $g + ib_{-1}$. Between 1981 (the last year

---

[2] The intergenerational effect of deficit financing can be shown by setting $bd = 0$ in equation (6.1) at some point in time and then solving for the resulting tax rate:
$$\tau_{(bd=0)} = \frac{g + ib_{-1}}{1 + ib_{-1}}.$$

before the 1982 recession and subsequent recovery) and 1990, net interest payments as a proportion of total outlays increased from 9.77% to 15.53%, which does not appear all that serious, but only because the deficit also increased: in 1981, $bd = 1.96\%$, while in 1990, $bd = 2.93\%$, using national-income calculations of the deficit in *ERP* for 1991, Table B-81.

As a counter-factual exercise, consider the longer-term effects of having a balanced budget in the years 1987-89, even though a surplus would have been even better in order to reduce aggregate demand during these years in which there existed excess demand in the labor market. The main benefits would have been much smaller interest payments in later years and more scope for extra expenditures on goods and services in the subsequent recession. Assuming the actual values for nominal GNP and the average interest rate paid on government debt held by the public, the following calculations are made:

Year	Actual ib_{-1}	Predicted ib_{-1}
1987	3.15%	3.15%
1988	3.11%	2.86%
1989	3.27%	2.77%
1990	3.37%	2.67%

The assumption behind the predicted value for ib_{-1} is that the value of federal government debt held by the public would remain at $1736.2 billion (*ERP*, 1991, Table B-76), the amount outstanding at the end of 1986 because the budget would be balanced for the next three years. Although the divergence between the two series does not appear to be large, by 1990 the difference between actual and predicted interest payments amounted to $37.8 billion; cumulatively, for 1988-90, the difference is $75.5 billion. This whole amount could have been spent on goods and services in 1990 to forestall the recession without making the overall deficit worse than it actually was. For comparison, the federal government purchased

---

(Footnote 2 continued) The longer the deficit was allowed to continue in the past, the larger is b_{-1} and this raises τ because

$$\frac{\partial \tau}{\partial b_{-1}} = \frac{i(1-g)}{(1+ib_{-1})^2} > 0.$$

$416.1 billion in that year; the saved-up interest payments would have allowed for an increase of 18.1%.

In summary, there seems to be a bias in favor of expansionary fiscal policy because there is also a bias in the calculated natural rate towards excess supply in the labor market. There are, however, instances where it is obvious that excess demand exists in the labor market and yet fiscal deficits continue. It is in these circumstances that it becomes obvious that budgetary decisions by the federal government are not aimed at stabilizing the economy; instead deficits are the short-run response of short-sighted governments to the many demands for net benefits by a heterogeneous population. The costs of these actions can always be postponed until tomorrow, but these costs are also much larger tomorrow which makes further postponement even more imperative. In the meantime, stabilization of the macroeconomy must rely more heavily on monetary policy which itself becomes more constrained by the mounting needs to finance the growing debt. Can anything be done to put fiscal policy back on its original track as a countercyclical instrument? The answer is probably no, but we must investigate a number of proposals before we can reach this conclusion.

6.4   Improving the Policy Apparatus

In order to allow surpluses to develop during economic boom periods, it would be necessary to change the incentive system now in place, but since legislators are in charge of this system they are unlikely to replace it with something that is not to their benefit. In simple terms, Congress and the executive branch cannot be forced to impose constraints on their own behavior and there is no outside body — not even the electorate — that can impose the necessary constraints. Nevertheless, there have been several attempts at self-restraint, or at least legislative initiatives have been drawn up or proposed that give the appearance of future success.

6.4.1   The Balanced Budget Act of 1985

The most prominent example of such legislation is the Balanced Budget and Emergency Deficit Control Act of 1985, commonly referred to as the Gramm-Rudman-Hollings bill. This legislation required that the deficit be reduced year-by-year until it was entirely eliminated in fiscal year 1991. The President's budget message to Congress and congressional budget resolutions would be bound by the constraints imposed on the maximum size of the deficit. Also stipulated was a formula that dictated how incompatible expenditure plans were to be resolved within the deficit targets. At the time that the legislation was implemented, there were many cynical assessments of its potential for success. For instance, Meyer (1986) wrote:

> Gramm-Rudman is not a credible policy. There are few who believe either Congress or the Administration has the stomach to impose the spending cuts required under the bill, even taking into account the use of static cuts and optimistic economic assumptions. Congress has seen Gramm-Rudman as providing the incentive required to secure the President's commitment to a tax increase. But without a consensus on a tax increase, few believe that Gramm-Rudman will be fully implemented. The lack of credibility of the deficit reduction program restrains the monetary authorities from moving aggressively to offset the potential fiscal restraint, threatening the close coordination of monetary and fiscal policies that is the key to the smooth transition to a balanced budget (p. 67).

The lack of consensus on tax increases did not take long to materialize. President Reagan stated bluntly in the 1986 *ERP*: "I reject the notion of increased taxes. Higher taxes would only encourage more Federal spending and limit the economy's ability to grow." (p. 7). Congress, on the other hand, was reluctant to cut spending in areas that were important to its constituents. This impasse was resolved by an important escape clause in the legislation. The deficit targets that were established for each fiscal year had to be consistent with *predicted* expenditures and taxes. As a result, if macroeconomic conditions were assumed to be optimistically rosy, tax revenues could be predicted to be quite large and cyclically-sensitive expenditures could be projected to be quite low. In fact, the economic forecasts presented by the Congressional Budget Office and the Office of Management and Budget as part of the Gramm-Rudman procedure have been accused of being nothing more than calculated growth rates that would be consistent with existing budget plans. When the deficit turns out to be larger than predicted or permitted by the legislation, the next target becomes even more difficult to reach and the need to obfuscate becomes stronger. With each passing year, the budget targets became more lax and the date for a balanced budget was postponed. Within the space of five years, the Gramm-Rudman bill had become a dead letter.

The successor legislation to the Balanced Budget Act of 1985 was the Budget Enforcement Act of 1990, which tried to contain expenditure increases rather than set targets for the deficit. It established separate ceilings on discretionary spending in the defense, domestic and international categories for fiscal years 1991-93 and introduced a sequester procedure in the event that the spending caps were violated. It also required a "pay-as-you-go" provision for any new entitlement programs that may be legislated. However, there are enough loopholes such as "emergency appropriations" to make these expenditure caps less than completely binding. Moreover, there is nothing in the new budget law that makes fiscal policy countercyclical, except that the enforcement provisions may be suspended during a recession.

6.4.2   Balanced Budget Constitutional Amendments

Even before the failure of Gramm-Rudman became evident, stronger measures to limit fiscal deficits had been proposed. President Reagan suggested in 1986 that, "We must direct our attention to a constitutional amendment providing for a permanently balanced budget ... [to] restrain future spending, and ensure that future fiscal decisions are prudent and responsive to the national interest." (*ERP*, 1986, p. 7). The argument in favor of constitutional remedies as opposed to ordinary legislation is the recognition that Congress and the administration would not willingly constrain their own behavior and that some higher authority is needed to perform this task. Once the constitution requires a balanced budget, it would be impossible for the political participants in the deficit "game" to continue to play by the old rules. Because the politicians would no longer have the power to dispense special privileges, lobbying would be reduced or perhaps even wither away. This would remove the disadvantage faced by future generations and the bias towards deficit finance would be eliminated. In cases of dispute, the Supreme Court would have to rule on the constitutionality of the issue and since the Justices are appointed for life, their susceptibility to lobbying would be much lower than politicians who must run for office rather frequently.

How would the Supreme Court, as the final arbiter, make macroeconomic policy choices? If decisions by the Supreme Court favored the strict construction of the balanced-budget amendment, countercyclical fiscal policy would by definition be unavailable and therefore its original purpose could not be re-established. On the other hand, if Supreme Court opinions allowed some latitude in interpretation, the door would be opened to the resumption of the current system. Moreover, it would probably prove impossible to define a budget balance that is constitutionally foolproof. It would then be possible for Congress or the President to conjure up expenditures that would not be part of the stipulated budget; even now, some items are treated as "off-line". From that perspective, it would be advisable to make the constitutional amendment in the form of a maximum debt outstanding, rather than as an arbitrarily defined budget balance. Even then, it should not be beyond the imagination of politicians to come up with a perfect substitute for government bonds that is not called "debt". Friedman (1986, p. 6) seems to favor spending limits in the constitutional amendment, to put pressure on lobbyists to consider the opportunity cost of their proposals. "That would pit one special interest against another and change the rules of the game in such a way that the legislator would now find it in his self-interest to operate in the public interest." Wildavsky (1964, pp. 160-65), however, has argued persuasively that legislators do not themselves propose new activities and must rely on bureaucrats to perform that function and to do it aggressively; in that environment, it will be easier to bend the constitutional rules through creative accounting than to disappoint too many of the bureaucrats.

The point is that Congress and the administration are jointly too powerful in the economic sphere to be controlled by other forces. At this stage, not even the electorate has counterveiling power, because both Democrat and Republican politicians are fundamentally similar in their approach to deficit spending. The 1992 presidential candidacy of Ross Perot did offer an alternative view on deficits and a sizable constituency supported his ideas of deficit reduction, but many politicians have made promises on this front without being able to keep them.

Even within a government that publicly commits itself to reductions in its expenditures, the forces that prefer more spending are more powerful and will ultimately prevail over those that prefer less spending. Bureaucrats in a government agency are not interested in the efficiency of their operation or whether the social benefits of their output exceeds the social costs; instead they are maximizing their own welfare. Bureaucratic theory has postulated a number of variables that bureaus try to maximize (e.g., budgets, employees, rents, clients), but it would be hard to imagine an official volunteering for budget cuts.[3] In that environment, various agencies in the government must be forced to accept arbitrarily chosen cuts because they will not provide the information necessary to make more rational choices. Even then, agencies will try to foil the intent of the government by threatening to harm an important constituency of the government. For example, Congressmen and Senators who make strong proposals for defense cuts are usually advised by the Pentagon that such cuts will be implemented by closing military bases in their districts or states. Such threats are usually more than sufficient to cancel the whole budget-cutting exercise. Friedman (1986, pp. 5-6) recommends that entire agencies be eliminated to prevent their future lobbying, but the possibility of eliminating and not just reducing budgets will elicit even more counterveiling pressure from the affected agency. Whatever the economic merit of closing the CIA at this time, that agency is well protected from such a threat by many embarrassing secrets that it keeps for such occasions.

6.4.3   Presidential Line-Item Veto

A more modest proposal for fiscal reform, but one that has some experience, is the line-item veto. Presently, an entire bill is either signed by the President or vetoed. It has been customary to add certain items of spending to totally unrelated bills, with a view that the President, wishing to see the major portion of the bill enacted,

---

[3] Niskanen (1973, p. 23, fn. 1) compares an economy-minded manager in a profit-maximizing business and in a bureau. He predicts that, "In a bureau, at best, this manager might receive a citation and a savings bond, a lateral transfer, the enmity of his former colleagues, and the suspicion of his new colleagues."

would not veto the bill merely to prevent minor extra expenditures. The end result is an accretion of pork-barrel projects that are cumulatively large and add to the problems of deficit spending. If the President had a line-item veto he could enforce some discipline on Congressional spending binges, without bringing the legislative process to a complete halt.

Such a system already exists in many state governments and Holtz-Eakin (1988) has analyzed its impact on spending decisions. He points out that, ". . . the line item veto alters the relative power of the governor versus the legislature." (p. 270). The governor and legislature have different views of the median voter that they must satisfy. "Each representative in the state legislature will reflect the preferences of the median voter of his or her district... If the legislature votes as a single body on spending proposal the bill which passes will be that favored by the median point in the distribution of *median* voters across the jurisdictions. The governor, in contrast, will reflect the tastes of the median voter in the statewide distribution of *all* voters ... Here there is a rationale for a line item veto: to restrict the influence of jurisdictions with either unusually high or unusually low tastes." (p. 272-73, italics in original). In other words, the governor can overcome the heterogeneity problem that gives rise to excess spending by using the line-item veto. The empirical results of the Holtz-Eakin study have a complicated interpretation, but he does conclude that in the long run the line-item veto does not affect budgetary decisions one way or the other (p. 270). Dixit and Nalebuff (1991), who suggest that such a veto would create a strategic game between the President and Congress, speculate that currently, ". . . compromises made in Congress will be honored without fear that the president will pick and choose what segments to keep. Once Congress predicts they will lose all of the parts that would not survive on their own, the process of agreeing on a budget will become more contentious, and a consensus compromise may not be found... Thus a president with a line-item veto might end up with less power, simply because the Congress is less willing (or able) to put proposals on his desk." (pp. 284-85). In any case, such power in the hands of a President who is not committed to using fiscal policy as a countercyclical weapon will lead to partisan use of this capability without an improved performance in the macroeconomy.

6.4.4   Reliance on Monetary Policy

If there is no hope of making fiscal policy respond to business cycles, greater reliance will have to be placed on monetary policy to do the job. After all, both of these policy instruments can and do influence the level of aggregate demand in the macroeconomy in fairly similar ways and to the extent that such control over aggregate demand by either method can mitigate the effects of other sources of demand instability, there is need for only one of these policies.

The issue here is not whether monetary policy can reduce the fluctuations in macroeconomic activity that arise from business cycles; in fact, the historical record discussed in Chapter 2 (see Chart 2-4) does not lead to optimism on this score. Instead, we are here concerned with the possibility that monetary policy, like fiscal policy, will be captured by special-interest groups who will subvert the intent of the policy to reach macroeconomic goals, arbitrary though they may be. There is certainly the probability of dispute over the appropriate level of interest rates from a private welfare perspective. If we divide the population into debtors and creditors, it is immediately obvious that the welfare of the former is enhanced by low interest rates while the latter group is better off with high interest rates. It is also possible to have different opinions about interest rates depending on whether you buy or sell abroad, because of the effects of interest rates on exchange rates. How these conflicting opinions influence the final decision made by the Board of Governors of the Federal Reserve Board or by the Federal Open-Market Committee[4] is certainly not obvious, but whatever the result, there is a major distinction between this decision-making process and the one used by Congress to determine budgetary revenues and expenditures. We saw earlier that politicians will try to satisfy two or more groups with different demands by giving them all something — in return for other favors. However, it is not possible for the monetary authorities to provide low interest rates to debtors and high interest rates to creditors. The Fed must make only one choice about interest rates, because market arbitrage would ensure that only one price prevails in the

---

[4] Henceforth, the nickname "Fed" will be used to represent the U.S. monetary authorities.

money market. Of course, there is a spread between interest rates paid by debtors and those received by creditors but the gap is accounted for by taxes and value added in the process of intermediation; the Fed is unlikely to be able to affect that spread to any extent, let alone reverse it. Because of the inability to satisfy a number of constituencies, the Fed is more able to concentrate on macroeconomic requirements. The recent history of tight monetary policy in the face of recession, not only in the United States but in Germany and Canada as well, gives some evidence that monetary authorities are not trying to win popularity contests. One may argue that a strong anti-inflation stance is misguided when unemployment rates are unusually high, but that debate is more concerned with the choice of stabilization-policy goals rather than about the policy apparatus itself.

Moreover, the apolitical nature of the Fed and its virtual independence from Congress gives it the power to make unpopular but necessary decisions. The seven Governors are appointed by the President and confirmed by the Senate for a period of fourteen years; the chairman from among them is appointed for four years starting half-way through a presidential term. Hence they all survive the administration that appointed them. According to the Full Employment and Balanced Growth Act of 1978, the Fed must transmit to Congress semiannual reports which contain an appraisal of past economic performance as well as the Fed's objectives with respect to targets for monetary aggregates and the projections on which they are based. There are, of course, no penalties applied if the Fed's predictions are incorrect and therefore these "Monetary Policy Reports" do not provide Congress with a lever on monetary-policy decisions. From an earlier episode of Congressional demands for a voice in monetary policy, Pierce (1978, p. 364) suggests that, "The Federal Reserve has succeeded in sidestepping the intent of Congressional resolution and public law alike and conducts its business in virtually the same ways that it always has." It is only with slight journalistic hyperbole that *The Economist* described Paul Volcker, the chairman of the Fed during the 1979-82 monetary-targeting era, as the "second most powerful man in the United States." (Sept. 22, 1984, p. 5). Such independence of political control is the antithesis of democratic government, but the irony is that socially optimal decisions are more likely to be made by groups like the Fed that are not elected by the public and are only indirectly accountable to politicians and the electorate.

While the monetary authorities are able to devote their attention to stabilization-policy requirements, the continuing deficits will erode the priority attached by the Fed to macroeconomic goals in order to finance the mushrooming debt. The pressure to maintain low interest rates from the most important debtor in the country may be too strong to resist, especially as interest payments encroach more and more on discretionary spending. The conflict between macroeconomic goals and the servicing of the federal debt will be strongest during a boom period when tighter policy is needed to restrict aggregate demand. If, at that time, the Fed succumbs to the demands of the Treasury, then both fiscal and monetary policies will be lost to the needs of macroeconomic stabilization.

In such confrontations about "appropriate" interest rates between the administration and the Fed, the historical record, as presented by Weintraub (1978, p. 351), favors the President over the Governors of the Fed and their chairman. He finds that the "thrust" of monetary policy from 1951 to 1977 differs markedly from one administration to another in concert with the desires of the President. From the Truman-Eccles dispute about interest rates to the appointment of Chairman Arthur Burns to a Nixon-administration post, Weintraub concludes that, ". . . it may reasonably be urged that the dominant guiding force behind monetary policy is the President. Congress plays only a 'watchdog' role." (p. 349).

On the whole, despite many proposals to improve the performance of fiscal policy or to rely more heavily on monetary policy, there is little evidence that stabilization of the macroeconomy is likely to receive the priority that is often promised by new administrations before they take office. The most urgently needed reform of making surpluses and deficits symmetrical is nowhere in sight. It is simply not in anyone's short-term interest to pursue this type of reform and the problem will be allowed to get worse.

6.5   Exploitation of Stabilization Policies

The fundamental difficulty facing macroeconomic policy is that rational economic agents have learned to take advantage of government intervention for their own benefit. The depression of the 1930s created the conditions necessary for the welfare state, with the consequence that macroeconomic policies to achieve "full employment" and "price stability" have been accepted as government responsibilities ever since. Once the authorities commit themselves unequivocally to these goals, individuals can benefit from that commitment by trying to become net beneficiaries of these policies. For example, a government-sponsored unemployment insurance scheme allows not only involuntarily unemployed persons to benefit but also those who are voluntarily unemployed but who work merely to make themselves eligible for the benefits. The aim of the unemployment insurance is to raise the welfare of the unemployed to the same level as those who are employed, but the government is unable to distinguish between the voluntary and involuntary groups and must make its benefits available to all. The policy itself leads to adaptive behavior whereby individuals begin to maximize their welfare based not only on their tastes and endowments but also on the benefits from the government policy. To continue the previous example, some individuals whose reservation wage was higher than the prevailing wage and were not members of the labor force may find that an unemployment insurance program that pays benefits to those who meet a minimum work-time requirement will cause them to enter the labor force just to meet the requirements for eligibility. In other words, the marginal disutility from working the number of hours needed to qualify is outweighed by the marginal utility of the extra consumption financed from the work and the unemployment benefits that come afterwards, the last item swinging the balance toward labor-force participation. At the same time, if the unemployment insurance plan is financed by a tax on wage income, some current workers will leave the labor force because their after-tax wage has fallen below their reservation wage. As a result, the revenues from the tax will be smaller than anticipated and the expenditures will be higher than planned, with the effect that the scheme must be restricted or financed from other sources. In either case, the original intent of the scheme is subverted.

More generally, individuals will avoid taxes and make themselves eligible for benefits available from government programs. As Buchanan has urged, economic agents should maximize their welfare from both private and public exchanges and this leads individuals to avoid taxes and attract benefits in their transactions with the government. But there is a fallacy of composition at work in this reaction when applied to public-choice decisions by all economic agents taken together. While it is possible for people to consume pure public goods without reducing the amount available to others, most government programs do not involve public-goods provision but instead are redistributive in nature and those who avoid being net losers from the redistribution prevent others from being net gainers. As was concluded earlier in this chapter, the only way for everyone to be a winner is to make future generations into losers.

Stabilization policy needs to be able to influence aggregate demand within a business cycle not between one generation and another. Therefore shifting the burden of deficit financing from the present time into the distant future is of no benefit when cycles repeat themselves every 4-7 years. What is needed is an incentive mechanism that will reduce the reluctance to pay taxes, to accept high real interest rates and to absorb lower government expenditures when the macroeconomy experiences boom conditions. But such a scheme probably cannot be devised. In the distant past, when tax rates were low, the need to raise taxes during a boom period was accepted, probably reluctantly, because the cost of fighting the change exceeded the cost of the change itself. However, as tax rates crept upward and the tax base became eroded, the inducements for tax avoidance and to marshall political forces against further rate increases became stronger. The state of the business cycle is of no consequence here; the private interest dictates that lower taxes are always beneficial. In fact, even in a boom period, individuals can claim altruism as the source for their reluctance to pay high taxes; the extra aggregate demand is needed to make jobs available for anyone who is still unemployed.

In the labor market, as aggregate demand from private sources falls in a recession, it is possible to maintain the existing employment level, if governments make up the missing demand for labor by direct hiring or through increased expenditures on goods and services. The person who previously produced "private" goods is just as happy now producing "government" services, especially since the alternative is unemployment. This is the great benefit of stabilization policy when properly conceived and executed. However, this process must be reversible when demand from consumers, investors and foreigners picks up again. Now, there must be an incentive for those who were temporarily given jobs through government intervention to go back to their previous employment. But as we saw in Chapter 5, this may involve moving from one industry to another, which is not a costless or riskless operation and, in addition, wages in government-related industries are higher than elsewhere. Hence, the incentive is to stay put. Any attempt to make government employment less attractive in a boom, such as making the wage in that sector move countercyclically, would be resisted by those who benefit from having the government wage rise whenever the private wage increases.

In macroeconomic policy decisions, we would want the median voter to shift preferences during a business cycle. Consider the possibility of ranking all potential voters from those who want the "tightest" to those who want the "easiest" policies from their own personal perspective and then isolating the median in that ranking. In order to obtain a collective choice for tight policy in a boom and easy policy in a recession, either the characteristics of the median person must change in accordance with that requirement or individuals must be added or subtracted to the ranking to provide a new median who favors the appropriate policy.

There is no strong presumption for people changing their attitude toward the policy stance. It is difficult to imagine anyone wanting higher taxes during a boom or at any other time. While there will be a group who wants lower government expenditures and another group that wants higher expenditures, as was shown in Chapter 5, it is not clear how these views will change systematically over a business cycle. Finally, as pointed out earlier, views about appropriate interest rates will differ depending on personal characteristics, but again these do not shift a great deal; instead, being a creditor or debtor depends more on one stage in the life cycle. Therefore, it is unlikely that the median voter's preferences for stabilization policy will adapt to the circumstances.

The size of the electorate and therefore the choice of the median voter depends on the issue involved in the "election" and on the amount of "voting costs". As Table 5-2 makes clear, symmetrical costs imposed on both sides in an adversarial situation do not necessarily lead to a symmetrical elimination of voters on both sides of the issue. Moreover, it is not obvious that these voting costs and their effect on the determination of the median voter are at all related to the state of the business cycle. There may be some exceptions. Although workers in government-related industries are likely to want to stay in their current employment regardless of the situation in the overall labor market, these workers will probably spend less on lobbying for the *status quo* when the labor market exhibits excess demand than during periods of excess supply.

In the end, it would take an enlightened despot to dictate that interest rates and tax rates should be procyclical and that government spending should be countercyclical because, in a democracy, debtors seem to outnumber creditors, those in favor of more government spending are more powerful than those that want less, and no one will ever find a good reason to raise their own taxes. Such a decision-making process goes counter to Buchanan's public-choice requirements, but the only way to reconcile democratically sustained macropolicy, is to insist on some self-denial in our collective choices. Governments cannot devise programs that discriminate between voluntarily and involuntarily unemployed people, but the individuals themselves can perform that function and if they categorize themselves accordingly, an unemployment insurance scheme can be actuarially sound. Similarly, we must stoically learn to accept tax increases when they are necessary and to acquiesce in government-spending cuts even if they affect us adversely. The only way in which we can convince ourselves that these sacrifices are necessary is to understand that the present system of macroeconomic policy decision making by adversarial means leads to results that are worse. In other words, we have to escape the prisoner's dilemma, but the odds of that occurring, for reasons explained above, are not optimistically high.

6.6　Conclusion

The crucial debate in macroeconomics over the past two decades has concerned itself with the ability of stabilization policy initiatives to influence aggregate demand in the face of rational expectations. The major thesis in this chapter has been that unbridled self-interest in these policy decisions will render such intervention inoperative even if it is needed to keep aggregate demand at a constant level. The challenge to neo-Keynesian macroeconomists is to convince everyone else not only that intervention is imperative, but also that a collective-choice mechanism will lead to monetary and fiscal policy decisions that are restricted to macroeconomic goals — arbitrary though they may be — and not to a vast, inter-related, inefficient, and self-sustaining redistribution system, derisively labelled as "pork-barrel" politics.

The irony of the situation is that the more we ask of government, the less it can achieve. As conflicting demands for government intervention in all sorts of circumstances multiply, the important goals will give way to the urgent ones. If we could collectively persuade ourselves to limit government involvement in economic activity to genuine public goods, including well-specified macroeconomic goals, we may be able to prevent inappropriate stabilization policies and mushrooming budget deficits. The inescapable difficulty with this advice is that if everyone else follows it, the incentive for anyone to exploit it becomes very large and the prisoner's dilemma is once again solved in a noncooperative fashion. Keynes (1980, Vol. 27, p. 388) once wrote: "Dangerous acts can be done safely in a community which thinks and feels rightly, which would be the way to hell if they were executed by those who think and feel wrongly." But how do we get people to think and feel rightly, when it is in their own self-interest to think and feel wrongly? In Keynes's time there may have been a certain amount of self-denial in public policy decisions, but Gresham's Law operates in this sphere as well and we now pride ourselves in our ability to answer the question: "What's in it for me?"

Epilogue

This book was written under a self-imposed constraint to concentrate on events before 1990 and to avoid topical policy advice, but I am unable to resist the temptation to put the Clinton administration macroeconomic plans in perspective.

At the beginning of 1993, the U.S. economy was still in the grip of a prolonged recession, with the unemployment rate at 7% compared to Gordon's (1993, p. A3) estimate of the natural rate at about 6%. Despite these current conditions, the main focus of President Clinton's macropolicy is the overwhelming need to get the deficit under control. In fact, many commentators are now arguing that the economic recovery is being stifled by the deficit. For example, Alan Greenspan, the Chairman of the Federal Reserve, called the deficit a "malignant force" which was depressing economic activity. It seems that the newly accepted dogma is that deficit reduction and economic recovery go hand-in-hand. What has been largely overlooked in this doctrinaire approach to government finance is that deficit spending during the recession added a great deal of aggregate demand to the economy and helped to keep the downturn in economic activity relatively mild. Instead of an obsession with the deficit without reference to its context, stabilization policy should lead to countercyclical budget balances, with deficits during a recession but also surpluses during the last stages of an upturn. It is the lack of symmetry in U.S. fiscal policy over the past two or more decades that is the real "malignant force". After a lot of initial agonizing over expenditure cuts and increased taxes, in two or three years, when the labor market is likely to experience excess demand, there will not be anything near a budget surplus of, say, $200 billion to help to stabilize the debt ratio and the burden on future generations.

According to estimates produced by the Office of Management and Budget in February 1993, the unemployment rate will fall to 6% in 1995 or 1996. After that time there will be excess demand in the labor market unless there is a dramatic reduction in the natural rate over the next few years. Despite a number of optimistic assumptions about growth of real output, inflation and interest rates, projected expenditures by 1997 will be 22% of GDP, while revenues are forecast to be about 19.5% of GDP, leaving a gap of about 2.5%. The Congressional Budget Office, with less rosy assumptions, has a higher outlay projection, a lower revenue projection and a larger gap of about 4.5%. Therefore, even in a best-case scenario, there will be a sizable budget deficit at a time when there should be a sizable surplus. The Clinton administration will make the same grave error made by the Reagan administration when it refused to raise taxes and/or lower expenditures during the latter half of the 1980s, at a time when the economy did not need the extra government demand for goods and services.[1]

Moreover, President Clinton is perpetuating the adversarial approach to macroeconomic policy by suggesting that a small group of "rich" persons can be made to pay a proportionately larger share of revenue by raising only the top personal income-tax rate. This measure is predicted to contribute about half of the cumulative increase in total revenue of $251 billion from all sources and is openly designed as retribution for the favorable treatment received by the wealthy during the Republican tenure in the White House. Instead, what is needed is a broad-based tax increase and a reluctant acceptance of the fact that it is virtually impossible to reduce expenditures by any significant amount, as documented in Chapter 5. Somehow, tax revenue must rise to approximately 22% of GDP on average and even higher during the boom phase of the business cycle. In other words, a major structural change is needed in the federal tax system to make it symmetrically countercyclical, with a budget balance over the cycle. Moreover, the tax system needs to affect as many people as possible, but as little as possible. To make such taxes politically acceptable requires that the lobbying costs against the changes must exceed the cost

---

[1] See Section 6.3 for a discussion of the earlier episode.

of the tax to the individual. By taking a little from everyone, there would be no special-interest groups that could mount a campaign to prevent the tax from being implemented. Finally, a general tax on a broad base has fewer distortionary effects than a higher tax on a narrower base.[2]

For all the reasons mentioned above, a value-added tax on consumption would be the best single tax measure that could be enacted at this time. First, even a very low rate of tax would generate a large amount of additional revenue for the federal government. Second, by its very nature, tax revenues would be countercyclical; in fact, a value-added tax should have approximately a unitary income elasticity. Third, by taxing all consumption expenditures, it would affect almost all citizens, unlike an increase in the income-tax rate which leaves out large groups of nonearning individuals. Finally, the only incentive effect of this tax is to make saving more desirable, but this may be considered a virtue if long-term growth is to be increased as well.

Unfortunately, there are never enough volunteers in the battle against budget deficits and therefore citizens must be "drafted" to perform this task, similar to military service during a major war. But there will always be pressures exerted to exempt some groups of individuals from the draft. As soon as even the smallest exemption is made, the system will appear to be "unfair" and other groups will demand equal treatment. In due course, there are not enough individuals left in the draft to pursue the war. The tax system of the 1990s will, without fundamental changes now, resemble the Selective Service System of the 1960s during the Vietnam war: discredited and ineffective. Somehow the Clinton administration must convince the public that everyone must contribute to the resolution of the deficit problem once the economy recovers from the recession. To do so requires an explicit threat: as long as we keep trying to find other groups to bear the burden, the only group that we will find is our children.

---

[2] Jean Baptiste Colbert long ago devised the "optimal" tax system: "The art of taxation consists in so plucking the goose as to obtain the largest amount of feathers with the least amount of hissing."

Bibliography

Adams, Charles and David T. Coe (1989), "A Systems Approach to Estimating the Natural Rate of Unemployment and Potential Output for the United States," *IMF Working Paper*, 89/89, Washington: International Monetary Fund.

Aizenman, Joshua and Jacob A. Frenkel (1985), "Optimal Wage Indexation, Foreign Exchange Intervention, and Monetary Policy, *American Economic Review*, 75, pp. 402–23.

Alesina, Alberto (1988), "Macroeconomics and Politics," *NBER Macroeconomics Annual*, pp. 13–52.

Arrow, Kenneth J. (1951), *Social Choice and Individual Values*, New York: Wiley.

Backus, David and John Driffill (1985), "Inflation and Reputation," *American Economic Review*, 75, pp. 530–8.

Bailey, Martin J. (1956), "The Welfare Cost of Inflationary Finance," *Journal of Political Economy*, 64, pp. 93–110.

Baldwin, Robert E. (1989), "The Political Economy of Trade Policy," *Journal of Economic Perspectives*, 3, pp. 119–35.

Barnett, Corelli (1972), *The Collapse of British Power*, London: Eyre Methuen.

Barro, Robert J. (1974), "Are Government Bonds Net Wealth?" *Journal of Political Economy*, 82, pp. 1095–117.

Barro, Robert J. (1979), "Second Thoughts on Keynesian Economics," *American Economic Review: Papers and Proceedings*, 69, pp. 54–63.

Barro, Robert J. and Donald B. Gordon (1983), "A Positive Theory of Monetary Policy in a Natural Rate Model," *Journal of Political Economy*, 91, pp. 589–610.

Bhagwati, Jagdish and Vangal K. Ramaswami (1963), "Domestic Distortions, Tariffs and the Theory of Optimum Subsidy," *Journal of Political Economy*, 71, pp. 44–59.

Bhagwati, Jagdish (1982), "Directly Unproductive, Profit-Seeking (DUP) Activities," *Journal of Political Economy*, 90, pp. 988–1002.

204 *Bibliography*

Blanchard, Olivier Jean and Peter Diamond (1989), "The Beveridge Curve," *Brookings Papers on Economic Activity*, 1989:1, pp. 1–76.

Blanchard, Olivier Jean and Stanley Fischer (1989), *Lectures on Macroeconomics*, Cambridge, Mass.: MIT Press.

Blinder, Alan S. (1981), *Economic Policy and the Great Stagflation*, New York: Academic Press.

Blinder, Alan S. (1988), "The Fall and Rise of Keynesian Economics," invited paper at the 1988 Australian Economics Congress, Australian National University, Canberra.

Brown, E. Cary (1956), "Fiscal Policy in the 'Thirties: A Reappraisal," *American Economic Review*, 46, pp. 857–79.

Buchanan, James M. (1987), "The Constitution of Economic Policy," *American Economic Review*, 77, pp. 243–50.

Carter, Jimmy (1982), *Keeping Faith: Memoirs of a President*, New York: Bantam Books.

Commission on Money and Credit (1961), *Money and Credit*, Englewood Cliffs, N.J.: Prentice Hall.

Corden, W. Max (1974), *Trade Policy and Economic Welfare*, Oxford: Oxford University Press.

Dixit, Avinash K. and Barry J. Nalebuff (1991), *Thinking Strategically*, New York: W. W. Norton & Co.

Dobell, A. Rodney and Y.C. Ho (1967), "An Optimal Unemployment Rate," *Quarterly Journal of Economics*, 81, pp. 675–83.

Dunlop, John T. (1938), "The Movement of Real and Money Wage Rates," *Economic Journal*, 48, pp. 413–34.

Eckstein, Otto (1981), *Core Inflation*, Englewood Cliffs N.J.: Prentice-Hall.

Enzler, Jared, Lewis Johnson and John Paulus (1976), "Some Problems of Money Demand," *Brookings Papers on Economic Activity*, 1976:1, pp. 261–82.

Fischer, Stanley (1984), "The Benefits of Price Stability," unpublished working paper, Cambridge, Mass.: Massachusetts Institute of Technology.

Fischer, Stanley and Franco Modigliani (1978), "Towards an Understanding of the Real Effects and Costs of Inflation," *Weltwirtschaftliches Archiv*, 114, pp. 810–33.

Fishlow, Albert (1974), "Indexing Brazilian Style: Inflation Without Tears," *Brookings Papers on Economic Activity*, 1:1974, pp. 261–80.

Friedman, Milton (1957), *A Theory of the Consumption Function*, Princeton, N.J.: Princeton University Press.

Friedman, Milton (1968), "The Role of Monetary Policy," *American Economic Review*, 58, pp. 1–17.

Friedman, Milton (1969), "The Optimum Quantity of Money," in *idem*, *The Optimum Quantity of Money and Other Essays*, Chicago: Aldine.

Friedman, Milton (1986), "Economists and Economic Policy," *Economic Enquiry*, 24, pp. 1–10.

Friedman, Milton and Anna J. Schwartz (1963), *A Monetary History of the United States*, Princeton: Princeton University Press.

Gordon, Robert J. (1973), "The Welfare Costs of Higher Unemployment," *Brookings Papers on Economic Activity*, 1:1973, pp. 133–205.

Gordon, Robert J. (1984), "Unemployment and Potential Output in the 1980s," *Brookings Papers on Economic Activity*, 2:1984, pp. 537–68.

Gordon, Robert J. (1990), *Macroeconomics*, 5th edition, Glennview, Illinois: Scott, Foresman.

Gordon, Robert J. (1993), *Macroeconomics*, 6th edition, New York: HarperCollins.

Hamermesh, Daniel S. (1986), "The Demand for Labor in the Long Run," in Orley Ashenfelter and Richard Layard, editors, *Handbook of Labor Economics*, Vol. I, Amsterdam: North Holland.

Halperin, Daniel and Eugene Steuerle (1988), "Indexing the Tax System for Inflation," in Henry J. Aaron *et al.* editors, *Uneasy Compromise: Problems of a Hybrid Income-Consumption Tax*, Washington: The Brookings Institution.

Harris, Richard G. (1989), "The New Protectionism Revisited," *Canadian Journal of Economics*, 22, pp. 751–78.

Heller, Walter W. (1967) *The New Dimensions of Political Economy*, New York: W.W. Norton & Co.

Hession, Charles H. (1984), *John Maynard Keynes*, New York: Macmillan Publishing Company.

Holtz-Eakin, Douglas (1988), "The Line Item Veto and Public Sector Budgets," *Journal of Public Economics*, 36, pp. 269–92.

Howitt, Peter (1990), "Zero Inflation as a Long-Term Target For Monetary Policy," in Richard G. Lipsey, editor, *Zero Inflation*, Toronto: C.D. Howe Institute.

Keynes, John Maynard (1936), *The General Theory of Employment, Interest, and Money*, New York: Harcourt, Brace & World.

Keynes, John Maynard (1980), *Collected Writings*, Cambridge: Cambridge University Press.

Kirman, Alan P. (1992), "Whom or What Does the Representative Individual Represent?" *Journal of Economic Perspectives*, 6 pp. 117–36.

Kramer, Gerald H. and Susan J. Lepper (1972), "Congressional Elections," Chapter 5 in William O. Aydelotte *et al.* editors, *The Dimensions of Quantitative Research in History*, Princeton: Princeton University Press.

Lucas, Robert E. Jr. (1981), *Studies in Business-Cycle Theory*, Cambridge, MA: MIT Press.

MacRea, C. Duncan (1977), "A Political Model of the Business Cycle," *Journal of Political Economy*, 85, pp. 239–63.

Maital, Shlomo and Irwin Lipnowski (1985), "Hanging Together or Separately: A Game Theoretic Approach to Macroeconomic Conflict," in *idem*, editors, *Macroeconomic Conflict and Social Institutions*, Cambridge, MA: Ballinger Publishing Co.

Mankiw, N. Gregory (1990), "A Quick Refresher Course in Macroeconomics," *Journal of Economic Literature*, 28, pp. 1645–60.

McCandless, George T. (1991), *Macroeconomic Theory*, Englewood Cliffs: Prentice Hall.

Meyer, Laurence H. (1986), "The Political Economy and Macroeconomic Effects of Deficit Reduction in the U.S.," in Martin F. J. Prachowny, editor, *Policy Forum on the February 1986 Federal Budget*, Kingston, Ontario: John Deutsch Institute for the Study of Economic Policy, pp. 63–77.

Modigliani, Franco and Albert Ando (1963), "The 'Life Cycle' Hypothesis of Saving: Aggregate Implications and Tests," *American Economic Review*, 53, pp. 55–84.

Mundell, Robert A. (1962), "The Appropriate Use of Monetary and Fiscal Policy for Internal and External Stability,' *International Monetary Fund Staff Papers*, 9, pp. 70–9.

Mundell, Robert A. (1963), "On the Selection of a Program of Economic Policy with an Application to the Current Situation in the United States," *Banca Nazionale Del Lavoro Quarterly Review*, 16, pp. 262–84.

Mussa, Michael (1974), "Tariffs and the Distribution of Income: The Importance of Factor Specificity, Substitutability and Intensity in the Short and Long Run," *Journal of Political Economy*, 82, pp. 1191–203.

Niskanen, William A. (1973), *Bureaucracy: Servant or Master?*, London: The Institute of Economic Affairs.

Okun, Arthur M. (1970), "Potential GNP: Its Measurement and Significance," in *idem*, *The Political Economy of Prosperity*, Washington: The Brookings Institution; reprinted from: American Statistical Association, *Proceedings of the Business and Economic Statistics Section* (1962).

Okun, Arthur M. (1975), "Inflation: Its Mechanics and Welfare Costs," *Brookings Papers on Economic Activity*, 2:1975, pp. 351–401.

Olson, Mancur (1965), *The Logic of Collective Action*, Cambridge, MA: Harvard University Press.

Phelps, Edmond (1967), "Phillips Curves, Expectations of Inflation and Optimal Unemployment over Time," *Economica*, 34, pp. 254–81.

Pierce, James L. (1978), "The Myth of Congressional Supervision of Monetary Policy," *Journal of Monetary Economics*, 4, pp. 363–70.

Pindyck, Robert S. and Daniel L. Rubinfeld (1991), *Econometric Models and Economic Forecasts*, 3rd edition, New York: McGraw Hill.

Prachowny, Martin F.J. (1981), "Sectoral Conflict over Stabilization Policies in Small Open Economies," *Economic Journal*, 91, pp. 671–84.

Prachowny, Martin F.J. (1985), *Money in the Macroeconomy*, New York: Cambridge University Press.

Prachowny, Martin F.J. (1987), "Macroeconomic Policy in a Conflict Environment," *Zeitschrift für die gesamte Staatswissenschaft*, 143, pp. 244–60.

Prachowny, Martin F.J. (1987a), "Conflict in the Labor Market: Seniority Rules and Unemployment," *Journal of Macroeconomics*, 9, pp. 527–43.

Reuber, Grant L. (1964), "The Objective Function of Canadian Monetary Policy, 1949–61: Empirical 'Trade Offs' and the Reaction Function of the Authorities," *Journal of Political Economy*, 72, pp. 109–32.

Schlesinger, Arthur M. Jr. (1959), *The Age of Roosevelt*, Vol. II: *The Coming of the New Deal*, Boston: Houghton Mifflin.

Schumpeter, Joseph A. (1954), *History of Economic Analysis*, New York: Oxford University Press.

Sheffrin, Steven M. (1989), *The Making of Economic Policy: History, Theory, Politics*, Oxford: Blackwell.

Stein, Herbert (1988), *Presidential Economics*, Second Edition, Washington: American Enterpise Institute.

Stern, I. (1975), "Industry Effects of Government Expenditures: An Input-Output Analysis," *Survey of Current Business*, 55 (5), pp. 9–23.

Stiglitz, Joseph E. (1992), "Capital Markets and Economic Fluctuations in Capitalistic Economies," *European Economic Review*, 36, pp. 269–306.

Tarshis, Lorie (1939), "Changes in Real and Money Wages," *Economic Journal*, 49, pp. 150–4.

Tinbergen, Jan (1952), *On the Theory of Economic Policy*, Amsterdam: North-Holland.

Topel, Robert (1993), "What Have We Learned from Empirical Studies of Unemployment and Turnover," *American Economic Review: Papers and Proceedings*, 83, pp. 110–15.

Truman, Harry S. (1955), *Memoirs*, Garden City, N.Y.: Doubleday & Co.

U.K. Committee on the Working of the Monetary System (Radcliffe Committee) (1959), *Report*, London: Her Majesty's Stationery Office.

U.S. Congress (1946), "The Employment Act of 1946," 79th Congress, 2nd Session, Chapter 33.

U.S. Congress (1978), "Full Employment and Balanced Growth Act of 1978," 95th Congress, Public Law 95–523.

U.S. President (1947–91), *Economic Report of the President*, Washington: Superintendent of Documents.

Weintraub, Robert E. (1978) "Congressional Supervision of Monetary Policy," *Journal of Monetary Economics*, 4, pp. 341–62.

Wildavsky, Aaron (1964), *The Politics of the Budgetary Process*, Boston: Little, Brown & Co.

Wiseman, Michael (1976), "Public Employment as Fiscal Policy," *Brookings Papers on Economic Activity*, 1:1976, pp. 67–114.

Young, Paula C. (1991), "Benchmark Input-Output Accounts for the U.S. Economy, 1982," *Survey of Current Business*, 71 (7), pp. 30–71.

Index

Accord of 1953 54
Adams, Charles 12, 39, 85, 87, 94, 111, 144, 180, 181
adaptive behavior 80, 193
adjustment costs 106, 118, 125, 132, 135
see also disequilibrium costs
aggregate demand 15, 56, 58, 73, 76, 83, 88, 116, 153, 179, 181, 183, 190, 194, 196, 199
and balance of payments 57
and inflation 50, 59, 67
Keynes on 9, 18–19
and unemployment 55, 118
aggregate-demand equation 76, 116
aggregate-demand policies 64, 66, 74, 75, 76
see also macroeconomic policy, stabilization policy
aggregate-demand shocks 2, 69
aggregate-supply curve 38, 40, 65, 69, 73, 76, 116
aggregate-supply relationship 114
aggregate-supply shock 74
see also oil-price shocks
aggregation 8
Aizenman, Joshua 14
Alesina, Alberto 29
anarchy 176
Ando, Albert 63
Arrow, Kenneth 15

automatic stabilizers 43, 50, 52, 54, 55, 58, 62
availability doctrine 54

Backus, David 29
balance-of-payments 26, 56
Balanced Budget and Emergency Deficit Control Act of 1985 184
Baldwin, Robert E. 174
Barnett, Corelli 18
Barro, Robert J. 27, 150, 179
barter trade 21
Beveridge curve 108
Bhagwati, Jagdish 29, 179
Blanchard, Olivier 24, 108
Blinder, Alan 77
Bolivia 35
Brazil 20
Brown, E. Cary 44
Brumberg, Richard 63
Buchanan, James 174, 175, 179, 196
budget constraint 96, 99, 155, 156
budget deficit 80, 84, 88, 155, 157, 159, 167, 169, 180, 197
Budget Enforcement Act of 1990 186
Bureau of Labor Statistics 167
Bureau of Management and Budget 173
bureaucratic parasites 178
bureaucratic theory 188
bureaucrats 146, 179, 188

Burns, Arthur 192
Bush administration 182
Bush, George 47, 83
business cycles 120, 152, 155, 180,
    194, 190, 195

Canada 191
capital 104, 143
  as a factor of production 153
  equipment 172
  intensity 170
  stock of 103, 105, 110, 118, 154
Carter administration 71–5, 73,
    117
Carter, Jimmy 48, 71, 73, 75, 85
Chow test 119, 143
Central Intelligence Agency
    (CIA) 188
Civil Works Administration 44
Clark, John D. 52
classical unemployment 118
  see also cyclical unemployment,
    involuntary unemployment,
    structural unemployment
Clinton administration 200
Clinton, Bill 199
Coe, David T. 12, 39, 85, 88, 94,
    111, 144, 180, 181
COLA clauses 75
  see also indexation
Colbert, Jean Baptiste 201
collective choices 4, 175, 195, 196
collective decisions 19, 156, 170,
    173
Commission on Money and Credit
    54
compensation schemes 123
conflict
  about policy choices 2, 29
  between full employment and
    price stability 57
  environment 19
Congressional Budget Office 185,
    200
conservative social welfare
    function 170

constitutional amendment 186–7
constitutional exchange 175
constitutional framework 29
constitutional reform 176
constitutional restraint 7, 30
consumption 98–9, 118, 128, 140,
    193
  of goods and services 96, 155
contractarian model 176
contracts 20, 93, 101, 112, 114,
    124, 136, 141, 145
Corden, W. Max 6, 170, 171
core inflation rate 35
cost functions 106, 108
cost of inflation 20
  of predictable inflation 37
costs of production 51
Council of Economic Advisers 46,
    52, 63, 65, 71, 77, 90, 173
countercyclicality 120–1, 184, 195
  of budgets 182, 199
  of employment policies 47, 121
  of fiscal policy 40, 51, 53, 80, 81,
    84, 181, 186, 187
  of government spending 152, 172
  see also stabilization policy
credibility 75, 79, 80, 82, 84, 86
"crowding in" 153–5, 157, 169,
    172
"crowding out" 158
cyclically-adjusted budget deficit
    181
cyclical unemployment 118
  see also classical unemployment,
    involuntary unemployment,
    structural unemployment

dead-weight loss 22
defense expenditures 50
deficits 152, 179
demand curve 124, 125, 126, 137
demand for labor 94, 104, 108–9,
    120, 135, 148, 149
Diamond, Peter 108
diminishing returns 109

direct hiring by government
116–17, 119
disequilibrium costs 107
see also adjustment costs
disequilibrium transactions 94,
134, 138, 140
disinflation 37–8
distortions 132–3
Dixit, Avinash 189
Dobell, A. Rodney 14
dominant strategy 178
Driffill, John 29
Dunlop, John T. 120

Eccles, Marriner 192
Eckstein, Otto 35
Economic Report of the President
45, 48, 49, 69, 142, 148, 181
Economist, The 16, 151, 191
effective market classification
56–7
Eisenhower administration 52–4
Eisenhower, Dwight D. 52, 68
elasticity of substitution 120
elasticity of the labor input 115
Emergency Employment Act of
1971 117
Employment Act of 1946 44–7,
51, 52, 53, 54, 59, 60, 64, 83
Employment and Earnings 167
entitlement programs 80, 186
exchange rates 190
expectations 68, 75, 85, 86
of inflation 18, 23, 27, 25, 37, 63,
64, 73, 82, 136, 142, 145
see also inflation
expenditures on goods and
services 160, 194
expropriation 176

factors of production 103, 106,
153, 158, 166
fallacy of composition 194
farm subsidies 16
Federal Open-Market Committee
190

Federal Reserve Act of 1913 33
Federal Reserve System 33, 47,
59, 77–8, 82, 83, 84, 173, 190,
191
fiscal and monetary policies 40,
43, 50, 56, 61, 67, 74, 77, 83,
88, 136, 173, 196
see also aggregate-demand
policies, stabilization policy
fiscal drag 60
fiscal policy 28, 46, 52, 57, 59, 65,
116, 136, 152, 170, 172, 179–80,
184, 190, 192, 199
Fischer, Stanley 24, 35
Fisher effect 22
Fishlow, Albert 20
fixed costs 93, 105
Ford administration 69
Ford, Gerald 85
free-rider problem 155, 175
frictional unemployment 9, 14,
55, 60, 62, 82, 117
see also structural
unemployment
Friedman, Milton 17, 22, 27, 33,
53, 63, 90, 111, 187, 188
full employment 9, 12, 14, 19, 23,
45, 66, 136, 139
as a goal 2, 18
policies 16
Full Employment and Balanced
Growth Act of 1978 46–8, 72,
79, 83, 191
full-employment budget surplus
40, 56, 61

game, strategic 6, 24, 28, 29, 177,
186
general-equilibrium model 153
Germany 191
GNP deflator 142
goods market 93, 115, 117, 136,
145
Gordon, Robert J. 12, 16, 27, 39,
40, 60, 62, 66, 70, 71, 88, 94,
119, 121, 142, 144, 181, 199

government benefits 177
government demand for goods and services 145, 152, 154, 157, 160
government demand for industry output 153, 158, 161, 167, 169, 172
government employment 120–1, 133, 134, 169
government expenditures 161, 170, 179, 182, 194, 195
Gramm-Rudman-Hollings bill 53, 81, 84, 184
 see also Balanced Budget and Emergency Deficit Control Act of 1985
grants-in-aid 160
Great Depression 5, 17, 44, 50, 51, 83, 118, 121
Greenspan, Alan 47, 199
Gresham's Law 197
Gross Domestic Product (GDP) 3, 200
Gross National Product (GNP) 3, 11, 13, 35, 38, 39, 72, 75, 80, 119, 120, 142, 183
 see also output
growth of monetary aggregates 22, 47, 60, 75, 78
"Guideposts" 59

Halperin, Daniel 36
Hamermesh, Daniel 119, 120
Harris, Richard G. 174
Heller, Walter W. 91
Hession, Charles 14
heterogeneity 15
 and conflict 30
 of individuals 2, 7, 103, 122, 174, 177, 180, 184
 in the labor market 109, 111
 and median voter 189
 of tastes or endowments 176
Ho, Y.C. 14
Holtz-Eakin, Douglas 189
home activity 12

Hopkins, Harry 44
hours of work 8, 11, 14–16, 94, 95, 96, 97, 99, 101–3, 104, 113, 120, 124, 128, 135, 140, 170
 fixed 16
 overtime 101, 104–5, 135
 standard 102, 105
Howitt, Peter 20, 21, 35
Humphrey-Hawkins bill 46, 74, 75, 86
 see also Full Employment and Balanced Growth Act of 1978
hyperinflation 17, 21, 35

impossibility theorem 15
income effect 97
income tax 28, 43, 53, 55, 59, 81, 182, 200
 see also taxes
indexation 20, 36
 see also COLA clauses
index of business failures 142
index of consumer confidence 144
indifference curves 26, 28, 99, 144
industry-by-commodity total requirements coefficient 161
inflation 17, 19
 see also expectations of inflation
inflation target 47
information 17
input-output accounts 159, 167, 169
interest payments 96, 182, 183, 192
interest rate 22, 157, 166, 183, 190, 192, 194, 195
intergenerational transfers of welfare 176
intermediation in financial markets 191
intertemporal consumption function 96
interventionists 1, 18
inventories 161
investment expenditures 157, 161, 167, 172

involuntary unemployment 3, 8,
13, 16, 55, 102, 121, 128, 137,
139–40, 145, 150, 193, 196
see also classical unemployment,
cyclical unemployment,
structural unemployment
involuntary exchange 15, 94, 101,
102, 113
IS-LM-AS model 2
IS-LM model 62
isoprofit curve 125, 136, 137
Israel 20

Johnson, Lyndon 58, 59
Joint Economic Committee 173

Kennedy, John F. 54
Kennedy-Johnson administration
54–60, 62, 63, 68, 91
Keynes, John Maynard 6, 9, 10,
14, 16, 18, 118, 197
Keynesian model 60
Keynesian revolution 174
Keynesians 1, 18, 23, 137, 196
Kirman, Alan 8
Korean war 50-1
Kramer, Gerald 144

labor force 11, 14, 98–9, 103, 111,
124, 128, 131, 133, 139–40, 166,
193
labor input 8, 11, 14, 104, 106,
113, 114, 116, 124, 126
labor market 11, 14, 19, 31, 85,
92, 97, 103, 107, 111–12, 116,
121, 148, 150, 174, 194, 196
disequilibrium in 1, 17, 59, 86,
88, 112–13, 136, 140, 180–1, 199
heterogeneity in 2, 15, 109, 141,
147
institutions 134–5
Keynes on 16, 118
participants in 19, 28, 174
and Phillips curve 26, 63, 64, 89,
142-4
property rights in 93–4

welfare analysis in 123–37
labor-supply curve 95, 99, 100,
102
slope of 97
labor-use curve 109, 110, 115,
116, 118, 119, 125, 126, 127,
130, 134, 136, 137, 141, 145,
146
Landon, Alfred 44
lay-offs 124, 128, 131, 135, 142,
149
leisure 40, 96, 99, 100, 128, 140,
150
Lepper, Susan 144
life-cycle hypothesis 63, 96
line-item veto 188
Lipnowski, Irwin 178
LM test for serial correlation 143
lobbying 7, 157, 159, 167, 168,
169, 172, 177, 186–8, 196
costs 178, 200
power 180
resources 178
long-run equilibrium 157
loss function 89
Lucas, Robert E. Jr. 120

M1 (monetary aggregate) 70, 71,
82, 119
MacRea, C. Duncan 29
macroeconomic goals 3, 5, 6, 8
macroeconomic theory 1, 5, 6, 30
macroeconomic policy 2, 6, 187
Maital, Shlomo 178
Mankiw, N. Gregory 6, 8
marginal disutility of work 14
marginal product 12, 13, 104,
105, 141
of labor 14, 40, 104, 109, 113,
119, 132, 143
marginal rate of transformation
156
marginal revenue 105
marginal utility 96, 193
of goods consumption 101
of leisure 98, 100

McCandless, George 8
median voter 135, 146, 151–2,
  155, 159, 166–7, 189, 195
 behavior of 143
 model of 7, 141
median worker 141, 144, 169
menu costs 20, 22
Meyer, Laurence 185
microeconomics 2, 5, 30, 60
minimum wage legislation 71
Modigliani, Franco 35, 63
monetary aggregates 42, 191
monetary authorities 22, 29
monetary policy 28, 42, 46, 52–4,
  56, 58, 59, 69, 71, 80, 116, 136,
  184, 190, 192
Monetary Policy Reports 191
monetary targeting 84
money illusion 21
money market 93, 116, 117, 136,
  145
money wages 19
 see also real wages, reservation
 wages
monopolist 105
monopoly power 114
moral hazard 132, 140, 171
Mundell, Robert 56
Mussa, Michael 153

Nalebuff, Barry 189
National Recovery
  Administration (NRA) 48
natural rate of unemployment 1,
  3, 24, 28, 49, 60, 69, 87, 94,
  111–12, 113, 115, 117, 118, 121,
  133–7, 141, 142, 144–7, 180–1,
  184, 199
 development of 17
 as a goal 23, 62–3, 83, 90, 139
 history of 45, 49, 66, 68, 71, 79,
  85, 131
natural rate output 115
 see also potential output
neoclassical economists 23, 27, 52,
  137

Net National Product (NNP) 36
New Deal 33
New Economic Policy, The 64
Niskanen, William 188
Nixon administration 64–6, 192
Nixon, Richard 64, 67, 92
nominal wage 15, 17, 19, 105,
  113, 114, 117, 137, 142
 see also real wage, reservation
 wage
nonearned income 96, 125
noninterventionists 1, 18
nonwage income 19, 96, 98, 100,
  110, 124, 128
NOW accounts 71

objective function 23–5
Office of Management and Budget
  185, 200
oil prices 40, 66, 69, 71, 76, 77,
  78, 85, 142
 shock 2, 34, 64, 72, 73, 77, 81,
  119
 see also supply shocks
Okun, Arthur 10, 14, 16, 21, 91
Okun coefficient 12
Okun's Law 11–12, 14, 55, 91
Olson, Mancur 157
"Operation Twist" 57
opinion polls 144
optimal hours of work 14, 16
optimal inflation rate 22, 25, 35,
  49
optimal intervention 6, 29, 31,
  131, 134, 136
optimal money holdings 22
optimality of equilibrium 3
optimum tariff 5, 6, 173
Organization of Petroleum
  Exporting Countries (OPEC)
  34, 68
output 114, 115, 116, 118, 121,
  130, 152, 154, 155, 158, 160,
  161, 168
output gap 38, 40, 43, 71
overtime premium 101, 106

Pareto condition 15, 30, 171
Pareto improvement 5, 16, 17,
    123, 132, 133, 134, 136, 138,
    139, 150, 173, 176
Pareto optimality 2, 19, 131
Pareto superiority 10, 19, 178
pay-off, in games 178, 180
peace dividend 151
Pentagon 188
permanent-income hypothesis 55,
    63, 96
Perot, Ross 187
Phelps, Edmond 17, 27, 90
Phillips curve 3, 23, 25, 55, 56,
    62, 89, 145
  estimates of 60, 63, 65, 68, 142–3
  slope of 23, 25, 63, 84, 87, 89
  stability of 59, 68–9, 78–88
Pierce, James L. 191
Pindyck, Robert 38, 119
policy makers 60, 63, 71, 89–90
political business cycle 24, 29, 30
political pressure group 8
potential output 16, 33, 38, 39,
    40, 62–3, 69, 71, 77
Prachowny, Martin 29, 116, 144
price and wage controls 48, 50,
    65, 66, 68, 79, 89, 136
price stability 19, 54, 139
prisoner's dilemma 4, 174, 178,
    196–7
private goods 155, 179
private or self-interest 18, 149,
    174, 196
production function 103, 114,
    115, 119
production possibility frontier 21,
    156
profit function 108, 126
profit maximization 69, 103, 105,
    113-14, 120, 121, 188
profits 97, 113, 125–6
property rights 93, 123
public debt 50, 179, 187
public goods 151, 155, 175, 179,
    194, 197

public-choice decision 7, 146, 152,
    159, 167, 174–6, 194, 196
public interest 174
public-sector industry 152
public service employment 47, 73,
    117
Public Works Administration
    (PWA) 44
public works projects 53, 55
purchasing power 96

quits 106–9, 118, 133

Radcliffe Committee Report
    (UK) 54
Ramaswami, Vangal 29
rational expectations 3, 6, 17, 18,
    28, 196
reaction functions 24, 26
Reagan administration 88, 166,
    181, 182, 200
Reagan-Bush administrations
    78–85
Reagan, Ronald 47, 78, 85, 185–6
Reaganomics 86
real business cycles 2
real money balances 33, 42, 76,
    116
real wage 3, 20, 38, 78, 96, 99,
    100, 118, 132
  and demand for labor 9, 103,
    109, 112–13, 116–17, 120–1,
    125–7
  and equilibrium in labor market
    17, 114
  and welfare 13-14, 15, 19,
    127–31, 134, 136–7, 139, 141–2,
    144–7
  see also nominal wage,
    reservation wage
referendum 146, 159
relative prices 20, 34, 70, 155
relative wages 169
rents 103, 112, 124, 128, 146, 150,
    154, 157
representative agent 2, 8, 30, 103

reputation model 29–30
reservation wage 3, 111, 150,
  and supply of labor 98–103, 110,
  125
  and welfare 122, 124, 127–8, 146,
  193
  see also nominal wage, real wage
returns to scale 119
Reuber, Grant 26
Ricardian equivalence 179
risk aversion 79, 141, 144, 147,
  171
risk premium 142
rolling regressions 37
Roosevelt administration 33
Rubinfeld, Daniel 38, 119

Schlesinger, Arthur M. Jr. 44
Schumpeter, Joseph 10, 17
Schwartz, Anna 33
search costs 133
second-best solution 29, 97, 99
security of employment 124, 127,
  130, 131, 140, 142, 145, 147,
  149, 154
Selective Service System 201
seniority 109, 127, 135, 142, 147,
  150
seniority rights 112, 153
seniority rules 148
"shoe-leather" costs 35
social choices 15
social insurance system 171
social welfare function 5, 24
Solow, Robert 149
South Carolina 151
Spearman rank correlation 167
  special interest 187
special-interest group 7, 30, 139,
  174, 187, 190, 201
stabilization policies 1, 12, 43, 51,
  55, 115, 117, 137–40, 145–6,
  174, 182, 194, 196
  goals for 180, 191
state and local government 160
Stein, Herbert 48, 54, 66–7, 86, 92

Stern, I. 160
Steuerle, Eugene 36
Stiglitz, Joseph 1
Stolper-Samuelson theorem 7, 153
structural unemployment 73–4,
  91, 117
  see also cyclical unemployment,
  involuntary unemployment
subsidies 7, 132–4
substitution effect 97
supply curve 125, 133
  of labor 94, 130
supply of workers 128, 136, 154
supply shocks 66, 69–70, 74, 76–7,
  88, 119
supply-side economics 86
Supreme Court 186
Survey of Current Business 40

tariffs 7
Tarshis, Lorie 120
tastes 152, 193
taxes 7, 79, 155, 157, 175, 177,
  191, 193–5
  and budget deficits 152, 172,
  179, 185, 195
  changes to 50–1, 55, 58, 63, 70
  collections 73
  on consumption 81
  and expenditure policies 56
  on money holdings 22
  rates 56, 78, 84, 86, 182
  surcharge 60
  tax system 36, 52
  on wages 133–4
tax-based incomes policies 75
Tax Reform Act of 1986 36
terms of trade 156
Thurmond, Strom 151
Tinbergen, Jan 24
Tobin's *q* 144
Topel, Robert 94
trade policy 6
trade theory 7
trade-off 144

transactions costs 20, 21, 157, 159, 167, 168, 171, 175
transfer payments 160, 177
Treasury, U.S. Department of the 192
Truman administration 49–52
Truman, Harry 45, 50–1, 53, 192

unanimity 175
unemployment compensation 28, 71
unemployment insurance 10, 16, 19, 43, 53, 55, 111, 139, 193
utility 141, 154, 174, 179
utility function 95

vacancies 106–10, 112, 113, 117, 125, 132, 141
value-added tax 201
velocity of money 43, 70–1, 80, 82
Vietnam war 35, 58
Vinson, Fred M. 45
Virginia 151
Volcker, Paul 47, 191
voluntary exchange 175
voluntary guidelines 60, 73, 74
voters 30, 92, 166, 195
voting process 141

wage differentials 154
wage tax 133
Wall Street Journal, The 35
War on Poverty 57
Warner, John 151
weekly wage 11, 16, 119–20
Weintraub, Robert E. 192
welfare 121, 139, 157–8, 170, 190, 193
    calculations 152
    comparisons 123, 131
    effects 137
    of factors of production 102–3, 127–8, 145–6, 152, 155, 193
    improvement 156
    maximization 112, 179
welfare economics 92, 123
welfare reform 73
welfare state 193
Wildavsky, Aaron 187
Wiseman, Michael 117
workers 93
    number of 8, 104
    productivity of 127
work-leisure choice 94, 125

zero-sum games 176–8